Lecture Notes in Artificial Intelligence 5244

Edited by R. Goebel, J. Siekmann, and W. Wahlster

Subseries of Lecture Notes in Computer Science

Ralph Bergmann   Gabriela Lindemann
Stefan Kirn   Michal Pěchouček (Eds.)

Multiagent
System Technologies

6th German Conference, MATES 2008
Kaiserslautern, Germany, September 23-26, 2008
Proceedings

 Springer

Volume Editors

Ralph Bergmann
University of Trier
Department of Business Information Systems II
Trier, Germany
E-mail: bergmann@uni-trier.de

Gabriela Lindemann
Humboldt-University Berlin, Institute for Computer Science
Berlin, Germany
E-mail: lindeman@informatik.hu-berlin.de

Stefan Kirn
University of Hohenheim, Stuttgart, Germany
E-mail: wi2office@uni-hohenheim.de

Michal Pěchouček
Czech Technical University, Department of Cybernetics
Prague, Czech Republic
E-mail: pechouc@labe.felk.cvut.cz

Library of Congress Control Number: Applied for

CR Subject Classification (1998): I.2.11, I.2, C.2.4, D.2.12, D.1.3, J.1

LNCS Sublibrary: SL 7 – Artificial Intelligence

ISSN   0302-9743
ISBN   978-3-540-87804-9 Springer Berlin Heidelberg New York

Typesetting: Camera-ready by author, data conversion by Scientific Publishing Services, Chennai, India
Printed on acid-free paper   SPIN: 12530519   06/3180   5 4 3 2 1 0

Preface

For the sixth time, the German special interest group on Distributed Artificial Intelligence in cooperation with the Steering Committee of MATES organized the German Conference on Multiagent System Technologies – MATES 2008. This conference, which took place during September 23–26, 2008 in Kaiserslautern, followed a series of successful predecessor conferences in Erfurt (2003, 2004, and 2006), Koblenz (2005), and Leipzig (2007). MATES 2008 was co-located with the 31st German Conference on Artificial Intelligence (KI 2008) and was hosted by the University of Kaiserslautern and the German Research Center for Artificial Intelligence (DFKI).

As in recent years, MATES 2008 provided a distinguished, lively, and interdisciplinary forum for researchers, users, and developers of agent technology to present and discuss the latest advances of research and development in the area of autonomous agents and multiagent systems. Accordingly, the topics of MATES 2008 covered the whole range: from the theory to applications of agent and multiagent technology. In all, 35 papers were submitted from authors from 11 countries. The accepted 16 full papers included in this proceedings volume and presented as talks at the conference were chosen based on a thorough and highly selective review process. Each paper was reviewed and discussed by at least three Program Committee members and revised according to their comments. We believe that the papers of this volume are a representative snapshot of current research and contribute to both theoretical and applied aspects of autonomous agents and multiagent systems.

The conference program also included two invited talks by Sascha Ossowski (University Rey Juan Carlos, Madrid, Spain) and Michael Wooldridge (University of Liverpool, UK). In his talk, Sascha Ossowski examined different stances on coordination and outlined various research issues related to coordination in multiagent systems. Michael Wooldridge's talk put a focus on knowledge representation and reasoning related to the specification and verification of social choice mechanisms and coordination mechanisms such as social laws.

Additionally, MATES 2008 also provided a doctoral mentoring program, dedicated to PhD students at advanced stages of their research. This program gave students an opportunity to interact closely with established researchers in their fields, to receive feedback on their work, and to get advice on managing their careers.

Particular thanks goes to the Program Committee and additional reviewers for their efforts and hard work in the reviewing and selection process. We thank all the authors who submitted papers to the conference, making this program successful. We express our special thanks to the two invited speakers Sascha Ossowski and Michael Wooldridge. Finally, we like to thank the organization team of KI 2008 for providing valuable support and for all the effort involved in the local organization of MATES.

This volume was produced using the EasyChair system[1]. We would like to express our gratitude to its author Andrei Voronkov. Finally, we thank Springer for their continuing support in publishing this series of conference proceedings.

July 2008

Ralph Bergmann
Gabriela Lindemann
Stefan Kirn
Michal Pěchouček

---

[1] http://www.easychair.org

Organization

General Co-chairs

Stefan Kirn   Universität Hohenheim, Germany
Michal Pĕchouček   Czech Technical University, Czech Republic

Program Co-chairs

Ralph Bergmann   Universität Trier, Germany
Gabriela Lindemann   Humboldt Universität zu Berlin, Germany

Steering Committee

Hans-Dieter Burkhard   Humboldt-Universität zu Berlin, Germany
Stefan Kirn   Universität Hohenheim, Germany
Matthias Klusch   DFKI, Germany
Jörg P. Müller   TU Clausthal, Germany
Rainer Unland   Universität Duisburg-Essen, Germany
Gerhard Weiss   SCCH Hagenberg, Austria

Program Committee

Klaus-Dieter Althoff   Universität Hildesheim, Germany
Bernhard Bauer   Universität Augsburg, Germany
Federico Bergenti   Università degli Studi di Parma, Italy
Michael Berger   Siemens AG, Germany
Ralph Bergmann   Universität Trier, Germany
Lars Braubach   Universität Hamburg , Germany
Gerhard Brewka   Universität Leipzig, Germany
Hans-Dieter Burkhard   Humboldt-Universität zu Berlin, Germany
Monique Calisti   Whitestein Technologies, Switzerland
Mehdi Dastani   Universiteit Utrecht, The Netherlands
Jörg Denzinger   University of Calgary, Canada
Jürgen Dix   Technische Universität Clausthal, Germany
Torsten Eymann   Universität Bayreuth, Germany
Jean-Pierre George   Université Paul Sabatier, France
Paolo Giorgini   Università degli Studi di Trento, Italy
Heikki Helin   TeliaSonera, Finland
Stefan Kirn   Universität Hohenheim, Germany
Matthias Klusch   DFKI, Germany

Franziska Klügl	Universität Würzburg, Germany
Ryszard Kowalczyk	Swinburne University of Technology, Australia
Daniel Kudenko	University of York, UK
Winfried Lamersdorf	Universität Hamburg, Germany
Jürgen Lind	iteratec GmbH, Germany
Gabriela Lindemann	Humboldt-Universität zu Berlin, Germany
Stefano Lodi	Università di Bologna, Italy
Beatriz Lopez	Universitat de Girona, Spain
Mirjam Minor	Universität Trier, Germany
Heinz-Jürgen Müller	Berufsakademie Mannheim , Germany
Jörg P. Müller	Technische Universität Clausthal, Germany
Volker Nissen	Technische Universität Ilmenau, Germany
Andrea Omicini	Università di Bologna, Italy
Michal Pěchouček	Czech Technical University, Prague
Wolfgang Renz	HAW Hamburg, Germany
Abdel Badeh Salem	Ain Shams University, Egypt
Von-Wun Soo	National Tsing Hua University, Taiwan
Steffen Staab	Universität Koblenz-Landau, Germany
Ingo Timm	Universität Frankfurt, Germany
Robert Tolksdorf	Freie Universität Berlin, Germany
Adelinde Uhrmacher	Universität Rostock, Germany
Rainer Unland	Universität Duisburg-Essen, Germany
Wiebe Van der Hoek	University of Liverpool, UK
Laszlo Zsolt Varga	MTA SZTAKI, Hungary
Danny Weyns	Katholieke Universiteit Leuven, The Netherlands
Cees Witteveen	TU Delft, The Netherlands
Georg Weichhart	Profactor, Austria

Additional Reviewers

Sameh Abdel Naby	Dirk Bade	Tina Balke
Tristan Behrens	Ralf Berger	Lars Braubach
Didac Busquets	Thomas Hubauer	Stefan König
Andreas Lattner	Christoph Niemann	Peter Novak
Alexander Pokahr	Meike Reichle	Christoph Ringelstein
Thorsten Schoeler	Fernando Silva Parreiras	Sergej Sizov
Danny Weyns	Sonja Zaplata	

Table of Contents

Invited Talks

Research Papers

Logic for Automated Mechanism Design and Analysis

Michael Wooldridge

University of Liverpool
Department of Computer Science
Liverpool L69 3BX, UK
mjw@liv.ac.uk

Abstract. Recent years have witnessed an explosion of interest in the issues surrounding the use of social choice mechanisms and economic resource allocation mechanisms in settings where the participants are computer programs. Algorithmic mechanism design, and the recent emergence of computational social choice theory are two examples of this growth of interest. If we take seriously the idea that computational agents will participate in economically inspired mechanisms, then it is natural to consider the questions of knowledge representation and reasoning for them. In this talk, we describe our work in this area, particularly as it relates to the specification and verification of social choice mechanisms, and coordination mechanisms such as social laws. We motivate and introduce the main research issues in the area, discussing, for example, the succinct representation of social choice rules, the complexity of reasoning with such representations, and the handling of preferences. We conclude by showing discussing the relationship of our work to mechanism design as it is understood in economics. The talk will report joint work with Thomas Agotnes (Bergen), Wiebe van der Hoek (Liverpool), Marc Pauly (Stanford), and Paul E. Dunne (Liverpool).

R. Bergmann et al. (Eds.): MATES 2008, LNAI 5244, p. 1, 2008.

Coordination in Multi-Agent Systems: Towards a Technology of Agreement

Sascha Ossowski

Centre for Intelligent Information Technologies (CETINIA),
Universidad Rey Juan Carlos,
Calle Tulipán s/n,
28933 Móstoles (Madrid), Spain
sascha.ossowski@urjc.es

Abstract. It is commonly accepted that coordination is a key characteristic of multi-agent systems and that, in turn, the capability of coordinating with others constitutes a centrepiece of agenthood. However, the key elements of coordination models, mechanisms, and languages for multi-agent systems are still subject to considerable debate. This paper provides a brief overview of different approaches to coordination in multi-agent systems. It will then show how these approaches relate to current efforts working towards a paradigm for smart, next-generation distributed systems, where coordination is based on the concept of agreement between computational agents.

1 Introduction

Most current transactions and interactions at business level, but also at leisure level, are mediated by computers and computer networks. From email, over social networks, to virtual worlds, the way people work and enjoy their free time has changed dramatically in less than a generation time. This change has made that IT research and development focuses on aspects like new Human-Computer Interfaces or enhanced routing and network management tools. However, the biggest impact has been on the way applications are thought and developed. These applications require components to which more and more complex tasks can be delegated, components that show higher levels of intelligence, components that are capable of sophisticated ways of interacting, as they are massively distributed, sometimes embedded in all sort of appliances and sensors. In order to allow for an efficient design and implementation of systems of these characteristics, it is necessary to effectively enable, structure, and regulate their communications in different contexts.

Such an enterprise raises a number of technological challenges. Firstly, the open distributed nature of such systems adds to the *heterogeneity* of its components. The system structure may evolve at runtime, as new nodes may appear or disappear at will. There is also a need for on-the-fly alignment of certain concepts that interactions relate to, as the basic ontological conventions in such systems will be very limited. The *dynamicity* of the environment calls for a continuous *adaptation* of the structures that regulate the components' interactions, so as to achieve and sustain desired functional properties. But also non-functional issues related to *scalability*, *security*, and

R. Bergmann et al. (Eds.): MATES 2008, LNAI 5244, pp. 2–12, 2008.

usability need to be taken into account. When designing mechanisms that address these challenges, the notion of *autonomy* becomes central: components may show complex patterns of activity aligned with the different goals of their designers, while it is usually impossible to directly influence their behaviour from the outside.

Coordination in multi-agent system (MAS) aims at harmonising the interactions of multiple autonomous components or agents. Therefore, it appears promising to review different conceptual frameworks for MAS coordination, and to analyse the potential and limitations of the work done in that field with regard to some of the aforementioned challenges.

This paper is organised as follows. Section 2 provides a brief overview of coordination in MAS. Section 3 proposes the notion of *agreement* as a centrepiece of an integrated approach to coordination in open distributed systems, and outlines some research topics related to the vision of a technology of agreement. Some conclusions are drawn in Section 4.

2 Coordination in Multi-agent Systems

Maybe the most widely accepted conceptualisation of coordination in the MAS field originates from Organisational Science. It defines coordination the *management of dependencies* between organisational activities [21]. One of the many workflows in an organisation, for instance, may involve a secretary writing a letter, an official signing it, and another employee sending it to its final destination. The interrelation among these activities is modelled as a *producer/consumer* dependency, which can be managed by inserting additional *notification* and *transportation* actions into the workflow.

It is straightforward to generalise this approach to coordination problems in multi-agent systems. The subjects whose activities need to be coordinated are the agents, while the entities between which dependencies arise are usually goals, actions or plans. Depending on the characteristics of the MAS environment, a taxonomy of dependencies can be established, and a set of potential coordination actions assigned to each of them (e.g. [36], [26]). Within this model, the *process* of coordination is to accomplish two major tasks: first, a *detection* of dependencies needs to be performed, and second, a *decision* respecting which coordination action to apply must be taken. A coordination *mechanism* shapes the way that agents perform these tasks [24].

The *result* of coordination, and its *quality*, is conceived differently at different levels of granularity. Understanding coordination as *a way of adapting to the environment* [36] is quite well suited to address the issue from a *micro-level* (agent-centric) perspective. This is particularly true for multi-agent settings. If new acquaintances enter an agent's environment, coordination amounts to re-assessing its former goals, plans and actions, so as to account for the new (potential) dependencies between itself and other agents. If a planning agent, for instance, is put into a multi-agent environment, it will definitely have to accommodate its individual plans to the new dependencies between its own prospective actions and potential actions of others, trying to exploit possible synergies (others may free certain relevant blocks for it), and avoiding harmful dependencies (making sure that others do not unstack intentionally constructed stacks etc). At this level, the result of coordination, the agent's adapted individual plan, is the better the closer it takes the agent to the achievement of its goals in the multi-agent environment.

From a *macro-level* (MAS-centric) perspective, the outcome of coordination can be conceived a "global" plan (or decision, action etc.). This may be a "joint plan" [29] if the agents reach an explicit agreement on it during the coordination process, or just the sum of the agents' individual plans (or decisions, actions etc. – sometimes called "multi-plan" [27]) as perceived by an external observer. Roughly speaking, the quality of the outcome of coordination at the macro-level can be evaluated with respect to the agents' joint goals or the desired functionality of the MAS as a whole. If no such notion can be ascribed to the MAS, other, more basic features can be used instead. A good result of coordination, for instance, often relates to "efficiency", which frequently comes down to the notion of Pareto-optimality. The amount of resources necessary for coordination (e.g. the number of messages necessary) is also sometimes used as a measure of efficiency.

The dependency model of coordination appears to be particularly adequate for *representing* relevant features of coordination problems in MAS. Frameworks based on this model have been used to capture coordination requirements in a variety of interesting MAS domains (e.g. [11]). It is also useful to rationalise observed coordination behaviour in line with a knowledge-level perspective [22]. Still, dependency detection may become a rather knowledge intensive task, which is further complicated by incomplete and potentially inconsistent local views of the agents. Moreover, making timely decisions that lead to efficient coordination actions is also everything but trivial. The problem becomes even more difficult when agents pursuing partially conflicting goals come into play [26]. In all but the simplest MAS, the instrumentation of these tasks gives rise to complex patterns of interactions among agents.

From a design perspective, coordination is probably best conceived as the effort of *governing the space of interaction* [6] of a MAS, as the basic challenge amounts to how to make agents converge on interaction patterns that adequately (i.e. instrumentally with respect to desired MAS features) solve the dependency detection and decision tasks. A variety of approaches that tackle this problem can be found in the literature, shaping the interaction space either directly, by making assumptions on agent behaviours and/or knowledge, or indirectly, by modifying the *context* of the agents in the MAS environment. The applicability of these mechanisms depends largely on the number and type of assumptions that one may make regarding the possibility of manipulating agent programs, agent populations, or the agents' environment. This, in turn, is dependent on the characteristics of the coordination problem at hand.

The RICA-J framework [31], for instance, provides an ontology of interaction types, together with their associated protocols. Agents can choose to play or abandon certain roles within an interaction but, when using the framework, an agent programmer is limited to using protocol compliant actions.

Governing coordination infrastructures make a clear separation between the *enabling* services that they provide (e.g. communication channel or blackboard-based communication primitives) and the *governing* aspects of interaction, which are usually described within a declarative language (e.g. programmable tuple spaces) [25]. The access regulations for the elements of the MAS environment (resources, services, etc) expressed in such a language are often termed *environment laws* [30].

Electronic Institutions (EI) [23] use organisational abstractions to shape the interactions of the agents participating in them. Agents play different roles in the (sub-) protocols that, together with additional rules of behaviour, determine the sequences of illocutions that are permitted within a particular instance of a scene. Scenes, in turn, are interconnected and synchronised by means of transitions within a performative structure. Norms, as additional institutional abstractions, express further behaviour restrictions for agents. In the EI framework, agents can only interact with each other through specific institutional agents, called governors [13], which assure that all behaviour complies with the norms and that it obeys the performative structure. So, different from the aforementioned approaches, the governing or regulating responsibility is transferred from the infrastructure to specialized middle agents.

From the point of view of an individual agent, the problem of coordination boils down to finding the sequence of actions that, given the regulations within the system (or, if possible in a certain environment, the expected cost of transgressing them), best achieves its goals. In practice, this implies a series of non-trivial problems. Models of coalition formation determine when and with whom to form a team for the achievement of some common (sub-) goal, and how to distribute the benefits of synergies that arise from this cooperation [32]. Distributed planning approaches [12] may determine how to (re-)distribute tasks among team members and how to integrate results. From an individual agent's perspective, the level of trustworthiness of others is central to almost every stage of these processes, so as to determine whether other agents are likely to honour the commitments that have been generated [33].

An appealing way to tackle both the system-level and the agent-level requirements is to take an organisation-oriented tack towards the problem of MAS coordination. Organisational models underlying approaches such as Agent-Group-Role [14], MOISE [18], EI [23], or RICA [31] provide a rich set of concepts to specify and structure mechanisms that govern agent interactions through the corresponding infrastructures or middleware. But they can also facilitate the agents' local decision-making tasks. For instance, role and interaction taxonomies can be used to find suitable interactions partners, by providing additional information regarding the usability of services in a certain interaction context [15]. Structural information about roles can also be used for the bootstrapping of reputation mechanisms, when only very limited information about past interactions is available in the system [5]. Role hierarchies, and other types of structural information, can also be extended on-the-fly to improve system performance [17]. In general, the fact that organisational structures may dynamically evolve, shifts the attention from their traditional use as a *design-time* coordination mechanism for mainly closed distributed problem-solving systems, to an adaptive *run-time* coordination mechanism also applicable to open MAS [24].

3 Towards a Technology of Agreement

The previous section has given a brief overview of work on coordination mechanisms that has been carried in the MAS field. Even though an attempt has been made to structure and present it in some coherent manner, the reader will have noticed that several quite different approaches and mechanisms coexist under the "umbrella" of the term coordination. Not all of them are relevant to the challenges for the design of open distributed systems outlined in the introduction. For instance, the whole set of *coupled* coordination mechanisms [35] are effectively useless for the purpose of this paper, as they require having a direct influence on the agent programs. On the other hand, the problem of semantic interoperability is usually outside the scope of MAS coordination models and languages.

The notion of *agreement* among computational agents appears to be better suited as the fundamental notion for the proposal outlined in this paper. Until recently, the concept of agreement was a domain of study mainly for philosophers, sociologists and was only applicable to human societies. In recent years, the growth of disciplines such as social psychology, socio-biology, social neuroscience, together with the spectacular emergence of the information society technologies, have changed this situation. Presently, agreement and all the processes and mechanisms implicated in reaching agreements between different kinds of agents are a subject of research and analysis also from technology-oriented perspectives.

The process of agreement-based coordination can be designed based on two main elements:

(1) a normative context, that determines the rules of the game, i.e. interaction patterns and additional restrictions on agent behaviour; and
(2) a call-by-agreement interaction method, where an agreement for action between the agents that respects the normative context is established first; then the actual enactment of the action is requested.

The techniques based on organizational structures discussed in the previous section will be useful to specify and design such systems. In addition, semantic alignment, norms, argumentation and negotiation, as well as trust and reputation mechanisms will be in the "agreement technology sandbox".

Semantics

Semantic technologies constitute a centrepiece of the approach as semantic problems pervade all the others. Solutions to semantic mismatches and alignment of ontologies (e.g. [4]) are needed to have a common understanding of norms or of deals, just to put two examples. In particular, it is interesting to look into how far policies and measures of trust can be used to decide which alignments and mappings between heterogeneous formats to apply, assuming that data, alignments, as well as trust-relevant meta-data is published and reusable by agents on the Web. Such published alignments shall allow combinations of knowledge bases based on static mapping rules, dynamic service calls and allow partial revocations of data published by other agents. Semantic-alignment protocols and algorithms interweaving alignment and negotiation in cooperation are needed, so as to analyse and design basic resource management mechanisms for locating adequate services in open, large-scale, decentralized systems. The following challenges around semantic alignment appear particularly relevant:

- Integration of Ontologies and nonmonotonic Rules: Nonmonotonicity seems inevitable for ontological agreement between agents in order to deal with consistent, but closed subsets of ontologies in open environments which would otherwise involve logically inconsistent superfluous ontological information.
- Querying over distributed ontologies involving alignments: Queries for data, grounded in distributedly published ontologies and mapping/alignment rules, impose new challenges. The right tradeoffs between expressivity and efficiency for ontology, mapping and query languages are to be found.

- Alignment with standards: it must be explored how existing standardization efforts in the area can be enhanced to cater for agreement relevant information such as trust, provenance and policies and how these additions can be exploited for open, distributed access to heterogeneous data and service.

Norms

Normative systems need to be specified so that they may be properly implemented and one may reason about them for a variety of purposes. Reasoning about the system is necessary for the designer of the system to assure that the system has adequate properties. It is also essential for the designer of agents whose interactions will be regulated to assure that they conform to the rules. Reasoning about the normative system may also be necessary at run-time because complex multiagent systems usually need dynamic regulations. The problem is interesting, from an individual agents' perspective, because norm adoption and compliance involve complex decision-making, and is also conceptually significant because currently available formalisms tend to be heavy and consequently there are few practical implementations [16]. Major issues to be addressed include:

- Normative reasoning and negotiated flexibility. A serious challenge is the fact that norms need to be interpreted and instantiated in specific situations; second, that norms (especially when applied to a specific case) can be in conflict; third, that it is possible that to work well, to fulfil the assigned mission of the role, and to be loyal with the organization, agents may need to violate a given rule or procedure. Any organization has such a problem (and it is one of the internal reasons for its adaptation and evolution). So agents must not only be norm-sensitive; they also need to be able to interpret and compare norms, and to negotiate and reach agreements about norm interpretation, application, and violation.
- Usability of norms. The adoption of formal, non-ambiguous, and machine understandable norms should not prevent end users from understanding thoroughly the norms and their effects, therefore suitable interfaces are needed to enhance user understanding and awareness of the current norms. Also, advanced norm explanation techniques are needed to enhance user awareness of (and control on) the norms enforced by the systems that the user is interacting with.

Organizations

Techniques of *virtual organisations* specify how to solve a complex task/problem by a number of agents in a declarative way. The agents participating in an organisation can work together and form teams for the solution of a particular task within the scope of the organisational objectives. The particular organisation of the group of agents will thus be the answer to the complexity of the problem. For instance, in a hierarchical organisation when not enough agents are found at a certain level to solve a problem, a reorganisation of the hierarchy is to be made that flattens the structure. Methods to support organizational change will play a critical role to this respect. As systems grow to include hundreds or thousands of agents, it is necessary to move from an agent-centric view of coordination and control to an organization-centric one [3]. Social structures can be explicitly expressed and shaped through organisational concepts, and can be exploited by the agents to cope with the difficulties of solving complex tasks in a coherent and efficient manner. Challenges include:

- Organisational Teamwork: The processes of team formation, coordination and dissolution are all based upon dynamic agreements that are forged and maintained within the limits imposed by organisational structures. Mechanisms are needed that create joint plans to carry out a set of tasks by means of a collaborative process among agents, deciding which agreement each agent is committed to. In this type of planning, the "assignments" of tasks or parts of a plan are not fully specified and need to be further developed by the agent. This creates interesting problems of trust regarding plan sharing and the assembly sub-plans.
- Organisational change: In open environments, organisational structures must continuously evolve so as to efficiently promote effective teamwork. Planning, case-based reasoning and learning models may be used to detect and implement these changes.
- Design methodologies and tools: To sow the seeds for industrial take-up, effective guidelines for the design of organisational structures with regard to certain types of problems need to be investigated. These guidelines need to be supported by tools that help programmers in the development of agents and organizations.

Argumentation and negotiation

Decision-making processes need to be investigated that are useful to develop a variety of agreement management methods to try and reach satisfactory agreements, good enough with respect to the needs and requirements of agents. Classical works in the field of negotiation methods, based on purely economic/game theoretical grounds, have proved to be limited in modelling real life exchanges. However, some formal guarantees are indeed required, especially in the realm of sensitive data, privacy preservation, and security – which calls for convergence of different approaches currently pursued in different areas. Frameworks that integrate argumentation in negotiation are needed, so as to supply the negotiating parties with additional information and help them convince each other by adequate arguments [2] [7]. Key topics to be addressed include:

- Argumentation in negotiation: The basic idea behind an argumentation-based approach is that by exchanging arguments, the mental states of agents may evolve, and consequently, the status of offers may change. It is worthwhile to explore how formal properties of argumentation frameworks can be identified, interpreted and exploited in a negotiation context.
- Strategies for bounded interactions: Negotiation, argumentation and contracting need practical bounds to fit practical requirements arising, for instance, from computational limitations of pervasive computing scenarios. Proper mechanisms need to be studied to meet these bounds and simultaneously preserve good properties (e.g. related to negotiation success, information disclosure minimization and the like) overcoming horizon effects that are not tackled by the existing approaches.

Trust

Trust is a critical prerequisite of any agreement process, as it helps to reduce the complexity of decisions that have to be taken in the presence of many risks. Trust can be built based on a range of different kinds of evidence, each having different strength and reliability [33]. For instance, trust will permit to model social security, e.g., a probabilistic security model that agents can use for decision making by fixing thresholds of trust for the acceptance of agreements. Norms as *a priori* restrictions for agreement acceptance should be complemented by trust-based mechanisms that analyse interactions *a posteriori* so as to draw conclusions for future behaviour. Particularly relevant challenges to this respect include:

- Scalability: When trust is based on other agents' opinions its computation does not scale on large societies. The use of social network analysis techniques would permit the clustering of agents into organisations and thus allow for scalable solutions.
- Semantics: The quest for a common global ontology seems abandoned as an impossible job. Local ontologies are abundant and any trust model will need to take into account how to deal with erroneous behaviour that may be caused by misunderstandings.
- Similarity: The scarcity of exact past experiences for an agreement under discussion requires that agents use 'similar' cases from the past in order to assess whether trust can be put on a new agreement. Case-based reasoning techniques and similarity functions are central in trust models.
- Balance between norms and trust: Norms and trust can somehow be seen as two extremes in a continuum. The more norms that can be enforced the less risk in the opponent's behaviour and thus the less need to rely on trust measures. However, norm enforcement has an associated cost that is otherwise negligible when decisions are based on trust. Techniques for finding the right point in the continuum are needed, that determine how "normative" a interaction among a given set of agents should be.

One may conceive the aforementioned topics in a "tower structure", with semantic technologies at the bottom layer and trust mechanisms at the top, where each level provides functionality to the levels above [1]. Notice, however, that there is also a certain feedback from higher to lower layers as, for instance, reputation mechanisms may influence organisational structures such as role and interaction hierarchies [17]; and this information can as well be used for semantic alignment [4] and discovery [15].

4 Discussion

This paper has presented an overview of different approaches to coordination in the MAS field. It has been argued that the notion of agreement is essential to instil coordination in open distributed systems. Some existing technologies from the field of MAS coordination can be applied to this respect, but others – and in particular semantic technologies – need to be added. Several research efforts are currently ongoing that may contribute to the development of a "technology of agreement" in one or another way. The attempt to harmonise these efforts, which is currently being carried out at European level, promotes the emergence of a new paradigm for next generation distributed systems based on the notion of *agreement* between computational agents [9].

Acknowledgements

Many ideas reported in this paper draw upon joint work with Carles Sierra, Vicent Botti, and others, in the framework of a Spanish national project on "Agreement

Technology". This term was first mentioned by Mike Wooldridge in internal discussions at the AAMAS conference in 2004. It has also been used as a title for a conference by Nick Jennings. I am also thankful to Axel Polleres, Cristiano Castelfranchi, Leila Amgoud, and Piero Bonatti for their comments regarding the different technological challenges related to a computational notion of agreement, as well as to Andrea Omicini for our discussions on the different stances on coordination in multi-agent systems. This work was partially supported by the Spanish Ministry of Science and Innovation, grants TIN2006-14630-C03-02 and CSD2007-00022 (CONSOLIDER-INGENIO 2010).

References

[1] Agreement Technologies project homepage,
    http://www.agreement-technologies.org/
[2] Amgoud, L., Dimopolous, Y., Moraitis, P.: A unified and general framework for argumentation-based negotiation. In: Proc. 6th Int. Joint Conference on Autonomous Agents and Multi-Agents Systems (AAMAS 2007) IFAAMAS, pp. 963–970 (2007)
[3] Argente, E., Julian, V., Botti, V.: Multi-Agent System Development based on Organizations. Electronic Notes in Theoretical Computer Science 150(3), 55–71 (2006)
[4] Atienza, M., Schorlemmer, M.: I-SSA - Interaction-situated Semantic Alignment. In: Proc Int. Conf. on Cooperative Information Systems (CoopIS 2008) (to appear, 2008)
[5] Billhardt, H., Hermoso, R., Ossowski, S., Centeno, R.: Trust-based Service Provider Selection in Open Environments. In: Proc. ACM Symposium on Applied Computing (SAC-2007), pp. 1375–1380. ACM Press, New York (2007)
[6] Busi, N., Ciancarini, P., Gorrieri, R., Zavattaro, G.: Coordination Models - A Guided Tour. In: Omicini, et al. (eds.) Coordination of Internet Agents: Models, Technologies, and Applications, pp. 6–24. Springer, Heidelberg (2001)
[7] Caminada, M., Amgoud, L.: On the evaluation of argumentation formalisms. Artificial Intelligence Journal 171(5-6), 286–310 (2007)
[8] Castelfranchi, C., Dignum, F., Jonker, C., Treur, J.: Deliberative Normative Agents - Principles and Architecture. In: Jennings, N.R. (ed.) ATAL 1999. LNCS, vol. 1757, pp. 364–378. Springer, Heidelberg (2000)
[9] COST Act. IC0801, http://www.cost.esf.org/index.php?id=110&action_number=IC0801
[10] Debenham, J., Sierra, C.: Merging intelligent agency and the Semantic Web. Knowledge-Based Systems 21(3), 184–191 (2008)
[11] Decker, K.: TAEMS: A Framework for Environment Centered Analysis and Design of Coordination Mechanisms. In: O'Hare, Jennings (eds.) Foundations of Distributed Artificial Intelligence, pp. 119–138. John Wiley and Sons, Chichester (1996)
[12] Durfee, E.: Distributed Problem Solving and Planning. In: Luck, M., Mařík, V., Štěpánková, O., Trappl, R. (eds.) ACAI 2001 and EASSS 2001. LNCS (LNAI), vol. 2086, pp. 118–149. Springer, Heidelberg (2001)
[13] Esteva, M., Rosell, B., Rodríguez-Aguilar, J.A., Arcos, J.L.: AMELI - An agent-based middleware for electronic institutions. In: Proc. of the Third Int. Joint Conference on Autonomous Agents and Multiagent Systems (AAMAS-2004), pp. 236–243. ACM Press, New York (2004)
[14] Ferber, J., Gutknecht, O., Fabien, M.: From Agents to Organizations - An Organizational View of Multi-agent Systems. In: Giorgini, P., Müller, J.P., Odell, J.J. (eds.) AOSE 2003. LNCS, vol. 2935, pp. 214–230. Springer, Heidelberg (2004)

[15] Fernández, A., Ossowski, S.: Exploiting Organisational Information for Service Coordination in Multiagent Systems. In: Proc. of the Int. Conf. on Autonomous Agents and Multiagent Systems (AAMAS-2008), pp. 257–264. IFAAMAS (2008)

[16] Gaertner, D., García-Camino, A., Noriega, P., Rodríguez-Aguilar, J.A., Vasconcelos, W.: Distributed norm management in regulated multiagent systems. In: Proc. Int. Joint Conference on Autonomous Agents and Multiagent Systems (AAMAS-2007), pp. 624–631. IFAAMAS (2007)

[17] Hermoso, R., Centeno, R., Billhardt, H., Ossowski, S.: Extending Virtual Organizations to improve trust mechanisms (Short Paper). In: Proc. of the Int. Conf. on Autonomous Agents and Multiagent Systems (AAMAS-2008), pp. 1489–1492. IFAAMAS (2008)

[18] Hubner, J., Sichman, J., Boissier, O.: Developing organised multiagent systems using the MOISE+ model: programming issues at the system and agent levels. Int. Journal of Agent-Oriented Software Engineering 1(3/4), 370–395 (2006)

[19] Klusch, M., Sycara, K.: Brokering and matchmaking for coordination of agent societies: a survey. In: En Coordination of Internet Agents: Models, Technologies, and Applications (Omicini y otros), pp. 197–224. Springer, Heidelberg (2001)

[20] Klusch, M., Fries, B., Sycara, K.: Automated Semantic Web Service Discovery with OWLS-MX. In: Proceedings of 5th International Conference on Autonomous Agents and Multi- Agent Systems (AAMAS-2006), pp. 915–922. ACM Press, New York (2006)

[21] Malone, T., Crowston, K.: The Interdisciplinary Study of Co-ordination. Computing Surveys 26(1), 87–119 (1994)

[22] Newell, A.: Reflections on the Knowledge Level. Artificial Intelligence 59, 31–38 (1993)

[23] Noriega, P., Sierra, C.: Electronic Institutions – Future Trends and Challenges. In: Klusch, M., Ossowski, S., Shehory, O. (eds.) CIA 2002. LNCS (LNAI), vol. 2446, pp. 14–17. Springer, Heidelberg (2002)

[24] Omicini, A., Ossowski, S.: Objective versus Subjective Coordination in the Engineering of Agent Systems. In: Klusch, et al. (eds.) Intelligent Information Agents – The European AgentLink Perspective, pp. 179–202. Springer, Heidelberg (2003)

[25] Omicini, A., Ossowski, S., Ricci, A.: Coordination Infrastructures in the Engineering of Multiagent Systems. In: Bergenti, Gleizes, Zambonelli (eds.) Methodologies and software engineering for agent systems – The Agent-Oriented Software Engineering Handbook, pp. 273–296. Kluwer, Dordrecht (2004)

[26] Ossowski, S.: Co-ordination in Artificial Agent Societies. LNCS (LNAI), vol. 1535. Springer, Heidelberg (1999)

[27] Ossowski, S.: Constraint Based Coordination of Autonomous Agents. Electronic Notes in Theoretical Computer Science 48, 211–226 (2001)

[28] Ossowski, S., Menezes, R.: On Coordination and its Significance to Distributed and Multi-Agent Systems. Journal of Concurrency and Computation - Practice and Experience 18(4), 359–370 (2006)

[29] Rosenschein, J., Zlotkin, G.: Designing Conventions for Automated Negotiation. AI Magazine 15(3), 29–46 (1995)

[30] Schumacher, M., Ossowski, S.: The governing environment. In: Weyns, D., Van Dyke Parunak, H., Michel, F. (eds.) E4MAS 2005. LNCS (LNAI), vol. 3830, pp. 88–104. Springer, Heidelberg (2006)

[31] Serrano, J.M., Ossowski, S.: On the Impact of Agent Communication Languages on the Implementation of Agent Systems. In: Klusch,, et al. (eds.) Cooperative Information Agents VIII. LNCS, vol. 2782, pp. 92–106. Springer, Heidelberg (2004)

[32] Shehory, O., Sycara, K., Somesh, J.: Multi-agent Coordination through Coalition Forma-
        tion. In: Singh,, Rao,, Wooldridge (eds.) Intelligent Agents IV - Agent Theories, Archi-
        tectures and Languages. LNCS, vol. 1365, pp. 143–154. Springer, Heidelberg (1998)
[33] Sabater, J., Sierra, C.: Review on Computational Trust and Reputation Models. Artificial.
        Intelligence Review 24(1), 33–60 (2005)
[34] Sierra, C., Debenham, J.: Information-Based Agency. In: Proc Int. Joint Conference on
        AI (IJCAI-2007), pp. 1513–1518. AAAI Press, Menlo Park (2007)
[35] Tolksdorf, R.: Models of Coordination. In: Omicini, Zambonelli, Tolksdorf (eds.) Engi-
        neering Societies in an Agent World, pp. 78–92. Springer, Heidelberg (2000)
[36] Von Martial, F.: Co-ordinating Plans of Autonomous Agents. LNCS (LNAI), vol. 610.
        Springer, Heidelberg (1992)

Optimistic-Pessimistic Q-Learning Algorithm for Multi-Agent Systems

Natalia Akchurina

International Graduate School of Dynamic Intelligent Systems,
University of Paderborn, Warburger Str. 100, 33098 Paderborn, Germany
anatalia@mail, uni-paderborn.de

Abstract. A reinforcement learning algorithm OP-Q for multi-agent systems based on Hurwicz's optimistic-pessimistic criterion which allows to embed preliminary knowledge on the degree of environment friendliness is proposed. The proof of its convergence to stationary policy is given. Thorough testing of the developed algorithm against well-known reinforcement learning algorithms has shown that OP-Q can function on the level of its opponents.

Keywords: Algorithmic game theory, multi-agent reinforcement learning.

1 Introduction

Reinforcement learning turned out to be a technique that allowed robots to ride a bicycle, computers to play Backgammon on the level of human world masters and solve such complicated tasks of high dimensionality as elevator dispatching. Can it come to rescue in the next generation of challenging problems like playing football or bidding on virtual markets? Straightforward answer - no. The convergence of reinforcement learning algorithms is only guaranteed under the conditions of stationarity of the environment that is violated in multi-agent systems. Several algorithms [1], [2], [3], [4], [5] were proposed to extend this approach to multi-agent systems. The convergence was proved either for very restricted class of environments (strictly competitive or strictly cooperative) [1], [2], [5] or against very restricted class of opponents [3]. Convergence to Nash equilibrium was achieved only by Nash-Q [3] in self play for strictly competitive and strictly cooperative games under additional very restrictive condition that all equilibria encountered during learning stage are unique [2]. In this paper we propose an algorithm based on Hurwicz's optimistic-pessimistic criterion that will always converge to stationary policies (proved formally) but to best-response only if we guessed the criterion correctly.

Section 2 is devoted to formal definition of stochastic games — framework for multi-agent reinforcement learning, and presents the theorems that we will use while proving the convergence of our method in Sect. 3. Section 4 is devoted to analysis of the results of thorough testing of our algorithm against other reinforcement learning algorithms.

R. Bergmann et al. (Eds.): MATES 2008, LNAI 5244, pp. 13–24, 2008.

2   Preliminary Definitions and Theorems

Definition 1. *A 2-player stochastic game Γ is a 6-tuple $\langle S, A^1, A^2, r^1, r^2, p \rangle$, where S is the discrete state space $(|S| = m)$, A^k is the discrete action space of player k for $k = 1, 2$, $r^k : S \times A^1 \times A^2 \to \mathbb{R}$ is the payoff function for player k, $p : S \times A^1 \times A^2 \to \Delta$ is the transition probability map, where Δ is the set of probability distributions over state space S.*

Every state of a stochastic game can be regarded as a bimatrix game.

It is assumed that for every $s, s' \in S$ and for every action $a^1 \in A^1$ and $a^2 \in A^2$, transition probabilities $p(s'|s, a^1, a^2)$ are stationary for all $t = 0, 1, 2, \dots$ and $\sum_{s'=1}^{m} p(s'|s, a^1, a^2) = 1$.

A policy $\pi = (\pi_0, \dots, \pi_t, \dots)$ is defined over the whole course of the game. $\pi_t = (\pi_t(s_0), \dots, \pi_t(s_m))$ is called the *decision rule* at time t, where $\pi_t(s)$ is a mixed policy in state s. A policy π is called a *stationary policy* if $\pi_t = \overline{\pi}$ for all t (the decision rule is fixed over time).

Each player k $(k = 1, 2)$ strives to learn policy by immediate rewards so as to maximize its expected discounted cumulative reward (players do not know state transition probabilities and payoff functions):

$$v^k(s, \pi^1, \pi^2) = \sum_{t=0}^{\infty} \gamma^t E(r_t^k | \pi^1, \pi^2, s_0 = s)$$

where $\gamma \in [0, 1)$ is the discount factor, π^1 and π^2 are the policies of players 1 and 2 respectively and s is the initial state.

Definition 2. *A 2-player stochastic game Γ is called zero-sum when $r^1(s, a^1, a^2) + r^2(s, a^1, a^2) = 0$ for all $s \in S$, $a^1 \in A^1$ and $a^2 \in A^2$.*

2.1   Convergence Theorem

Theorem 1. *[6] Let $\mathcal{X}$ be an arbitrary set and assume that $\mathcal{B}$ is the space of bounded functions over $\mathcal{X}$ and $T : \mathcal{B}(\mathcal{X}) \to \mathcal{B}(\mathcal{X})$ is an arbitrary mapping with fixed point v^*. Let $U_0 \in \mathcal{B}(\mathcal{X})$ be an arbitrarily value function and $\mathcal{T} = (T_0, T_1, \dots)$ be a sequence of random operators $T_t : \mathcal{B}(\mathcal{X}) \times \mathcal{B}(\mathcal{X}) \to \mathcal{B}(\mathcal{X})$ such that $U_{t+1} = T_t(U_t, v^*)$ converges to Tv^* uniformly over $\mathcal{X}$. Let V_0 be an arbitrary value function, and define $V_{t+1} = T_t(V_t, V_t)$. If there exist random functions $0 \leq F_t(x) \leq 1$ and $0 \leq G_t(x) \leq 1$ satisfying the conditions below with probability 1, then V_t converges to v^* with probability 1 uniformly over $\mathcal{X}$:*

1. for all U_1 and $U_2 \in \mathcal{B}(\mathcal{X})$, and all $x \in \mathcal{X}$,

$$|T_t(U_1, v^*)(x) - T_t(U_2, v^*)(x)| \leq G_t(x)|U_1(x) - U_2(x)|$$

2. for all U and $V \in \mathcal{B}(\mathcal{X})$, and all $x \in \mathcal{X}$,

$$|T_t(U, v^*)(x) - T_t(U, V)(x)| \leq F_t(x) \sup_{x'} ||v^*(x') - V(x')||$$

3. $\sum_{t=1}^{n}(1 - G_t(x))$ converges to infinity uniformly in x as $n \to \infty$
4. there exists $0 \le \gamma < 1$ such that for all $x \in \mathcal{X}$ and large enough t

$$F_t(x) \le \gamma(1 - G_t(x))$$

2.2 Stochastic Approximation

Let $M(x)$ denote the expected value at level x of the response to a certain experiment. It is assumed that to each value x corresponds a random variable $Y = Y(x)$ with distribution function $Pr[Y(x) \le y] = H(y|x)$, such that $M(x) = \int_{-\infty}^{\infty} y dH(y|x)$ is the expected value of Y for the given x. Neither the exact nature of $H(y|x)$ nor that of $M(x)$ is known to the experimenter. It is desired to estimate the solution $x = \theta$ of the equation $M(x) = \alpha$, where α is a given constant by making successive observations on Y at levels $x_1, x_2, \ldots$

Let define a (nonstationary) Markov chain $\{x_n\}$ by taking x_1 to be an arbitrary constant and defining

$$x_{n+1} - x_n = \alpha_n(\alpha - y_n)$$

where y_n is a random variable such that

$$Pr[y_n \le y | x_n] = H(y|x_n)$$

Theorem 2. [7] If $\{\alpha_n\}$ is a fixed sequence of positive constants such that $0 < \sum_{n=1}^{\infty} \alpha_n^2 = A < \infty$ and $\sum_{n=1}^{\infty} \alpha_n = \infty$, if $\exists C > 0 : Pr[|Y(x)| \le C] = \int_{-C}^{C} dH(y|x) = 1$ for all x and $M(x)$ is nondecreasing, $M(\theta) = \alpha$, $M'(\theta) > 0$ then $\lim_{n\to\infty} E(x_n - \theta)^2 = 0$.

3 Optimistic-Pessimistic Q-Learning Algorithm

Competitive or cooperative environments are just extreme cases. In most cases the environment where our agent will function is competitive / cooperative to some degree. In this section we are proposing a reinforcement learning algorithm (OP-Q) based on Hurwicz's optimistic-pessimistic criterion [8] that allows us to embed preliminary knowledge of how friendly the environment will be. For example, parameter $\lambda = 0.3$ means that we believe that with 30% probability the circumstances will be favourable and the agents will act so as to maximize OP-Q's reward and in 70% will force it to achieve the minimum value. The algorithm is presented for 2-player stochastic game but without difficulty can be extended for arbitrary number of players.

Lemma 1. Let $Q, Q_1, Q_2 : S \times A^1 \times A^2 \to \mathbb{R}$ then for Hurwicz's criterion:

$$H(Q(s)) = \max_{a^1}[(1 - \lambda) \min_{a^2} Q(s, a^1, a^2) + \lambda \max_{a^2} Q(s, a^1, a^2)]$$

where $0 \le \lambda \le 1$ the following inequality holds:

$$|H(Q_1(s)) - H(Q_2(s))| \le \max_{a^1, a^2} |Q_1(s, a^1, a^2) - Q_2(s, a^1, a^2)|$$

Algorithm 3.1. Optimistic-Pessimistic Q-learning Algorithm (*for player 1*)

Input: parameters λ, α (see Theorem 3)
for all $s \in S$, $a^1 \in A^1$, and $a^2 \in A^2$ **do**
    $Q(s, a^1, a^2) \leftarrow 0$
    $V(s) \leftarrow 0$
    $\pi(s, a^1) \leftarrow 1/|A^1|$
end for
loop
    Choose action a^1 from s using policy $\pi(s)$ (with proper exploration)
    Take action a^1, observe opponent's action a^2, reward r^1 and succeeding state s'
    provided by the environment
    $Q(s, a^1, a^2) \leftarrow (1 - \alpha)Q(s, a^1, a^2) + \alpha(r^1 + \gamma V(s'))$
    $\pi(s, a^1) \leftarrow \begin{cases} 1 & a^1 = \arg\max_{a^{1'}} [(1 - \lambda) \min_{a^{2'}} Q(s, a^{1'}, a^{2'}) + \lambda \max_{a^{2'}} Q(s, a^{1'}, a^{2'})] \\ 0 & otherwise \end{cases}$
    $V(s) \leftarrow \max_{a^{1'}} [(1 - \lambda) \min_{a^{2'}} Q(s, a^{1'}, a^{2'}) + \lambda \max_{a^{2'}} Q(s, a^{1'}, a^{2'})]$
end loop

Proof.

$$|H(Q_1(s)) - H(Q_2(s))| =$$
$$= |\max_{a^1}[(1 - \lambda) \min_{a^2} Q_1(s, a^1, a^2) + \lambda \max_{a^2} Q_1(s, a^1, a^2)]$$
$$- \max_{a^1}[(1 - \lambda) \min_{a^2} Q_2(s, a^1, a^2) + \lambda \max_{a^2} Q_2(s, a^1, a^2)]|$$
$$\leq \max_{a^1} |(1 - \lambda)(\min_{a^2} Q_1(s, a^1, a^2) - \min_{a^2} Q_2(s, a^1, a^2))$$
$$+ \lambda(\max_{a^2} Q_1(s, a^1, a^2) - \max_{a^2} Q_2(s, a^1, a^2))|$$
$$\leq \max_{a^1}[|(1 - \lambda)(\min_{a^2} Q_1(s, a^1, a^2) - \min_{a^2} Q_2(s, a^1, a^2))|$$
$$+ |\lambda(\max_{a^2} Q_1(s, a^1, a^2) - \max_{a^2} Q_2(s, a^1, a^2))|]$$
$$\leq \max_{a^1}[(1 - \lambda) \max_{a^2} |Q_1(s, a^1, a^2) - Q_2(s, a^1, a^2)|$$
$$+ \lambda \max_{a^2} |Q_1(s, a^1, a^2) - Q_2(s, a^1, a^2)|]$$
$$= \max_{a^1} \max_{a^2} |Q_1(s, a^1, a^2) - Q_2(s, a^1, a^2)|$$

The above holds due to the triangle and the following inequalities [6]:

$$|\max_{a^k} Q_1(s, a^1, a^2) - \max_{a^k} Q_2(s, a^1, a^2)| \leq$$
$$\leq \max_{a^k} |Q_1(s, a^1, a^2) - Q_2(s, a^1, a^2)|$$

$$|\min_{a^k} Q_1(s, a^1, a^2) - \min_{a^k} Q_2(s, a^1, a^2)| \leq$$
$$\leq \max_{a^k} |Q_1(s, a^1, a^2) - Q_2(s, a^1, a^2)|$$

where $k = 1, 2$ □

Now we are ready to prove the convergence of our algorithm in a usual way [6], [1], [2].

Theorem 3. *If $\{\alpha_t\}$ is a sequence, such that: $\alpha_t > 0$, $\sum_{t=1}^{\infty} \chi(s_t = s, a_t^1 = a^1, a_t^2 = a^2)\alpha_t = \infty$[1] and $\sum_{t=1}^{\infty} \chi(s_t = s, a_t^1 = a^1, a_t^2 = a^2)\alpha_t^2 < \infty$ with probability 1 uniformly over $S \times A^1 \times A^2$ then OP-Q algorithm converges to stationary policy defined by fix point of operator*[2]:*

$$[TQ](s, a^1, a^2) = r^1(s, a^1, a^2) + \gamma \sum_{s'} p(s'|s, a^1, a^2)H(Q(s'))$$

Proof.
Let Q^* be fixed point of operator T and

$$M(x) = x - r^1(s, a^1, a^2)$$
$$- \gamma \sum_{s'} p(s'|s, a^1, a^2)H(Q^*(s')))$$

It's evident that conditions of Theorem 2 on M are fulfilled. $M(Q^*) = \alpha = 0$
The random approximating operator:

$$T_t(Q_t, Q^*)(s, a^1, a^2) = \begin{cases} (1 - \alpha_t)Q_t(s_t, a_t^1, a_t^2) + \alpha_t(r^1(s_t, a_t^1, a_t^2) + \gamma H(Q^*(s_t'))) \\ \quad if \ s = s_t \ and \ a^1 = a_t^1 \ and \ a^2 = a_t^2 \\ \\ Q_t(s, a^1, a^2) \ otherwise \end{cases}$$

where $y_t(s, a^1, a^2) = Q_t(s_t, a_t^1, a_t^2) - r^1(s_t, a_t^1, a_t^2) - \gamma H(Q^*(s_t'))$ if $s = s_t$ and $a^1 = a_t^1$ and $a^2 = a_t^2$.

It is evident that the other conditions will be satisfied if s_t' is randomly selected according to the probability distribution defined by $p(\cdot|s_t, a_t^1, a_t^2)$

Then according to Theorem 2 T_t approximates the solution of the equation $M(x) = 0$ uniformly over $\mathcal{X} = S \times A^1 \times A^2$. In other words, $T_t(Q_t, Q^*)$ converges to TQ^* uniformly over $\mathcal{X}$.

Let $G_t(s, a^1, a^2) = \begin{cases} 1 - \alpha_t & if \ s = s_t \ and \ a^1 = a_t^1 \ and \ a^2 = a_t^2 \\ 1 & otherwise \end{cases}$

and $F_t(s, a^1, a^2) = \begin{cases} \gamma\alpha_t & if \ s = s_t \ and \ a^1 = a_t^1 \ and \ a^2 = a_t^2 \\ 0 & otherwise \end{cases}$

Let's check up conditions of Theorem 1:

1. when $s = s_t$ and $a^1 = a_t^1$ and $a^2 = a_t^2$:

$$|T_t(Q_1, Q^*)(s, a^1, a^2) - T_t(Q_2, Q^*)(s, a^1, a^2)| =$$
$$= |(1 - \alpha_t)Q_1(s_t, a_t^1, a_t^2) +$$
$$+ \alpha_t(r^1(s_t, a_t^1, a_t^2) + \gamma H(Q^*(s_t')))$$

---

[1] χ denotes the characteristic function here.
[2] We assume here that OP-Q plays for the first agent.

$$- (1 - \alpha_t)Q_2(s_t, a_t^1, a_t^2) -$$
$$- \alpha_t(r^1(s_t, a_t^1, a_t^2) + \gamma H(Q^*(s_t')))|$$
$$= G_t(s, a^1, a^2)|Q_1(s, a^1, a^2) - Q_2(s, a^1, a^2)|$$

when $s \neq s_t$ or $a^1 \neq a_t^1$ or $a^2 \neq a_t^2$ it is evident that the condition holds.

2. when $s = s_t$ and $a^1 = a_t^1$ and $a^2 = a_t^2$:

$$|T_t(Q_1, Q^*)(s, a^1, a^2) - T_t(Q_1, Q_2)(s, a^1, a^2)| =$$
$$= |(1 - \alpha_t)Q_1(s_t, a_t^1, a_t^2) +$$
$$+ \alpha_t(r^1(s_t, a_t^1, a_t^2) + \gamma H(Q^*(s_t')))$$
$$- (1 - \alpha_t)Q_1(s_t, a_t^1, a_t^2) -$$
$$- \alpha_t(r^1(s_t, a_t^1, a_t^2) + \gamma H(Q_2(s_t')))|$$
$$= F_t(s_t, a_t^1, a_t^2)|H(Q^*(s_t')) - H(Q_2(s_t'))|$$
$$\leq F_t(s, a^1, a^2) \max_{a^1, a^2} |Q^*(s', a^1, a^2) - Q_2(s', a^1, a^2)|$$

The last inequality holds due to lemma 1.

when $s \neq s_t$ or $a^1 \neq a_t^1$ or $a^2 \neq a_t^2$ it is evident that the condition holds.

3. $\sum_{t=1}^n (1 - G_t(x))$ converges to infinity uniformly in x as $n \to \infty$ (see the assumption of the theorem)

4. the fourth condition evidently holds. □

4   Experiments

We tested OP-Q algorithm on 14 classes of 10-state 2×2 stochastic games derived with the use of Gamut [9] and on 1000 random 10-state 6-agent 2-action stochastic games (with uniformly distributed payoffs). Transition probabilities were derived from uniform distribution. For the sake of reliability we derived 1000 instances of each game class and made 10000 iterations. The agent plays as both the row agent and the column agent.

Below in this section we will present the average rewards (including exploration stage) of the developed OP-Q algorithm against the following well-known algorithms for multi-agent reinforcement learning:

– Q-learning [10] was initially developed for single-agent environments. The algorithm learns by immediate rewards a tabular function $Q(s, a)$ that returns the largest value for the action a that should be taken in each particular state s so as to maximize expected discounted cumulative reward. When applied to multi-agent systems Q learning algorithm ignores totally the presence of other agents though the later naturally influence its immediate rewards.

– $MinimaxQ$ [1] was developed for strictly competitive games and chooses the policy that maximizes its notion of the expected discounted cumulative reward believing that the circumstances will be against it.

- *FriendQ* [2] was developed for strictly cooperative games and chooses the action that will bring the highest possible expected discounted cumulative reward believing that the circumstances will favor it.
- *JAL* [4] believes that the average opponent's strategy very well approximates the opponent's policy in the future and takes it into account while choosing the action that maximizes its expected discounted cumulative reward.
- *PHC* [5] in contrast to Q learning algorithm changes its policy gradually in the direction of the highest Q values.
- *WoLF*[5] differs from PHC only in that it changes its policy faster when losing and more slowly when winning.

Because of the limitation on space we present the analysis only of the main game classes that though allows to gain the general notion of interaction between the developed OP-Q and the above presented multi-agent reinforcement learning algorithms. The test classes are presented in general form, where A, B, C, D are uniformly distributed in the interval $[-100, 100]$ payoffs and $A > B > C > D$. We will analyze the result as though OP-Q played for the row agent. For all games we chose neutral parameter $\lambda = 0.5$ for OP-Q, except random zero-sum games, and matching pennies. For these two classes we embedded our preliminary knowledge and set parameter λ to a more cautious value 0.3.

It should be noted that the results are being analyzed after the exploration stage that is why the small distinction from the figures can be easily explained by the fact that the later represent the average rewards including exploration phase. Q, PHC, WoLF, JAL turned out to have very similar final behaviour. Small difference in the performance of these algorithms is due to a bit different manner of tuning the policy and underlying mechanism.

4.1 Battle of the Sexes

After a short exploration phase OP-Q chooses the first strategy. Indeed Hurwicz's criterion for the first and the second strategies are:

$$H_1 = 0.5 \cdot (A + V) + 0.5 \cdot (C + V)$$

$$H_2 = 0.5 \cdot (C + V) + 0.5 \cdot (B + V)$$

where V is the OP-Q's notion of the expected discounted cumulative reward that it will get starting from the next step.

- *Q, PHC, WoLF* get the impression that in their environment (where OP-Q agent constantly plays the first strategy) the first strategy is much more profitable than the second one (B against C, where $B > C$) and play it. As a result OP-Q gets A as average reward after exploration stage and Q, PHC, WoLF only — B.
- *MinimaxQ* plays mixed policy $(\pi^2(a_1^2), \pi^2(a_2^2))$ with greater probability to play the first action $\pi^2(a_1^2) > \pi^2(a_2^2)$. And that is why OP-$Q$ gets $\pi^2(a_1^2)A + \pi^2(a_2^2)C$ in average (A more often than C) and MinimaxQ gets $\pi^2(a_1^2)B + \pi^2(a_2^2)C$ (B more frequently).

Table 1. Battle of the sexes

A,B	C,C
C,C	B,A

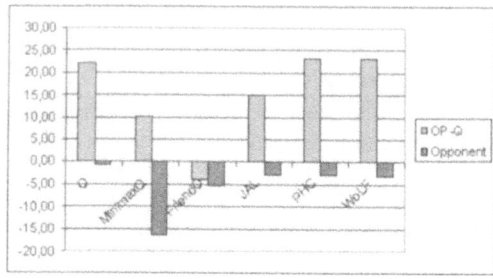

Fig. 1. Battle of the sexes

- *FriendQ* developed for cooperative environments believes that when it gets the best reward so do the other agents in the environment and that is why it is the most profitable for them to play the other part of the joint action that brings the largest reward to FriendQ. In battle of the sexes it is constantly playing the second action. As a result OP-Q and FriendQ both get very low C reward.
- *JAL* taking into account OP-Q's stationary $(1,0)$ policy chooses also the first more profitable for it action $(B > C)$. They respectively get A and B as average rewards.

4.2 Coordination Game

Sometimes Hurwicz's criterion is better for strategy 1 and sometimes for strategy 2. These events occur with equal probabilities for OP-Q agent with parameter $\lambda = 0.5$ and the second strategy is preferable more frequently for OP-Q agent with parameter $\lambda = 0.3$ for it is more sensitive to bad rewards than to good rewards.

- Q, *PHC*, *WoLF* also choose after some exploration the first strategy when OP-Q plays the first strategy. That leads to a very good reward for them both — A. When $\lambda \cdot A + (1 - \lambda) \cdot D < \lambda \cdot B + (1 - \lambda) \cdot C$, OP-$Q$ agent chooses the second strategy and then Q, PHC, WoLF choose also the second action. Then they get payoffs (B, B) correspondingly.
- *MinimaxQ* plays some mixed policy. They both get some combination of A and D rewards when OP-Q regards the first policy as a more profitable or B and C when the second one is preferable.

Table 2. Coordination game

A,A	D,D
C,C	B,B

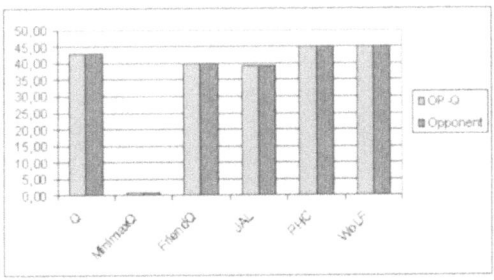

Fig. 2. Coordination game

- *FriendQ* being always sure that circumstances will be favorable plays the first action from the very beginning. Its assumption is correct when OP-Q plays the chooses the first action but leads to poor rewards otherwise.
- *JAL* though based on different mechanism acts in a similar way as Q, PHC, WoLF.

Because of its fear of low rewards OP-Q with $\lambda = 0.3$ plays the second strategy much more often than OP-Q with $\lambda = 0.5$ and that is why gets lower rewards in general.

4.3 Matching Pennies

OP-Q on the phase of exploration and further phase plays the first and the second strategies alternately.

- Q, *PHC*, *WoLF* on starting to get worse results switch the policy but OP-Q is more sensitive to bad results. Its higher average profit is explainable by the speed of its reactions. *PHC*, *WoLF* do not switch actions but tune policies — and their average rewards are higher.
- *MinimaxQ* plays $(0.5, 0, 5)$. They both get average rewards around zero after exploration.
- *FriendQ* plays the first or the second strategy. OP-Q upon exploring that the action it is playing is no more profitable switches its policy. That's why OP-Q gets much higher rewards.
- *JAL'* reactions are even slower because it takes into account average policy and it is difficult to notice a change in the current policy by it and that is why worse results than PHC, WoLF.

Table 3. Matching pennies

100,-100	-100,100
-100,100	100,-100

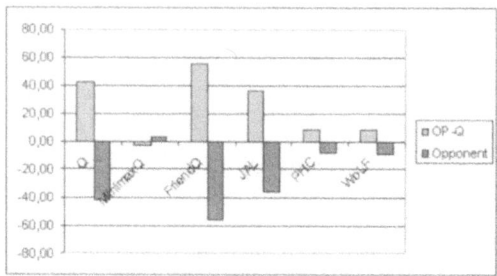

Fig. 3. Matching pennies game

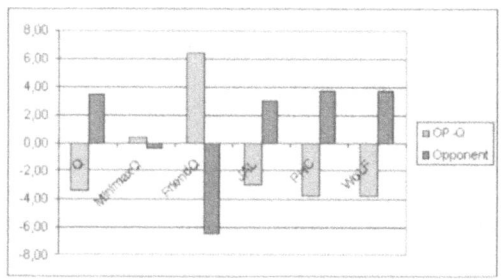

Fig. 4. Random zero game

4.4 Random Zero-Sum Game

- *Q, PHC, WoLF.* To analyze results we have to consider all the cases (16) of distribution of sign among payoffs. In 7 cases when OP-*Q* chooses his strategy both payoffs independently of the opponent's choice will be positive. For the gain for OP-*Q* is the loss for the opponent, the opponent will try to minimize the OP-*Q* reward. As in the majority of cases $\frac{9}{16}$ in the worst case OP-*Q* gets negative reward so the average is a small negative number.
- *MinimaxQ* plays mixed policy. Their average rewards are around zero.
- *FriendQ* loss is equal to OP-*Q*'s win, Friend*Q* will choose strategy with the smallest possible value *D*. If we just consider 24 cases how the payoffs can be ordered and what strategy in this case OP-*Q* will play it is easy to calculate that the average reward for OP-*Q* will be positive in 56% cases. That's why it is in average for OP-*Q* positive.
- *JAL*'s results can be explained in the same way as *Q*, PHC, WoLF but the mechanism is different.

4.5 Random Game

In Fig. 5 the average gains in the contest between OP-*Q*, *Q*, Friend*Q*, JAL, PHC and WoLF are presented. The results are averaged among 1000 games (10000 iterations each).

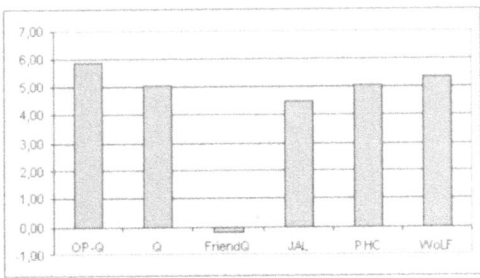

Fig. 5. Random game

5   Discussion and Conclusion

This paper is devoted to an actual topic of extending reinforcement learning approach for multi-agent systems. An algorithm based on Hurwicz's optimistic-pessimistic criterion is developed. Hurwicz's criterion allows us to embed initial knowledge of how friendly the environment in which the agent is supposed to function will be. A formal proof of the algorithm convergence to stationary policy is given. Thorough testing of the developed algorithm against Q, PHC, WoLF, Minimax$Q$, Friend$Q$, JAL showed that OP-Q functions on the level of its non-convergent opponents in the environments of different level of amicability by making its opponents follow more profitable for it policy.

References

1. Littman, M.L.: Markov games as a framework for multi-agent reinforcement learning. In: ICML, pp. 157–163 (1994)
2. Littman, M.L.: Friend-or-foe q-learning in general-sum games. In: Brodley, C.E., Danyluk, A.P. (eds.) ICML, pp. 322–328. Morgan Kaufmann, San Francisco (2001)
3. Hu, J., Wellman, M.P.: Multiagent reinforcement learning: theoretical framework and an algorithm. In: Proc. 15th International Conf. on Machine Learning, pp. 242–250. Morgan Kaufmann, San Francisco (1998)
4. Claus, C., Boutilier, C.: The dynamics of reinforcement learning in cooperative multiagent systems. In: AAAI 1998/IAAI 1998: Proceedings of the fifteenth national/tenth conference on Artificial intelligence/Innovative applications of artificial intelligence, pp. 746–752. American Association for Artificial Intelligence, Menlo Park (1998)
5. Bowling, M.H., Veloso, M.M.: Multiagent learning using a variable learning rate. Artificial Intelligence 136(2), 215–250 (2002)
6. Szepesvári, C., Littman, M.L.: Generalized markov decision processes: Dynamic-programming and reinforcement-learning algorithms. Technical report, Providence, RI, USA (1996)
7. Robbins, H., Monro, S.: A stochastic approximation method. Annals of Mathematical Statistics 22(3), 400–407 (1951)
8. Arrow, K.: Hurwiczs optimality criterion for decision making under ignorance. Technical Report 6, Stanford University (1953)

9. Nudelman, E., Wortman, J., Shoham, Y., Leyton-Brown, K.: Run the gamut: A comprehensive approach to evaluating game-theoretic algorithms. In: AAMAS 2004, pp. 880–887. IEEE Computer Society, Los Alamitos (2004)
10. Watkins, C.J.C.H.: Learning from Delayed Rewards. PhD thesis, King's College, Cambridge, England (1989)

How to Program Organizations and Roles
in the JADE Framework

Matteo Baldoni[1], Guido Boella[1], Valerio Genovese[1], Roberto Grenna[1],
and Leendert van der Torre[2]

[1] Dipartimento di Informatica. Università di Torino - IT
{baldoni,guido,grenna}@di.unito.it, valerio.click@gmail.com
[2] Computer Science and Communications, University of Luxembourg, Luxembourg
leon.vandertorre@uni.lu

Abstract. The organization metaphor is often used in the design and implementation of multiagent systems. However, few agent programming languages
provide facilities to define them. Several frameworks are proposed to coordinate
MAS with organizations, but they are not programmable with general purpose
languages. In this paper we extend the JADE framework with primitives to program in Java organizations structured in roles, and to enable agents to play roles
in organizations. Roles facilitate the coordination of agents inside an organization and offer new abilities (*powers*) in the context of organizations to the agents
which satisfy the *requirements* necessary to play the roles. To program organizations and roles, we provide primitives which enable an agent to enact a new role
in an organization to invoke powers.

1 Introduction

Organizations are the subject of many recent papers in the MAS field, and also among
the topics of workshops like COIN, AOSE, CoOrg and NorMAS. They are used for
coordinating open multiagent systems, providing control of access rights, enabling the
accommodation of heterogeneous agents, and providing suitable abstractions to model
real world institutions [10].

Many models have been proposed [13], applications modeling organizations or institutions [17], software engineering methods using organizational concepts like roles [21].
However, despite the development of several agent programming languages among
which 3APL [20], few of them have been endowed with primitives for modeling organizations and roles as first class entities. Exceptions are MetateM [12], J-MOISE+
[15], and the Normative Multi-Agent Programming Language in [19]. MetateM is BDI
oriented and not a general purpose language and is based on the notion of group.
J-MOISE+ is more oriented to programming how agents play roles in organizations,
while [19], besides not being general purpose, is more oriented to model the institutional structure composed by obligations than the organizational structure composed by
roles. On the other hand, frameworks for modelling organizations like SMoise+ [16]
and MadKit [14] offer limited possibilities to program organizations. The heterogeneity of solutions shows a lack of a common agreement upon a clear conceptual model of
what an organization is; the ontological status of organizations has been studied only

R. Bergmann et al. (Eds.): MATES 2008, LNAI 5244, pp. 25–36, 2008.

recently and thus it is difficult to translate the organizational model into primitives for programming languages. Moreover, it is not clear how an agent can interact with an organization, whether the organization has to be considered like an object, a coordination artifact, or as an agent [11]. The same holds for the interaction with a role. Thus, in this paper, we address the following research questions: *How to program organizations? How to introduce roles? How agents interact with organizations by means of the roles they play?* And as subquestions: *How to specify the interaction between an agent and its roles? How to specify the interaction among roles?* Moreover, *How can an agent start playing a role?* and, finally, *What is the behaviour of an agent playing a role?*

We start from the ontological model of organizations developed in [6], since it provides a precise definition of organizations and specifies their properties, beyond the applicative needs of a specific language or framework, and allows a comparison with other models. Moreover, this model has been successfully used to give a logical specification of multiagent systems and to introduce roles in object oriented languages [2]. This approach, due to the agent metaphor, allows to model organizations and roles using the same primitives to model agents, like in MetateM [11]. Despite the obvious differences with agents, like the lack of autonomy and of an independent character in case of roles, the agent metaphor allows to understand the new concepts using an already known framework. In particular, interaction between agents and organizations and the roles they play can be based on *communication protocols*, which is particularly useful when agents and organizations are placed on different platforms.

For the description of the interaction among players, organizations and roles we adopt the model of [5]. For what concerns the modeling of how an agent plays a role we take inspiration from [9]. We implement this conceptual model with JADE (Java Agent DEvelopment framework) [3], providing a set of classes which extends it and offer the primitives for constructing organizations when programming multiagent systems. We extend JADE not only due to its large use, general purpose character and open-source philosophy, but also because, being developed in Java, it allows to partly adopt the methodology used to endow Java with roles in the language powerJava [2]. Given the primitives for modeling agents and their communication abilities, transferring the model of [6] in JADE is even more straightforward than transferring it in Java. The extension of JADE consists in a new library of classes and protocols. The classes provide the primitives used to program organizations, roles and player agents, by extending the respective class.

The paper is organized as follows. In Section 2, we summarize the model of organizations and roles we take inspiration from. In Section 3, we describe how the model is realized by extending JADE, and in Section 4 we describe the communication protocols which allow the interaction of the different entities. In Section 5 we underline related and future work.

2   A Model for Organizations and Roles

In [6] a definition of the structure of organizations given their ontological status is given, roles do not exist as independent entities but they are linked to organizations (in other words, roles are not simple objects). Organizations and roles are *not autonomous*, but act via *role players*, although they are description of complex behaviours: in the real world, organizations are considered legal entities, so they can even act like agents, albeit via their representative playing roles. So, they share some properties with agents, and, in some aspects, can be modelled using similar primitives. Thus, in our model roles are entities, which contain both state and behaviour: we distinguish the *role instance associated with a player* and the *specification of a role* (a role type). As recognized by [8] this feature is quite different from other approaches which use roles only in the design phase of the system, as, e.g., in [21].

Goals and beliefs, attributed to a role (as in [9]) describe the behaviour expected from the player of the role, since an agent pursues his goals based on his beliefs. The player should be aware of the goals attributed to the roles, since it is expected to follow them (if they do not conflict with other goals). Most importantly, roles work as "interfaces" between organizations and agents: they give "powers" to agents, extending the abilities of agents, allowing them to operate inside the organization and inside the state of other roles. If on the one hand roles offer powers to agents, they request from agents to satisfy a set of *requirements*, abilities that the agents must have [7].

The model presented in [6] focuses on the dynamics of roles in function of the communication process: role instances evolve according to the speech acts of the interactants. Where speech acts are powers, that can change not only the state of its role, but also the state of other roles (see [4]). For example, the commitments made by a speaker of a promise or by commands made by other agents playing roles which are empowered to give orders. In this model, sets of beliefs and goals (as [9] does) are attributed to the roles. They are the description of the expected behaviour of the agent. The powers of roles specify how the state of the roles changes according to the moves played in the interactions by the agents enacting other roles.

Roles are a way to *structure the organization*, to *distribute responsibilities* and a *coordination means*. Roles allow to encapsulate all the interactions between an agent and an organization and between agents in their roles. The powers added to the players can be different for each role and thus represent different affordances offered by the organization to other agents to interact with it [1].

However, this model leaves unspecified how, given a role, its player will behave. In [9], the problem of formally defining the dynamics of roles is tackled identifying the actions that can be done in an *open system* such that agents can enter and leave. In [9] four operations to deal with role dynamics are defined: *enact* and *deact*, which mean that an agent starts and finishes to occupy (play) a role in a system, and *activate* and *deactivate*, which mean that an agent starts executing actions (operations) belonging to the role and suspends the execution of the actions. Although is possible to have an agent with multiple roles enacted simultaneously, only one role can be *active* at the same time: when an agent performs a power, it is playing only one role in that moment.

3   Organizations, Roles, and Players in JADE

We introduce organizations and roles as first class entities in JADE, with behaviours, albeit not autonomously executed, and communication abilities. Thus, organizations and roles can be implemented using the same primitives of agents by extending the JADE

Agent class with the classes Organization and Role. Analogously, to implement autonomous agents who are able to play roles, the Player class is defined as an extension of the Agent class. The Role class and its extensions represent the *role types*. Their instances represent the role instances associated with an instance of the Agent.[1] Organizations and roles, however, differ in two ontological aspects: first roles are associated to players; second, roles are not independent from the organization offering them. Thus, the Role class is subject to an invariant, stating that it can be instantiated only when an instance of the organization offering the role is present. Conversely, when an organization is destroyed all its roles must be destroyed too.

A further difference of role classes is that to define "powers", they must access the state of the organization they belong too. To avoid making the state of the organization public, the standard solution offered by Java is to use the so-called "inner classes". Inner classes are classes defined inside other classes ("outer classes"). An inner class shares the namespace of the outer class and of the other inner classes, thus being able to access private variables and methods. The class Role is defined as an inner class of the Organization class. Class extending the Role class must be inner classes of the class extending the Organization class. In this way the role can access the private state of the organization and of the other roles. Since roles are implemented as inner classes, a role instance must be on the same platform as the organization instance it belongs to. Moreover, the role agent can be seen as an object from the point of view of the organization and of the other roles which can have a reference to it, besides sending messages to it. In contrast, outside an organization the role agent is accessed by its player (which can be on a different platform) only as an agent via messages, and no reference to it is possible. So not even its public methods can be invoked.

The inner class solution for roles is inspired to the use of inner classes to model roles in object oriented programming languages like in powerJava [2]. The use of inner classes is coherent with the organization of JADE, where behaviours are often defined as inner classes with the aim to better integrate them with the agent containing them.

3.1 Organizations

To implement an organization it's necessary to extend Organization, subclass of Agent, which offers protocols necessary to communicate with agents who want to play a role, and the behaviours to manage the information about roles and their players. Moreover, the Organization class includes the definition of the Role inner class that can be extended to implement new role classes in specific organizations. To support the creation and management of roles the Organization class is endowed with the (private) data structures and (private) methods to create new role instances and to keep the list of the AIDs (Agent IDs) of role instances which have been created, associated with the AIDs of their players. Since roles are Java inner classes of an organization, the organization code can be written in Java mostly disregarding what is a JADE application. Moreover, the inner class mechanism allows the programmer to access the role state and viceversa, while maintaining the modularity character of classes.

---

[1] Nothing prevents to have organizations which play roles in other organizations, like in [8], for this, and other combinations, it is possible to predefine classes and extend them.

The `Enact` protocol allows starting the interaction between player and organization. A player sends a message to an organization requesting to play a role of a certain type; if the organization considers the agent authorized to play that role type, it sends to the caller a list of powers (what the role can do) and requirements (what the role can ask to player what to do). At this point, the player can compare his requirements list with the one sent from the organization and communicate back if he can play the role or if he can't. The operation of leaving a role, *Deact*, is asked by the player to the role itself, so the class organization does not offer any methods or protocols for that.

For helping players to find quickly one or more organizations offering a specific role, Yellow Pages are used. They allow to register a pair *(Organization, RoleType)* for each role in each organization; the interested player will only have to query the Yellow Pages to obtain a list of these couples and choose the best for itself.

3.2 Roles

A role is implemented by extending the `Role` class which offers the protocols to communicate with the player agent. Notice that, since the *Role* class is an inner class of the *Organization* class, this class should be an inner class of the class that extends `Organization` as well. The protocols to communicate with the player agent allows: (*i*) To receive the request of invoking powers; (*ii*) To receive the request to deact the role; (*iii*) To send to the player the request to execute a requirement; (*iv*) To receive from the player the result of the execution of a requirement; (*v*) To notify the player about the failure of executing the invoked power or the failure to receive all the results of the requested requirements. The role programmer, thus, has to define the powers which can be invoked by the player, and to specify them in a suitable data structure used by the `Role` class to select the requests of powers which can be executed.

Allowing a player to invoke a power, which results in the execution of a method by the role, could seem a violation of the principle of autonomy of agents. However, the powers are the only way the players have to act on an organization and, the execution of an invoked power may request, in turn, the execution by the player of requirements needed to carry on the power.

Moreover, since the player may refuse to execute a requested requirement (see Section 3.3), and the requirements determine the outcome of the power, this outcome, thus, varies from request to request, and from player to player. Since role instances are not autonomous, the invocation of a power is not subordinated to the decision of the role to perform it or not. In contrast with powers, a requirement cannot be invoked. Rather it is requested by the role, and the player autonomously decides to execute it or not. In the latter case the player is not complying anymore with its role and it is deacted. To remark this difference we will use the term *invoking a power* versus *requesting a requirement*.

Requests for the execution of requirements are not necessarily associated with the execution of a power. They can be requested to represent the fact that a new goal has been added to the role. For example, this can be the result of a task assignment when the overall organization is following a plan articulated in subtasks to be distributed among the players at the right moments [16]. In case the new goal is a requirement of the player the method *requestRequirement* is executed, otherwise, if it is a power of the role, a *requestResponsibility* is executed. The method *requestResponsibility* asks to the player to invoke a power of the role, while the method *requestRequirement* invokes a requirement of the player. It returns the result sent by the player if he complies with the requirement. The failure of executing of a requirement results in the deactment of the role. Analogously to requirements when the role notifies its player about the responsibility, it cannot be taken for granted that it will invoke the execution of the power. Note that both methods can be invoked also by other roles or by the organization itself, due to the role's limited autonomy.

Other methods are available only when agents are endowed with beliefs, which could be represented, for instance, in Jess. The method *sendInform* is used to inform the player that the beliefs of the roles are changed. This does not imply that the player adopts the conveyed beliefs as well. Methods a*ddBelief* and *addGoal* are invoked by the role's behaviours or by other roles' to update the state of the role.

Besides the connection with its player, the role is an agent like any other, and it can be endowed with further behaviours and further protocols to communicate with other roles of the organization or even with other agents. At the same time it is a Java object as any other and can be programmed, accessing both other roles and the organization internal state to have a better coordination.

3.3 Players

Players of roles in organizations are JADE agents, which can reside on different platforms with respect to the organization. To play a role, a special behaviour is needed; for this reason the `Player` class is offered. An agent which can become a player of roles extends the *Player* class, which, in turn, extends the *Agent* class. This class defines the states of the role playing (enact, active, deactivated, deacted), the transitions from one state to the others, and offers the protocols for communicating with the organization and with the role. A player agent can play more than one role. The list of roles played by the agent, and the state of each role, is kept in an hashtable.

The enactment procedure takes the AID of an organization and of a role type and, if successful, it returns the AID of the role instance associated to this player in the organization. From that moment the agent can activate the role and play it. The activate state allows the player to receive from the role requests of requirement execution and responsibilities (power invocation). Analogously, the *Player* class allows an agent to deact and deactivate a role.

The behaviour of playing a role is modelled in the player agent class by means of a *finite state machine* (FSM) behaviour. The behaviour is instantiated for each instance of the role the agent wants to play, by invoking the method *enact* and specifying the organization AID and the role type. The states are inspired to the model of [9].

Enact: The communication protocol (which contains another FSM itself) for enacting roles is entered. If it ends successfully with the reception of the new role instance AID the deactivated state is entered. The hashtable containing the list of played roles is updated. Otherwise, the deacted state is reached.

Activate: This state is modelled as a FSM behaviour which listens for events coming from outside or inside the agent. If another behaviour of the agent decides to invoke a power of the role by means of the *invokePower* method (see below), the behaviour

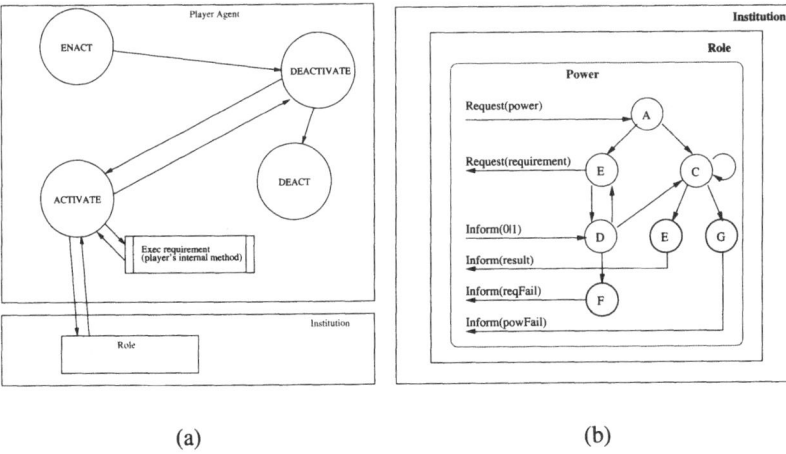

(a)   (b)

Fig. 1. (a) The states of role playing. - (b) The behaviour of roles - A: ManagePwRequest (manages the request from player); B: ManageReqRequest (if a requirement is needed); C: Execute (executes the called power); D: MatchReq (checks if all requirements are ok); E: InformResult (sends results to player); F: InformFail (sends fail caused by requirement missing); G: InformPowerFail (sends fail caused by power failure).

of the activated state checks if the power exists in the role specification and sends an appropriate message to the role agent. Otherwise an exception is raised. If another behaviour of the agent decides to deactivate the role the deactivated state is entered. If a message requesting requirements or invoke powers arrives from the role agent it plays, the agent will decide whether or not to comply with the new request sent by the role. First of all it checks that the required behaviour exists or there has been a mismatch at the moment of enacting a role. If the role communicates to its player that the execution of a power is concluded and sends the result of the power, this information is stored waiting to be passed back to the behaviour which invoked the power upon its request (see *receivePowerResult*). The cyclic behaviour associated with this state blocks itself if no event is present and waits for an event.

Deactivated: The behaviour stops checking for the invocation of requirements or powers from respectively the role and the player itself, and blocks until another behaviour activates the role again. The messages from the role and the power invocations from other behaviours pile up in the queue waiting to be complied with, until an activation method is called and the active state is entered.

Deact: The associated behaviour informs the role that the agent is leaving the role and cleans up all the data concerning the played role in the agent.

One instance of this FSM, that can be seen in Figure 1, is created for each role played by the agent. This means that for a role only one power at time is processed, while the others wait in the message queue. Note that the information whether a role is activated or not is local to the player: from the role's point of view there is no difference. However, the player processes the communication of the role only as long as it is activated, otherwise the messages remains in the buffer. More sophisticated solutions can be implemented as needed, but they must be aware of the synchronization problems.

The methods in the `Player` can be used to program the behaviours of an agent when it is necessary to change the state of role playing or to invoke powers. We assume that invocations of powers to be *asynchronous*. The call returns a call id which is used to receive the correct return value in the same behaviour. It is left to the programmer to stop of a behaviour till an answer is returned by JADE primitive *block*. This solution is coherent with the standard message exchange of JADE and allows to avoid using more sophisticated behaviours based on threads.

- *enact(organizationAID, roleClassName)*: to request to enact a role an agent has to specify the AID of the organization and the name of the class of the role. It returns the AID of the role instance or an exception is raised.
- *receivePowerResult(int)*: to receive the result of the invocation of a power.
- *deact(roleAID), activate(roleAID), deactivate(roleAID)* respectively deacts the role, activates a role agent that is in the *deactivate* state, and temporarily deactivates the role agent.
- *invokePower(roleAID, power)*: to invoke a power it is sufficient to specify the role AID and the name of the behaviour of the role which must be executed. It returns an integer which represent the id of the invocation.
- *addRequirement(String)*: when extending the *Player* class it is necessary to specify which of the behaviours defined in it are requirements. This information is used in the *canPlay* private method which is invoked by the *enact* method to check if the agent can play a role. This list may contain non truthful information, but the failure to comply with the request of a commitment may result in the deactment to the role as soon as the agent is not able to satisfy the request to execute a certain requirement.

Moreover, an agent, in order to be a player, has to implement an abstract method to decide whether to execute the requirements upon request from the roles. The method *adoptGoal* is used to preserve the player autonomy with reference to requirement requests from the role he's playing. The result is *true* if the player decides to execute the requirement.

4   Interaction

In this section we describe the different protocols used in the interaction between agents who want to play roles and organizations, and between players and their roles. All protocols use standard FIPA messages, to enable also non JADE agents to interact with organizations without further changes. Figure 2 describes the sequence diagram of the interaction.

4.1   Agents and the Organization

Behind the *enacting* state of the player described in the previous section, there is an *enactment protocol* inherited, respectively, as concern the initiator and the receiver, from the classes `Player` and `Organization`. It forwards from the player to the organization

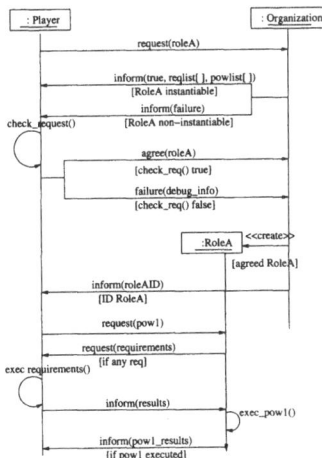

Fig. 2. The interaction protocol

the request of enacting a specified role, and manages the exchange of information: sending the specification of requirements and powers of the roles and checking whether the player complies with the requirements.

The organization listens from messages from any agent (even if some restrictions can be posed at the moment of accepting to create the role), while the subsequent communication between player and role is private. After a request from an agent the behaviour representing the protocol forks creating another instance of itself to be ready to receive requests of other agents in parallel.

The first message is sent by the player as initiator and is a `request` to enact a role. The organization, if it considers the agent authorized to play the role, returns to the candidate player a list of specifications about the powers and requirements of the requested role which are contained in its knowledge base, sending an `inform` message containing the list; otherwise, it denies to the player to play the role, answering with an `inform` message, indicating the failure of the procedure. In case of positive answer, the player, invoking the method *canPlay* using the information contained in the player about the requirements, decides whether to respond to the organization that it can play the role (`agree`) or not (`failure`).

The first answer results in the creation of a new role instance of the requested type and in the update of the knowledge base of the organization with the information that the player is playing the role. To the role instance the organization passes the AID of the role player, i.e., the initiator of the enactment, so that it can eventually filter out the messages not coming from its player. An `inform` is sent back to the player agent, telling him the played role instance's AID, The player, in this way, can address messages to the role and it can identify the messages it receives from the role it plays. Then the agent updates its knowledge base with this information, labeling the role as still deactivated. The protocol terminates in both the player and the organization. This completes the interaction with the organization: the rest of the interaction, including deacting the role, passes through the role instance only.

4.2 Players and Their Roles

The interaction between a player and its role is regulated by three protocols: the request by the role of executing a requirement, the invocation of a power by the player, and the request of the role to invoke a power. In all cases, the interaction protocol works only between a player and the role instances it plays. Messages following the protocol but which do not respect this constraint are discharged on both sides.

We start from the first case since it is used also in the second protocol during the execution of a power. According to Dastani et al. [9] if a role is activated, the player should (consider whether to) adopt its goals and beliefs. Since our model is distributed, the role is separated from its player: the goals (i.e., the requirements) and beliefs of the role have to be communicated from the role to its player by means of a suitable communication protocol. Each time the state of the role changes, since some new goal is added to it, the agent is informed by the role about it: either a requirement must be executed or a power must be invoked. In this protocol, the initiator is the role, which starts the behaviour when its method *requestRequirement* is invoked.

First of all, the agent checks if the requested requirement is in the list of the player's requirements, but this does not mean that it will be executed. Since the player agent is autonomous, before executing the requirement, it takes a decision by invoking the method *adoptGoal* which is implemented by the programmer of the player. The protocol ends by informing the role about the outcome of the execution of the requirement or the refusal of executing it, using an "inform" (see bottom of Figure 1 b).

This protocol is used inside the protocol initiated by the player for invoking a power of the role. After a request from the player, the role can reply with the request of executing some requirements which are necessary for the performance of the power. In fact, in the behaviour corresponding to the power, some invocation of the method *requestRequirement* can be present. The protocol ends with the role informing the agent about the outcome of the execution of the power.

A third protocol is used by the role to remind the agent about its responsibilities, i.e., the role asks its player to invoke a power executing the method *requestResponsibility*. In this case the object of the request is not a requirement executable by the player, but a power, i.e., a behaviour of the role. So the player has to decide whether and when to invoke the power.

In principle, the programmer could have invoked a power directly from the role, instead of requesting it by means of *requestResponsibility*. However, with this mechanism we want to model the case where the player is obliged to invoke the power but the decision of invoking the power is left to the player agent who can have more information about when and how invoke the power. It is left to the programmer of the organization to handle the violation of such obligations.

The final kind of interaction between a player and its role is the request of a player to deact the role. While deactivation is an internal state of the player, which is not necessarily communicated to the role, deacting requires that the role agent is destroyed and that the organization clears up the information concerning the role and its player.

5   Conclusions

In this paper we use the ontological model of organizations proposed in [6] to program organizations. We use as agent framework JADE since it provides the primitives to program MAS in Java. We define a set of Java classes which extends the agent classes of the JADE to have further primitives for building organizations structured into roles. To define the organizational primitives JADE offered advantages but also posed some difficulties. First of all, being based on Java, it allowed to reapply the methodology used to implement roles in powerJava [2] to implement roles as inner classes. Moreover, it provides a general purpose language to create new organizations and roles. Finally, being based on FIPA speech acts, it allows agents programmed in other languages to play roles in organizations, and viceversa, JADE agents to play roles in organizations not implemented in JADE. However, the decision of using JADE has some drawbacks. For example, the messages used in the newly defined protocols can be intercepted by other behaviours of the agents. This shows that a more careful implementation should use a more complex communication infrastructure to avoid this problem. Moreover, since JADE behaviours differently from methods do not have a proper return value, they make it difficult to define requirements and powers. Finally, due to the possible parallelism of behaviours inside an agent, possible synchronization problems can occur.

Few agent languages are endowed with primitives for modeling organization. MetateM [11] is one of these, and introduces the notion of group by enlarging the notion of agent with a context and a content. The context is composed by the agents (also groups are considered as agents like in our model organizations are agents) which the agent is part of, and the content is a set of agents which are included. The authors propose to use these primitives to model organizations, defining roles as agents included in other agents and players as agents included in roles. This view risks to leave apart the difference between the play relation and the role-of relation which have different properties (see, e.g., [18]). Moreover it does not distinguish between powers. Finally MetateM is a language for modeling BDI agents, while JADE has a wider applicability and is built upon on the Java general purpose language.

About S-Moise+ features [16], we will improve our system with agent sets and subset as particular inner classes in the Organization class. Very interesting is the matter of cardinality, constraint that we will implement considering both minimum than maximum cardinality allowed for each group.

The principles of permission will be implemented through a specific new protocol, called `Permissions`, which will allow to a role a call to another role's power, if and only if the first role's player can show (at the time of execution) his credentials (additional requirements); if no additional requirement is given, the other role's power invocation cannot be done.

Another future work is related to Obligations [16]; we are going to implement them by particular requirements that have to produce some result in a fixed time. If no result is produced, then a violation occours and this behaviour is sanctioned in some way. Planning goals too will be realized by requirements, that can be tested one after another to play single missions.

References

1. Baldoni, M., Boella, G., van der Torre, L.: Modelling the interaction between objects: Roles as affordances. In: Lang, J., Lin, F., Wang, J. (eds.) KSEM 2006. LNCS (LNAI), vol. 4092, pp. 42–54. Springer, Heidelberg (2006)
2. Baldoni, M., Boella, G., van der Torre, L.: Interaction between Objects in powerJava. Journal of Object Technology 6(2), 7–12 (2007)
3. Bellifemine, F.L., Caire, G., Greenwood, D.: Developing Multi-Agent Systems with JADE. Wiley, Chichester (2007)
4. Boella, G., Damiano, R., Hulstijn, J., van der Torre, L.: ACL semantics between social commitments and mental attitudes. In: Proc. of AC 2005 and AC 2006. LNCS (LNAI), vol. 3859, pp. 30–44. Springer, Heidelberg (2006)
5. Boella, G., Genovese, V., Grenna, R., der Torre, L.: Roles in coordination and in agent deliberation: A merger of concepts. In: Proc. of Multi-Agent Logics, PRIMA 2007 (2007)
6. Boella, G., van der Torre, L.: Organizations as socially constructed agents in the agent oriented paradigm. In: Gleizes, M.-P., Omicini, A., Zambonelli, F. (eds.) ESAW 2004. LNCS (LNAI), vol. 3451, pp. 1–13. Springer, Heidelberg (2005)
7. Cabri, G., Ferrari, L., Leonardi, L.: Agent roles in the brain framework: Rethinking agent roles. In: The 2004 IEEE Systems, Man and Cybernetics Conference, session on Role-based Collaboration (2004)
8. Colman, A., Han, J.: Roles, players and adaptable organizations. Applied Ontology (2007)
9. Dastani, M., van Riemsdijk, B., Hulstijn, J., Dignum, F., Meyer, J.-J.: Enacting and deacting roles in agent programming. In: Odell, J.J., Giorgini, P., Müller, J.P. (eds.) AOSE 2004. LNCS, vol. 3382, pp. 189–204. Springer, Heidelberg (2005)
10. Ferber, J., Gutknecht, O., Michel, F.: From agents to organizations: an organizational view of multiagent systems. In: Giorgini, P., Müller, J.P., Odell, J.J. (eds.) AOSE 2003. LNCS, vol. 2935, pp. 214–230. Springer, Heidelberg (2004)
11. Fisher, M.: A survey of concurrent metatem - the language and its applications. In: ICTL, pp. 480–505 (1994)
12. Fisher, M., Ghidini, C., Hirsch, B.: Organising computation through dynamic grouping. In: Objects, Agents, and Features, pp. 117–136 (2003)
13. Grossi, D., Dignum, F., Dastani, M., Royakkers, L.: Foundations of organizational structures in multiagent systems. In: Procs. of AAMAS 2005, pp. 690–697 (2005)
14. Gutknecht, O., Ferber, J.: The madkit agent platform architecture. In: Agents Workshop on Infrastructure for Multi-Agent Systems, pp. 48–55 (2000)
15. Huebner, J.F.: J-Moise$^+$ programming organizational agents with Moise$^+$ and Jason (2007), http://moise.sourceforge.net/doc/tfg-eumas07-slides.pdf
16. Huebner, J.F., Sichman, J.S., Boissier, O.: S-moise+: A middleware for developing organised multi-agent systems. In: Proc. of AAMAS Workshops. LNCS, vol. 3913, pp. 64–78. Springer, Heidelberg (2005)
17. Omicini, A., Ricci, A., Viroli, M.: An algebraic approach for modelling organisation, roles and contexts in MAS. Applicable Algebra in Engineering, Communication and Computing 16(2-3), 151–178 (2005)
18. Steimann, F.: On the representation of roles in object-oriented and conceptual modelling. Data and Knowledge Engineering 35, 83–848 (2000)
19. Tinnemeier, N., Dastani, M., Meyer, J.-J.C.: Orwell's nightmare for agents? programming multi-agent organisations. In: Proc. of PROMAS 2008 (2008)
20. van der Hoek, W., Hindriks, K., de Boer, F., Meyer, J.-J.C.: Agent programming in 3APL. Autonomous Agents and Multi-Agent Systems 2(4), 357–401 (1999)
21. Zambonelli, F., Jennings, N., Wooldridge, M.: Developing multiagent systems: The Gaia methodology. IEEE Transactions of Software Engineering and Methodology 12(3), 317–370 (2003)

Agent Models for Concurrent Software Systems

Lawrence Cabac, Till Dörges, Michael Duvigneau, Daniel Moldt,
Christine Reese, and Matthias Wester-Ebbinghaus

University of Hamburg, Department of Computer Science,
Vogt-Kölln-Str. 30, D-22527 Hamburg
http://www.informatik.uni-hamburg.de/TGI

Abstract. In this work we present modeling techniques for the development of multi-agent applications within the reference architecture for multi-agent system MULAN. Our approach can be characterized as model driven development by using models in all stages and levels of abstraction regarding design, implementation and documentation. Both, standard techniques from software development as well as customized ones are used to satisfy the needs of multi-agent system development. To illustrate the techniques and models within this paper we use diagrams created during the development of an agent-based distributed Workflow Management System (WFMS).

Keywords: High-level Petri nets, nets-within-nets, reference nets, net components, RENEW, modeling, agents, multi-agent systems, PAOSE.

1 Introduction

The agent metaphor is highly abstract and it is necessary to develop software engineering techniques and methodologies that particularly fit the agent-oriented paradigm. They must capture the flexibility and autonomy of an agent's problem-solving capabilities, the richness of agent interactions and the (social) organizational structure of a multi-agent system as a whole.

Many agent-oriented software development methodologies have been brought forward over the past decade, many of them already in a mature state. Here, we present our contribution to this rapidly evolving field of research by describing agent models and their usage during the development of multi-agent systems with MULAN (Multi-Agent Nets [7]). As a matter of course there exist many analogies to related agent-oriented development techniques and methodologies like Gaia [15], MaSE [4] or Prometheus [11]. This concerns development methods and abstractions like use cases, system structure (organization) diagrams, role models, interaction diagrams and interaction protocols as well as more fine-grained models of agents' internal events, data structures and decision making capabilities.

Our approach PAOSE (Petri net-based AOSE) facilitates the metaphor of multi-agent systems in a formally precise and coherent way throughout all aspects of software development as well as a concurrency-aware (Petri net-based) modeling and programming language. The metaphor of multi-agent systems is

R. Bergmann et al. (Eds.): MATES 2008, LNAI 5244, pp. 37–48, 2008.

formalized by the MULAN reference architecture, which is modeled using reference nets. We integrate several ideas from the methodologies mentioned above as well as concepts from conventional modeling techniques (UML). The result of those efforts is a development methodology that continuously integrates our philosophy of Petri net-based and model-driven software engineering in the context of multi-agent systems.

This paper focuses on the set of modeling techniques used within the PAOSE approach. Other aspects have already been presented, for example *the multi-agent system as a guiding metaphor* for development processes in [1]. In Section 2 we introduce the basic conceptual features of multi-agent application development with MULAN. The particular techniques, models and tools are presented in Section 3.

2   Concepts of Application Development with Mulan

Reference nets[1] and thus also MULAN run in the virtual machine provided by RENEW [9], which also includes an editor and runtime support for several kinds of Petri nets. Since reference nets may carry complex JAVA-instructions as inscriptions and thereby offer the possibility of Petri net-based programming, the MULAN models have been extended to a fully elaborated and running software architecture, the FIPA[2]-compliant re-implementation CAPA [5].

Reference nets can be regarded as a concurrency extension to *Java*, which allows for easy implementation of concurrent systems in regard to modeling (implementation) and synchronization aspects. Those – often tedious – aspects of implementation regarding concurrency are handled by the formalism as well as by the underlying virtual machine. In this aspect lies the advantage of our approach. We rely on a formal background, which is at the same time tightly coupled with the programming environment Java. MULAN can be regarded as a reference architecture for concurrent systems providing a highly structured approach using the multi-agent system metaphor.

We describe the internal components of the MULAN agent followed by an investigation of the interrelations between them, which results in the organizational structure of the system. For the details of further aspects of the MULAN architecture we refer to Rölke et al. [7].

2.1   The Mulan Agent

The reference net-based multi-agent system architecture MULAN (Multi Agent Nets) structures a multi-agent system in four layers, namely *infrastructure, platform, agent* and *protocol* [7,12]. Figure 1 shows a schematic net model of a MULAN agent. Several parts of the operational model, such as inscriptions, synchronous

---

[1] Reference nets [8] are high-level Petri nets comparable to colored Petri nets. In addition they implement the nets-within-nets paradigm where tokens are active elements (token refinement). Reference semantics is applied, so tokens are *references* to *net instances*. *Synchronous channels* allow for communication between net instances.

[2] Foundation for Intelligent Physical Agents http://www.fipa.org

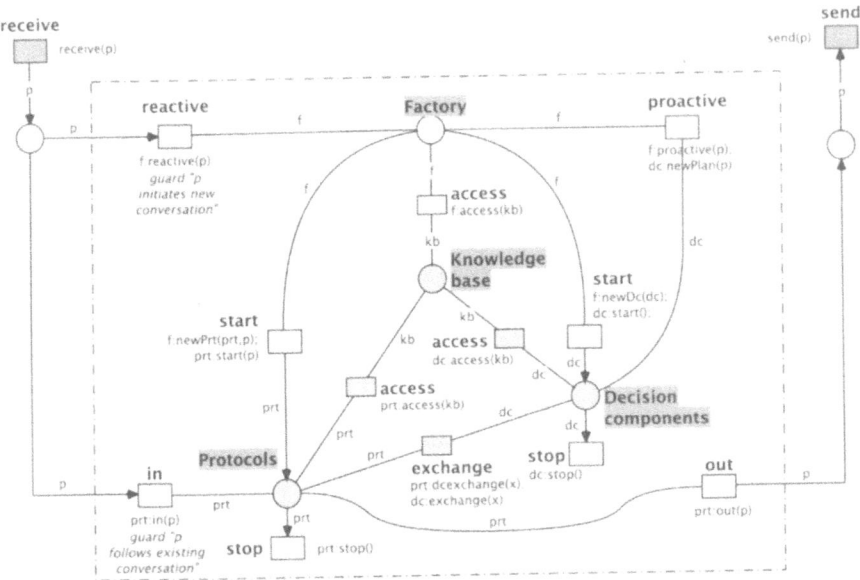

Fig. 1. Agent net

channels and initialization, are omitted for clearness. Instead, descriptive names have been given to the net elements representing synchronous channels or place contents. The model stresses that the agent is a communicating agent being able to receive and send messages. The labeled places store references to net instances that provide or refine the main functionality of the agent. These are the Factory, the Knowledge base, the Decision components, and the Protocols. Protocol and decision component nets comprise parts of the domain-specific agent behavior, the two corresponding places in the agent net may contain numerous net instances (compare *nets-within-nets* [14]).

The *factory* produces net instances from net patterns of protocols and decision components. It realizes reactive and proactive behavior by examining incoming messages and the agent's knowledge.

The *knowledge base* offers database functionality including atomic query, create, remove and modify operations to other subnets of the agent. It is used to store persistent information to be shared by protocol nets and decision components, for example the agent's representation of the environment. The knowledge base also stores the agent's configuration. It holds information about provided and required services, and a mapping of incoming messages to protocol nets.

Protocol nets implement domain-specific agent behavior. Each protocol net template models the participation of an agent role in a multi-agent interaction protocol. Instantiated protocol nets reside on the place Protocols of the agent, handle the processing of received messages and may generate outgoing messages. Protocol net instances are the manifestations of the agent's involvement in an interaction with one or more other agents. They can access the knowledge base and exchange information with decision components through the *exchange* channel.

Decision components implement, like protocol nets, domain-specific agent behavior. A decision component net instance can be queried by protocol net instances to add flexibility to the static, workflow-like character of protocol nets. Decision components can also initiate proactive agent behavior by requesting the factory to instantiate protocol nets. Thus an AI-like planning component can be attached to an agent as a decision component or the functionality can be implemented directly as reference nets. Decision components may also encapsulate external tools or legacy code as well as a graphical user interface whereby the external feedback is transformed into proactive agent behavior.

2.2 Organizational Structure

In a multi-agent application the organizational structure has to be defined, such that responsibilities for all aspects of the system are specified. The general perspectives in the area of a multi-agent systems are the structure, the interactions, and the terminology. These perspectives are orthogonal with connecting points at some intersections (compare Figure 2).

The structure of a multi-agent system is given by the agents, their roles, knowledge bases and decision components. The behavior of a multi-agent system is given by the interactions of the agents, their communicative acts and the internal actions related to the interactions. The terminology of a multi-agent system is given as a domain-specific ontology definition that enables agents and interactions to refer to the same objects, actions and facts. Without a common ontology successful interactions are impossible.

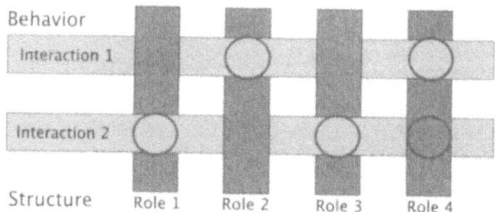

Fig. 2. Two dimensional matrix showing perspectives (*behavior, structure*)

A schematic two dimensional matrix is depicted in Figure 2 showing the independence and interconnection of agents and interactions. Neither is there any direct relationship between any pair of agents, nor between any pair of interactions. Thus these architectural elements are independent and depicted in parallel to each other. Agents and interactions are shown as orthogonal because each agent is involved in some interactions. The general case for any two structural and/or behavioral elements is independence, but interconnections exist. Coupled agents and interactions are marked by circles in the figure.

The terminology defined as ontology is the third dimension of perspectives (omitted in the diagram). It is orthogonal to the other two, but it tends to have many interconnecting points because each interaction and each agent uses parts of the ontology definition to fulfill its purpose.

Since the three perspectives are orthogonal to each other and independent within the perspective, it is easily possible to divide the tasks of design and implementation into independent parts. This means that different interactions can be developed by independent sub-teams and different agents can be designed by other independent sub-teams. Between agent teams and interaction teams, coordination is needed for the crucial parts only (circles in the diagram).

These three perspectives enable us to develop the parts of the system independently and concurrently – thus also distributedly – as long as there is enough coordination / synchronization between intersecting groups.

3   Techniques, Models and Development Tools

In this section we describe the techniques applied during the various stages of multi-agent application development with MULAN. An agent-based Workflow Management System serves as an example application to provide real-world models. However, since the WFMS is not the objective here, we will not go into detail of its design.

We present the applied techniques and resulting models starting with the coarse design giving an overview over the system, continuing with the definition of the structure of the multi-agent application, the ontology and the behavior of the agents.

3.1   Coarse Design

The requirements analysis is done mainly in open discussions. The results are captured in simple lists of system components and agent interactions. This culminates in a use case diagram as shown in Figure 3. Of course other methods to derive use cases can also be applied.

A use case diagram is especially useful to derive the multi-agent application matrix because we depict agent roles in the system as actors in the diagram. In contrast, usually in use case models the actors represent real world users.

Figure 3 shows the Account Manager (AM) role, the Workflow Data Base (WFDB) role, the Workflow Management System (WFMS) role and the User role together with several interactions. Already the use case diagram reveals the matrix structure in two dimensions. Agent roles form the multi-agent application structure while interactions form the behavior of the system. Arcs in the diagram correspond to the matrix interconnection points from Section 2.2. Use case diagrams are drawn directly in RENEW. The use case plugin provides the functionality by adding a palette of drawing tools to the editor.

The use case plugin (UC-Plugin) integrates a generator feature, which generates the complete folder structure of the application necessary for the implementation of a multi-agent application. This includes a standard source package folder structure, skeletons for all agent interactions, role diagram and ontology

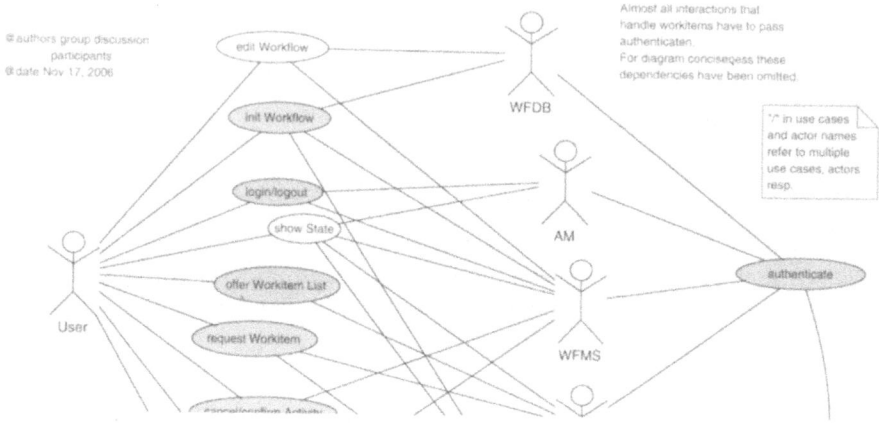

Fig. 3. Fragment of a use case diagram showing the system's coarse design

files as well as configuration files and build / start skripts. The generator utilizes the Velocity[3] template engine.

3.2 Multi-agent Application Structure

The structure of the multi-agent application is refined using a R/D diagram (role/dependency diagram). This kind of diagram uses features from class diagrams and component diagrams. Class diagrams provide inheritance arcs to denote role hierarchies. Component diagrams provide explicit nodes for services as well as arcs with *uses* and *offers* semantics to denote dependencies between roles. Initial values for role-specific knowledge bases are included through refinement of nodes.

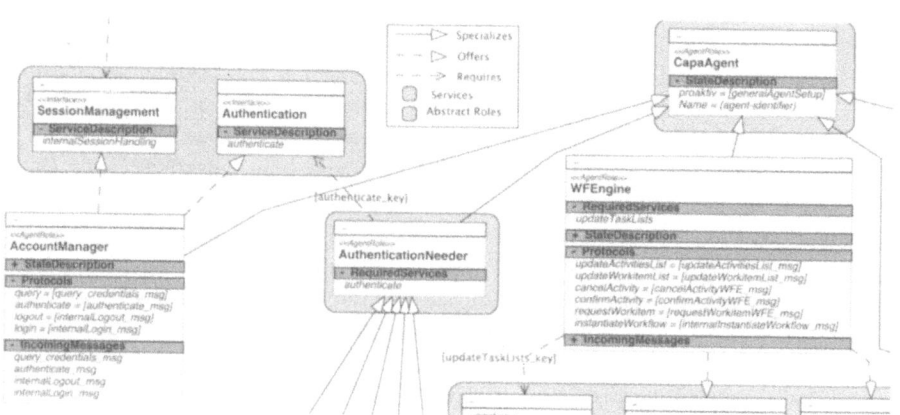

Fig. 4. Fragment of a R/D diagram (agents, roles, services)

---

[3] The Apache Velocity Project http://velocity.apache.org/

Figure 4 shows a fragment of the WFMS R/D diagram. The fragment depicts several roles marked **<AgentRole>**: CapaAgent, AuthenticationNeeder, Account-Manager and WFEngine. Also some services marked **<Interface>** are depicted: SessionManagement, Authentication etc. As an example, the service Authentication is offered by the AccountManager and used by each agent that holds the role AuthenticationNeeder.

The agent role descriptions are automatically generated from the R/D diagram. Role descriptions are combined to form agent descriptions (initial knowledge bases). Roles can easily be assembled to form the multi-agent application using the graphical user interface. The multi-agent application is started either from within the tool, by a startup script or by a Petri net.

3.3 Terminology

The terminology of a multi-agent system is used in a twofold way. First, it is used in form of an ontology definition by the agents to communicate with each other and for their internal representation of the environment. Second, it is used among the developers to communicate about the system and its design.

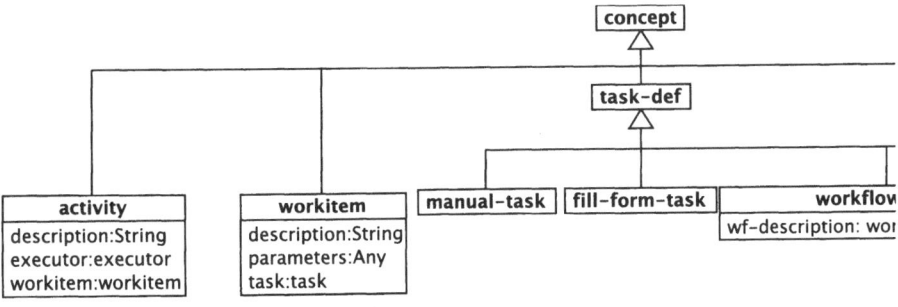

Fig. 5. Fragment of the WFMS ontology

To define the ontology of our multi-agent applications we have been using Protégé[4] for over two years now. Ontologies are defined in Protégé and then translated by a generator into Java classes. Protégé is a very powerful tool, but it features a completely different user interface design than RENEW.

The RENEW feature structure plugin allows to explicitly model the ontology as a concept diagram as shown in Figure 5. These are class diagrams restricted to inheritance and association. The concept diagrams can easily be understood by all sub-teams to capture the context of the concepts in use.

Up to now, the translation of models from the feature structure concepts to Protégé ontologies is a manual task. The Protégé model can then be used to generate the Java ontology classes. However, we have also developed a prototypical implementation of an ontology classes generator (directly) from concept diagrams. We are also working on transformations from and to Protégé models.

---

[4] Protégé http://protege.stanford.edu/

3.4 Knowledge and Decisions

While the agent's interactive behavior is defined in the interaction protocols (see next section), the facts about its environment are located in the agent's knowledge base. The initial knowledge of the agent is defined in its initial knowledge base file, constructed by joining information from the role definitions, which have been defined in the R/D diagram (introduced in Section 3.2). This XML document that can also be customized apart from the R/D diagram is parsed to build the initial knowledge of the agent during its initialization. Alternatively, a text file in the style of properties files suffices for the same purpose.

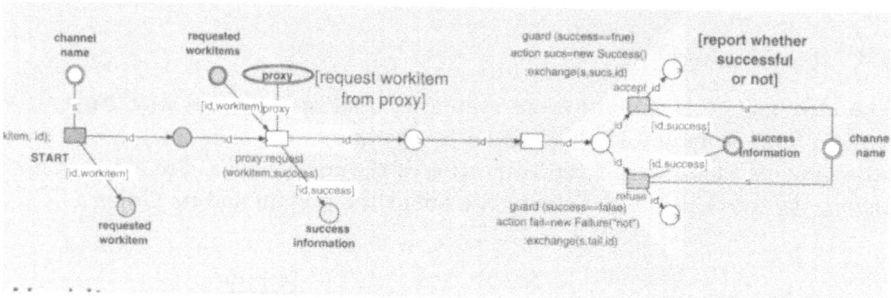

Fig. 6. Fragment of a decision component net: RequestWorkitemHandling

Decision components (DC) are constructed as reference nets. There exists a generalized form of a DC providing GUI interface connection. Also net components [2] for the development of DCs are provided.

Figure 6 shows a fragment of the DC net handling the request of a user for a workitem in the workitem dispatcher agent. The net holds the proxy net which implements the interface to the workflow engine. A request starts at the left of the image and is handed over to the proxy, which holds a list of available work items for the given user. The result of the request is handed back to the DC net and passed (via the *exchange* channel) on to the requester, a protocol net, which in turn sends an appropriate message to the requesting agent.

3.5 Behavior

The interactive behavior of the system components is specified using agent interaction protocol diagrams (AIP, introduced in [10], integrated in PAOSE in [3]).

Figure 7 depicts a fragment of an AIP involving the two roles AccountManager and WorkitemDispatcher in the authenticate interaction. Agent interaction protocol diagrams are integrated in our tool set through the RENEW Diagram plugin which is also capable of generating functional skeletons for protocol nets. As described in Section 2, protocol nets are reference nets that directly define the behavior of a MULAN agent.

Protocol nets are composed of *net components* [2]. Net components are also used for automatic generation of protocol net skeletons from agent interaction

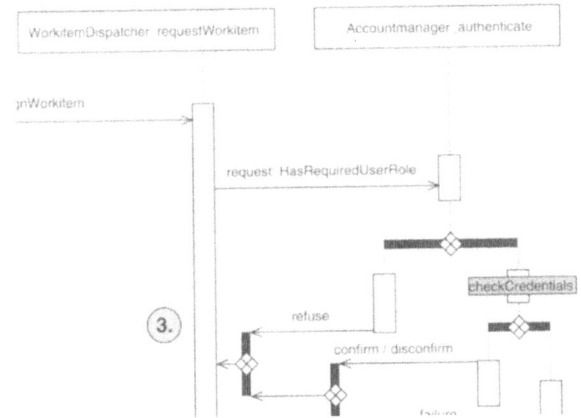

Fig. 7. Fragment of an agent interaction protocol diagram

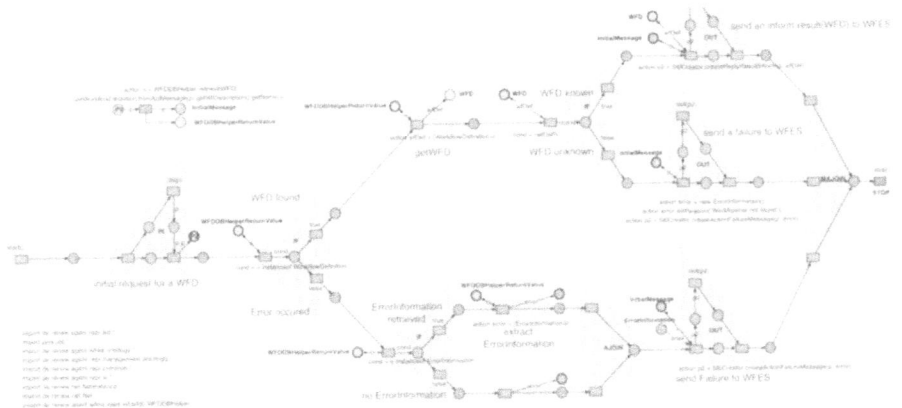

Fig. 8. A protocol net constructed with net components

protocol diagrams. The protocol nets are then refined during the implementation phase by adding inscriptions to the nets. Figure 8 shows an example protocol net.[5] Several decisions are made after receiving a request message. Finally, the appropriate answer is sent back.

With the implementation of interactions as protocol nets, the internal processes as decision components and the knowledge bases through the description of the role diagram, the whole multi-agent application is defined.

Additionally, all diagrams presented here serve as documentation elements and are included in the API-documentation of the system (MulanDoc Plugin).

3.6 Summary

In the context of MULAN and PAOSE we can identify three basic dimensions in which the perspectives on the system can be categorized. *Structure* relates

---

[5] The net components are recognizable and show the structure of the protocol net.

to roles and knowledge, which is functionally decomposed. *Behavior* relates to interactions and internal processes, which reflects the natural view via Petri nets onto systems with respect to behavior. *Terminology* is covered by ontologies and provides the glue between the different perspectives. Organizational embedding is covered by the matrix-like treatment, which provides the relationships between entities in the organizational context including the involved people. In addition, Table 1 shows a table of relations between task types, modeling techniques, applied tools and resulting artifact.

Table 1. Overview over the contiguous techniques

Task	Model	Tool	Result
Coarse Design	Use Case Diagram	UC Plugin	Plugin Structure
Ontology Design	Concept Diagram	FS-Nets/Protégé	Generated Classes
Role Design	R/D Diagram	KBE Plugin	Knowledge Bases
Internal Processes	Petri Net Diagram[6]	RENEW[6]	Decision Components
Interaction Design	AIP Diagram	Diagram Plugin	Protocol Nets

3.7 Experiences

The presented approach has been applied to several teaching projects consisting of twenty to forty students, tutors and lecturers. The approach has been further developed over the years, which resulted in better tool support and further elaboration of methods and techniques (many of which were presented earlier). After a phase of learning the concepts, methods and techniques, the students were able to design and construct rather complex concurrent and distributed software systems. For example, an agent-based workflow management system (compare with the diagrams of this paper) was developed using this approach.

The results of 5 weeks of teaching and 9 weeks of implementation include about 10 agent roles, more than 20 interactions and almost 70 concepts in the ontology. The outcome is a running prototype of an distributed agent based workflow management system, where a user is represented by an agent and the basic features are provided through a user GUI: Authentication, workflow instantiation, offering of available tasks according to application roles and task rules, accepting, cancellation and conclusion of tasks during the progress of a workflow. Workflows themselves are specified with Petri nets using a special task transition which provides cancellation (compare [6]). Thus synchronization and conflict solving are provided by the inherent features of the RENEW simulation engine. This example and our other previous projects show that PAOSE together with the guiding metaphor of a *multi-agent system of developers* [1] enable us to develop multi-agent applications with MULAN. The developed methods and the tool support have proven to be effective in supporting the development process.

---

[6] For the internal processes no abstract modeling technique has been presented. Several proposals exist, but have not resulted in tool support, yet. However, those processes can be modeled directly as reference nets in RENEW or can be externalized.

4   Conclusion

In this paper we present the modeling techniques used within the PAOSE approach to build agent models. The tools that are used during the development process support all tasks of development with modeling power, code generation and deployment facilities. Still some of the tools have prototypical character. Specifically, we have presented techniques to model structure, behavior and terminology of concurrent software systems in a coherent way following the multi-agent paradigm. All techniques and tools own semantics built upon the unique, concurrency-oriented modeling and programming language of reference nets, either directly or by referring to the MULAN reference architecture.

The concurrency-awareness in development process and modeling techniques distinguishes our approach from most of the methodologies mentioned in the introduction since they usually do not address true concurrency explicitly (compare [13]). The advantage of tight integration of abstract modeling techniques with the conceptual framework given through the formal model of MULAN is responsible for the clearness and the effectivity of our approach.

For the future, we follow several directions to refine the approach. On the practical side, we look into further developments, improvements and integration of tools and techniques. On the conceptual side, we work on expanding the multi-agent-oriented approach to other aspects of the development process like project organization and agent-oriented tool support. Following these directions, we want to achieve symmetrical structures in all three aspects of software development: the system, the development process and the project organization (compare [1]).

References

1. Cabac, L.: Multi-agent system: A guiding metaphor for the organization of software development projects. In: Petta, P., Müller, J.P., Klusch, M., Georgeff, M. (eds.) MATES 2007. LNCS (LNAI), vol. 4687, pp. 1–12. Springer, Heidelberg (2007)
2. Cabac, L., Duvigneau, M., Rölke, H.: Net components revisited. In: Moldt, D. (ed.) Fourth International Workshop on Modelling of Objects, Components, and Agents. MOCA 2006, pp. 87–102 (2006)
3. Cabac, L., Moldt, D., Rölke, H.: A proposal for structuring Petri net-based agent interaction protocols. In: van der Aalst, W.M.P., Best, E. (eds.) ICATPN 2003. LNCS, vol. 2679, pp. 102–120. Springer, Heidelberg (2003)
4. DeLoach, S.: Engineering organization-based multiagent systems. In: Garcia, A., Choren, R., Lucena, C., Giorgini, P., Holvoet, T., Romanovsky, A. (eds.) SELMAS 2005. LNCS, vol. 3914, pp. 109–125. Springer, Heidelberg (2006)
5. Duvigneau, M., Moldt, D., Rölke, H.: Concurrent architecture for a multi-agent platform. In: Giunchiglia, F., Odell, J.J., Weiss, G., Gerhard, W. (eds.) AOSE 2002. LNCS, vol. 2585. Springer, Heidelberg (2003)
6. Jacob, T., Kummer, O., Moldt, D., Ultes-Nitsche, U.: Implementation of workflow systems using reference nets – security and operability aspects. In: Jensen, K. (ed.) Fourth Workshop on Practical Use of Coloured Petri Nets. University of Aarhus, Department of Computer Science (August 2002)

7. Köhler, M., Moldt, D., Rölke, H.: Modelling the structure and behaviour of Petri net agents. In: Colom, J.-M., Koutny, M. (eds.) ICATPN 2001. LNCS, vol. 2075, pp. 224–241. Springer, Heidelberg (2001)

8. Kummer, O.: Introduction to Petri nets and reference nets. Sozionik Aktuell 1, 1–9 (2001)

9. Kummer, O., Wienberg, F., Duvigneau, M.: Renew – The Reference Net Workshop. Release 2.1 (March 2007), http://www.renew.de

10. Odell, J., Van Dyke Parunak, H., Bauer, B.: Extending UML for agents. In: Wagner, G., Lesperance, Y., Yu, E. (eds.) Proc. of the Agent-Oriented Information Systems Workshop at the 17th National conference on Artificial Intelligence, pp. 3–17 (2000)

11. Padgham, L., Winikoff, M.: Prometheus: A pragmatic methodology for engineering intelligent agents. In: Proceedings of the OOPSLA 2002 Workshop on Agent-Oriented Methodologies, pp. 97–108 (2002)

12. Rölke, H.: Modellierung von Agenten und Multiagentensystemen – Grundlagen und Anwendungen. Agent Technology – Theory and Applications, vol. 2. Logos Verlag, Berlin (2004)

13. Shehory, O., Sturm, A.: Evaluation of modeling techniques for agent-based systems. In: Agents, pp. 624–631 (2001)

14. Valk, R.: Petri nets as token objects - an introduction to elementary object nets. In: Desel, J., Silva, M. (eds.) ICATPN 1998. LNCS, vol. 1420, pp. 1–25. Springer, Heidelberg (1998)

15. Zambonelli, F., Jennings, N., Wooldridge, M.: Developing multiagent systems: The Gaia methodology. ACM Transactions on Software Engineering and Methodology 12(3), 317–370 (2003)

Filtering Algorithm for Agent-Based Incident Communication Support in Mobile Human Surveillance

Duco N. Ferro[1] and Catholijn M. Jonker[2]

[1] Almende B.V., Westerstraat 50,
3016 DJ Rotterdam, The Netherlands
duco@almende.org
[2] Man-Machine Interaction group, Delft University of Technology,
Mekelweg 4, 2628 CD Delft, The Netherlands
C.M.Jonker@tudelft.nl

Abstract. This paper presents an ontology and a filtering algorithm used in an agent-based system to support communication in case of incidents in the mobile human surveillance domain. In that domain reaching the right people as soon as possible is of the essence when incidents occur. The main goal of our efforts is to significantly reduce the response time in case of incidents by proposing and setting up the communication to the right people. Experimental results show that this can reduce the response time by more than 50%, e.g., from 40 to 20 minutes. To continuously improve the accuracy of the proposed communications, the agent-based system uses feedback mechanisms. An implementation of this system, ASK-ASSIST, has been deployed at a mobile human surveillance company.

Keywords: Mobile human surveillance, incident management, communication support, collaborative filtering, agent-based decision support.

1 Introduction

Efficient and effective communication is critical to timely align human and other resources capable of handling incidents. In domains such as security, crisis management, medical care, the military and traffic incident management, hundreds of individuals distributed over various groups and organizations perform several tasks at different places and move from one location to another over time. Such tasks are by nature urgent, localized and incident prone. As performing these tasks effectively typically depends on the activities and goals of other people, the activities and communication sessions need to be coordinated. Individuals that are not co-located need information and communication technology to coordinate their actions.

The leading case study of this paper is incident management during patrols in the domain of mobile human surveillance (MHS). In those domains patrols are planned in advance but may be disrupted by unforeseen events requiring immediate attention (e.g., in [9]). Managing incidents is complicated by a number of factors. The knowledge, information or support required for dealing with incidents is distributed across

R. Bergmann et al. (Eds.): MATES 2008, LNAI 5244, pp. 49–60, 2008.

the organizations involved. The availability of resources changes over time, and so does the context. In addition, due to organizational and legal requirements, incidents need to be resolved within a certain time limit. Due to these problems, individuals need to initiate and, possibly, anticipate the needed communication on the basis of incomplete and uncertain information.

Currently, central communication points (e.g., dispatch centers) are used to deal with these problems. Human operators at the central communication point respond to requests for support from the field. They propagate such requests across the network to find proper assistance. While this approach is effective, it is not efficient. Due to communication bottlenecks the response time to incidents can be too high [1].

To improve the efficiency of information provision in mobile human surveillance networks, we present an agent-based communication management architecture that is sustained by real-time self-organization. Analogous to recommendation system techniques, which are usually applied to recommend, for instance, books, movies or music to users, we propose an approach that ranks and recommends particular communication pairs/groups to actors that need assistance. For this we use information filters that exploit similarities between actors reporting incidents with those that handled incidents in the past and similarities between the incidents themselves and the contexts in which they occurred.

In this approach all entities in the application domain are associated to their own personal software agent. The idea is that each agent is capable of exploring potential links with other agents in a peer-to-peer manner that exceeds the network of the represented entity itself. Using these links the system can induce, rank and recommend communication groups according to the probability that these groups are capable of handling the incident at hand. Once a recommendation is made to the requesting actor, the result is evaluated using implicit and explicit feedback mechanisms. Implicit feedback is obtained by evaluating the time to solve the incident. Explicit feedback consists of feedback grades provided by the security actors themselves, after the incident is handled. Depending on these evaluations, the strength of the links among the agents is adjusted or new links are created to further improve the support the system offers.

The filtering algorithms and the multi-agent architecture have been implemented in the ASK-ASSIST system to set up context- and incident-sensitive phone and/or conference calls amongst the personnel in our case study domain. Experiments on the data of Trigion, a mobile security company, show that our approach produces prediction schemes that effectively and timely set up the communication network taking into account the context of the individuals and other aspects of the security network (e.g., feedback). The implemented system is currently in use by Trigion.

The remainder of this paper is organized as follows. In Section 2, we discuss related work and its potential in leveraging the communication bottleneck in incident management. Section 3 introduces and formalizes the mobile surveillance domain. The ASK-ASSIST system implementing the filtering algorithms and hosting the agents is described in Section 4. The filtering techniques essential for recommending the right communication are presented in Section 5. We discuss our work and lay out our plans for future work in Section 6.

2 Related Work

The potential of decision support systems (DSS) for incident management is shown in e.g., [11]. Although the literature describes ample work on decision support systems for incident management, research on decisions support systems is in the early stages. To facilitate the decision making process, the use of intelligent software agents, as an intermediate layer, is proposed in [8] and [2]. Hybrid human-agent systems enable such support, for instance, in health care [5].

The communication bottleneck is related to the problem of finding the right coalition of people. Robust matchmaking or coalition formation appears to occur at critical agent network scales. For example, in pair partnership matching an agent is satisfied with a coalition of itself and only one other agent as soon as a specific threshold of a value function is met or passed at a critical scale [7]. The effectiveness and efficiency of such groupings and, in particular, the value functions have to be accounted for and empirically tested.

In this paper we propose to use filtering techniques to find the most promising coalition to meet the requirements of the incident and the agent reporting the incident. In literature, different types of filtering techniques can be found:

- Content-based filtering [6] ,which allows the matching of an agent to an agent coalition. A corresponding task can be allocated to alleviate an incident on the basis of the similarity between an agent coalition given an incident and those of interest to one agent given the specific incident.

- Collaborative filtering, either memory-based [4] or model-based [10], which allows matching of an agent onto an agent coalition. A corresponding task can be allocated to alleviate an incident on the basis of the similarity between the coalition formation profile of an agent and those of other agents.

- Collaborative content-based filtering [3], which combines the above.

Although these techniques already allow filtering incident management data, to the best knowledge of the authors, no literature on collaborative content-based filtering techniques for this domain can be found. To solve the communication bottleneck we propose to use collaborative content-based filtering.

3 Mobile Human Surveillance and Its Formalization

In this section, we present a real world case study of the mobile human surveillance domain. First we illustrate our case study by showing some examples of the activities in the case domain. Then, we present a formalization of this domain, which will be used in the following section to describe the filtering algorithms. The main categories in the formalization refer to actors, shifts, communication, and incidents.

3.1 Introducing MHS Security

In the case of mobile surveillance, the security company plans frequent visits (i.e., the number and the nature of the visits are specified in the contract that was agreed on) by security guards to their client premises to deter and, possibly, observe inappropriate actions. While on patrol a security guard has to move by car from one location to another. Once the guard arrives at a location, there may be one or more tasks to perform (possibly in a specific order). A typical course of events during a work shift of a security guard does not only include the acts of transportation and performing location specific tasks, but also frequent contacts over the phone with, for example, an operator of the dispatch center or with a team leader. This communication need is particularly important if an incident such as a fire alarm occurs.

Now, assume that a member of the dispatch centre confronted with an alarm occurring at object 643221, situated at route 240, initially tries to assign that alarm to route 240. Suppose that after 5 minutes route 240 still does not respond (or actually refuses to perform the alarm check). The assignment task is then delegated to a team leader. The team-leader calls the guard at route 245. That is the route closest to the alarm. The guard at this route does not respond. After 15 minutes, route 275 is requested and responds positively. The guard at route 275 goes to the object and arrives 20 minutes later. So after 40 minutes there is a guard present at the object. In simulated experiments, we show that the arrival time can be strongly reduced.

Having illustrated surveillance security, we formalize the entities, logistic network, communication network and incidents for the mobile human surveillance security case.

3.2 Formalization of MHS Security

While modeling the entities in the domain of mobile human surveillance security, we make a distinction between two types of entities. The first type of entities we call actors (e.g., guards). Actors are ascribed individual preferences and are capable of exerting these preferences to when and which groups are formed.

Definition 3.1 (MHS Security Actors). *The set of actors A is the union of mobile surveillance security guards G , team-leaders TL and dispatch centre operators D.*

The second type concerns passive entities (e.g. tasks). Typically, passive elements represent contextual information such as a location where an actor is at or a task that the actor is performing. We define the passive entities as follows:

Definition 3.2 (MHS Security Passive Entities). *The set of passive entities P is the union of:*

1) *T ,the set of tasks: {opening_round, closing_round, regular_surveillance}*
2) *R, the set of route identifiers such that $R \subset \mathbb{N}$,*
3) *O, the set of identifiers for a security object (e.g., for a bank or a supermarket),*
4) *DEVICE, the set of communication device identifiers (e.g., for a PDA device),*
5) *INCIDENT_TYPE:={burglary_alarm, fire_alarm, assault, medical_alarm},*
6) *S, the set of work shifts identifiers, where $s \in S$ is a tuple $<r, t_{start}, t_{end}>$. such that $r \in R$, identifying the route number of the shift, and $t_{start} \in \mathbb{R}$, denoting the start the time window of the shift, and $t_{end} \in \mathbb{R}$, denoting the end of the time window of a shift,*
7) *I, the set of incident identifiers such that $i \in I$ is a tuple $<incident\_type, o, t>$, such that $incident\_type \in INCIDENT\_TYPE$, identifying the type of incident, and $o \in O$, identifying the object related to the incident, and $t \in \mathbb{R}$, denoting the start of the incident,*

8) *C, the set of communication meetings(i.e. calls and conference calls), where c ∈ C is a tuple <n, t_{start},t_{end}, REASON>, such that n ∈ N, a set of unique identifier for each call, t_{start} ∈ R, denoting the start the time window of the call, and t_{end} ∈ R, denoting the end of the time window of the call, and REASON ∈ I ∪ {regular}, denoting whether the call is considered regular communication or related to incident I,*

9) *GRADE := {1,..,9}, the set of feedback grades on incident support provided.*

Among the different elements, either active or passive, different relations exist. In section 3.1, we have illustrated the MHS security domain. Essential to mobile surveillance are the security patrols on each work shift. A work shift is a sequence of visits preceded by a login and followed by a logout. Formally we define a work shift as follows:

Definition 3.3 (MHS Security Work Shifts). *A mobile human surveillance security work shift w is described by a member of the union set W containing planned shifts, active shifts and finished shifts, such that:*

1) *planned_shift ⊆ S × login × (planned_visit)* × logout,*
2) *finished_shift ⊆ login × (finished_visit)* × logout*
3) *active_shift ⊆ login × (finished_visit)* × [active_visit] × (planned_visit)*× logout*

Generally, we will be interested in the state of the work shifts at some time point. We define a function *state: S ×R → W*, which allows us to retrieve the current state of a work shift. The mean travel time between two objects is defined in Definition 3.4:

Definition 3.4 (MHS Security Travel Time). *The mean travel time $\overline{\delta}^{travel}$ from one object o_1 to another o_2 is defined by the following function:*

$$\overline{\delta}^{travel}(o_1,o_2) = \frac{\sum_{v \in V_{finished}} t_{arrival} - t_{goto}}{|\text{ finished\_visit }|} \qquad (1)$$

In the next section, we show what specific problem we provide a solution for in this paper.

3.3 Communication Support for Alarm Handling

An important problem in mobile surveillance is the assignment of route to alarms (see previous section). This process can be very time consuming. The average of the amount of time it takes for a team-leader to assign an alarm can be estimated using log data. We determined the alarm assignment delays using the log data from 9 months. On a total of 12694 alarm assignments in that period, the average assignment time is about 19 minutes. The amount of alarms that is assigned after 10 minutes is 75.6%. About 12.7 % of the alarms are assigned after one hour.

To speed up this process, we developed a dynamic conference call that allows the personnel to setup a multi-party phone call. Given a request for support re-quest_support($a_{incident}$,<*incident_type*,$o_{incident}$,$t_{incident}$>,t_0), the problem is how to setup a call setup_incident_call($a_{incident}$, <*incident_type*,$o_{incident}$,$t_{incident}$>,{a_1,...,a_n}, t_{setup}) most suitable for handling an incident of type incident_type at object $o_{incident}$ for this specific actor $a_{incident}$.

Having defined and exemplified different element of the mobile human surveillance security environment and the problem focus, in the next section we discuss the MHS incident communication support problem in more detail and show how multi-agent support can improve the performance in this environment.

4 The Ask-Assist System

To increase the speed of handling an incident, we propose an agent-based incident communication support system: Ask-Assist. The system consists of multiple agents. Each agent is mapped to either an actor or passive entities as defined in the previous section, see figure 1.

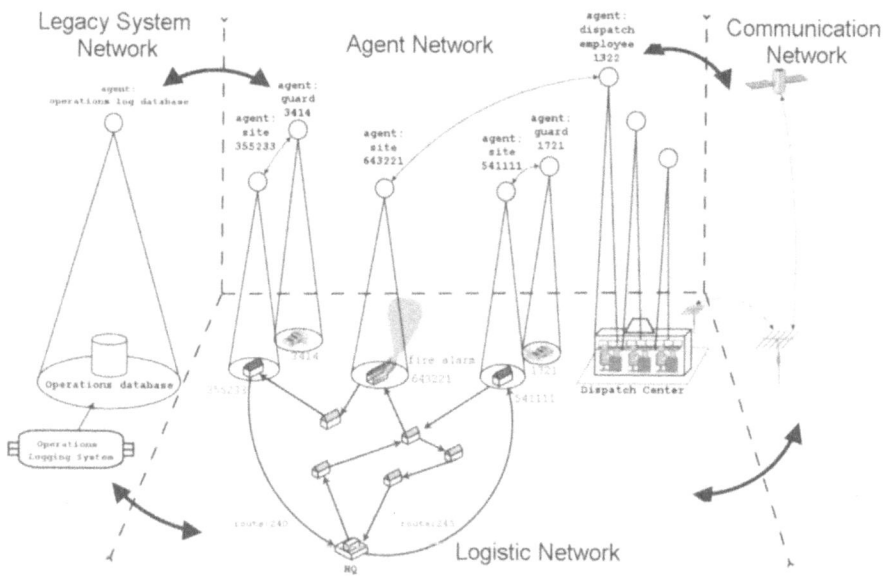

Fig. 1. A schematic overview of the mobile security environment and its mapping to the agent layer

Definition 4.1 (MHS Security Agents). *Let $\mathcal{A}$ be the set of agents and represent:*

$\mathcal{A} \rightarrow (A \cup P)$ *a function that maps each agent $\alpha \in \mathcal{A}$ to an entity in the environment. For example, we can each of the following type of entities to a corresponding agent:*

- *Operations log database agent α_{log}, where represent(α_{log}) = operations_log_system, and*
- *Guard agents α_g, where represent (α_g) = g | g ∈ G*

These agents represent the entities enabling the system as a whole to explore and extend potential communication connections in the real world. Agents recommend connections that may not exist in the network on the basis of their analyses of the data available on real world phenomena.

Each agent has different capabilities with respect to processing data that is retrieved on real world processes. In the next section, we will discuss the functionality of setting up a multi-party phone call for incident (i.e., alarms) handling by matchmaking based on logged data.

5   Algorithm for Self-organizing Incident Communication Support

We propose a collaborative content-based filtering approach to recommend communication when mobile human surveillance personnel are confronted with incidents. More specifically, we focus on the handling of alarms as described in section 3.3.

Both collaborative and content-based filtering are typically used in e-commerce recommendation systems to elicit user preferences on things like books, movies or music. But also in research there has been a growing interest in filtering techniques as an intelligent mechanism to deal with large amounts of data.

The idea is that in order to predict the preferences (e.g., by user ratings) of a set of users U over a set of items I, the filtering mechanism exploits either similarities between the preference schemes of users over items or the similarities between the items. If we define a utility function v measuring the value of an item i to a user u, i.e., $v: U \times I \rightarrow \mathbb{R}$, then to each user $u \in U$, we would like to recommend item $i \in I$ that maximizes the user's utility:

$$\forall u \in U, i = \arg\max_{i \in I} v(u,i) \qquad (2)$$

Similarly, we define the problem of finding the right person(s) $a \in 2^A$ to contact in case an alarm incident, $<\text{alarm\_type}_{incident}, o_{incident}, t_{incident}> \in INCIDENT$ is notified by a dispatch operator $d \in D$ and requests support, as follows:

$$\forall incident \in INCIDENT = \arg\max_{a \in 2^A} v(incident, a) \qquad (3)$$

where v is utility function, INCIDENT $\times 2^A \rightarrow \mathbb{R}$ that measure the utility of setting up communication with one or more persons a for an incident. While commonly most filtering algorithms are based on ratings provided by the users, we identify some additional factors that determine the utility of the support that is recommended.

5.1   Factors for Predicting the Success of Alarm Handling

We define a number of factors that are used to determine the expected success of communication aimed at handling alarms in mobile human surveillance:

• Incident similarity

The similarity between two incidents i_1 and i_2 is dependent on the nature of incident. This can be considered as a simple content-based similarity measure. We provide a function δ^i: INCIDENT $\times$ INCIDENT $\rightarrow [0,1]$ that allows us to propagate the utilities of handling different incident types. The function δ^i is described by the following table based on an expert opinion:

Table 1. Similarity table of the different incident types in mobile human surveillance

incident_types	burglary_alarm	fire_alarm	assault	medical_alarm
burglary_alarm	1.0	0.5	0.8	0.2
fire_alarm	0.5	1.0	0.6	0.3
assault	0.8	0.6	1.0	0.7
medical_alarm	0.2	0.3	0.7	1.0

- Explicit feedback

Each individual that has acted on a particular recommendation is contacted at a later time point to provide feedback on the systems recommendation, i.e., a number in the range of 1 to 9. This is a rating that measures whether the right people where suggested for handling the incident at hand., i.e., r:D × INCIDENT × A → GRADE, where a dispatch operator $d \in D$ evaluates the utility of actor $a \in A$ in handling an incident ∈ INCIDENT. To enrich the utility space of the feedback provided, we define a normalized feedback function φ: D× INCIDENT × A × 2^D→ [0,1] taking into account the ratings of a set of dispatch operators(i.e., the neighborhood), as follows:

$$\varphi(d, <q, o, t>, a, D') = \forall d \in D' \frac{\sum_{<q',o',t'>\in INCIDENT} r(d', <q', o', t'>, a) \times \delta^a(d, d') \times \delta^i(q, q')}{\sum_{<q',o',t'>\in INCIDENT} |\delta^a(d, d') \times \delta^i(q, q')|} \qquad (4)$$

where δ^a: $D \times D$ → [0,1] is a similarity function between two guards and $q \in$ INCIDENT_TYPE the type of the incident. We implemented δ^a by the standard Pearson correlation ρ [4]. The ratings of all guards in the guard agents neighborhood D' are weighted according to δ^a and δ^i.

- Experience

Some security objects are visited by particular guards more than other guards. We argue that these guards are therefore more experienced with these objects. We define the experience of an actor $a \in A$ in dealing with a particular type of incidents $q \in$ INCIDENT_TYPE with respect to a particular security object $o \in O$ and a decay ∈ ℝ as weight for the recentness of the alarm handling as a function ε:A × INCIDENT_TYPE × O × ℝ × 2^O → [0,1], taking into account the experience of a at similar object in the set 2^O, described by the following algorithm:

Algorithm 1:   ε (a,q,o,decay,O') → [0,1]

```
1:  t₀ = currentTime()
2:  total = 0
3:  result = 0
4:  for ∀o' ∈ O' do
```

```
 5:    for ∀incident ∈ INCIDENT do
 6:        if leave(a,<r',t_start,t_end>,<q',o',t_i>,t_j) ∈  incident
           then
 7:              result += (2^(-(tj-t0)/decay)) × 𝒮(o,o') × 𝒮(q,q')
 8:        endif
 9:        total+=1
10:    endfor
11: endfor
12: return result/total
```

where $\mathcal{S}: O \times O \to [0,1]$ is similarity function between two objects in terms of the guards by which they are visited. We implemented this by a kendall correlation τ on by ordering the guards by visiting frequencies to a particular location weighted by the recentness of the visit.

• Local rerouting costs

The rerouting of a actor $a \in A$ to an incident location $o_{incident} \in O$ is determined locally by a function $\gamma A \times O \to [0,1]$:

Algorithm 2 : $\gamma(a,o) \to [0,1]$

```
1:  t_0 = currentTime()
2:  r ← onRoute(a)
3:  active_shift_r ← state(<r,t_begin,t_end>,t_0) | t_begin < t_0 < t_end
4:  o_from ← current_position(active_shift_r)
5:  return 1/δ^travel (o_from,o_incident)
```

5.2 Recommendation and Adaptation Cycle

Setting up communication support involves a number of steps. First, the system needs to be initialized in to order directly provide the support in the field. This is realized by bootstrapping some part of the already available past data and initializing the neighborhood D' of each dispatch operator agent and the neighborhood O' of each object agent.

After having bootstrapped the agents, the following algorithm is used to produce a recommendation. This happens when the system receives a request for support (request_support).

Algorithm 3: SUPPORTALARMINCIDENT (request_support) → setup_incident_call

description: *this algorithm determines what call should be setup up, when an request for support for handling an alarm incident comes in.*

input: request_support($a_{incident}$,$<q_{incident},o_{incident},t_{incident}>$,$t_0$):
output: setup_incident_call($a_{incident}$, $<q_{incident},o_{incident},t_{incident}>$,$\{a_1,...,a_n\}$, t_{setup})

```
1:  candidate[] <- ∅
2:  for ∀a'∈ A | a' ≠ a_incident
3:     candidate[a'] = φ( a_incident , <q_incident,o_incident,t_incident>,a',D')
4:     candidate[a'] *= ε(a', q_incident,o_incident, decay, O')
5:     candidate[a'] *= γ(a', o_incident)
```

```
6:  end for
7:  candidate_sorted ← sort(candidate) by value
8:  group_to_call ← ∅
9:  for j = 0; j < n-best; j++ do
10:     group_to_call ← group_to_call ∪ candidate[j]
11: end for
12: return <a_incident, <q_incident, o_incident, t_incident>, group_to_call, t_now>
```

where for a particular incident the utility for each possible actor is determined and the *n-best* are picked for a conference meeting.

5.2 Learning by Iteration

Recommendations will result in particular behavior. First, implicitly, the new log events will show whether the recommendation was justified or not. Those new log events are processed and then utilized for future recommendation. In addition, explicit feedback may be received. These are processed as well, such that the agent links can be updated by replacing peers with low correlation or adding new peers that have a higher correlation. By allowing constant adaptation and a growth of incident related data, sparse events will be better handled as the amount of support request grows.

5.3 Experimental Results

We evaluated the potential of our filtering approach, which gave us some promising preliminary results. In the setting without any support, 62.45% of the alarm incidents is handled within the time limit of 30 minutes. By simulating the security domain based on a part of the logged data (n-best=3, decay=90 days), we found that for a bootstrapping period of 6 months, 72.2% could arrive within 30 minutes. Training the system on 9 months of log data gives a simulated result of 78.78%(see figure 2)

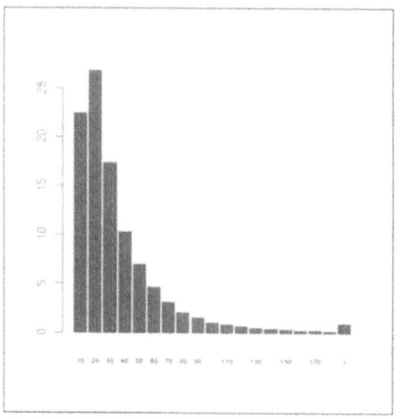

Real distributions of alarm handling times

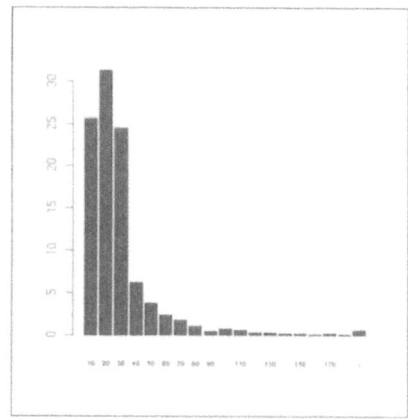

Simulated result when using Ask-Assist

Fig. 2. Distributions of the times to alarm handling

6 Discussion

In this paper we present a filtering approach for handling incidents in mobile human surveillance. Ask-Assist, the system that implements these algorithms, offers support to personnel of the Trigion security company. For this paper we concentrate on alarm incidents. Information on other incidents can be obtained from the authors. In simulated experiments on logged data made available to us by Trigion, we find that we can increase the amount of incidents that is handled in time (30 minutes) from 62.45% to 72.2% with an acceptable amount of training data. This means that roughly an extra 10% of the incidents, currently heavily delayed can be handled within 30 minutes. The results will be analyzed more thoroughly in future work, especially the dependency on different values for parameters such as *n-best, decay*.

Currently, a prototype of the system is being used by a security company in the Netherlands. The amount of human actors involved is around 60 guards and 5 team-leaders concerning 1318 sites. Ask-Assist has been developed by Almende B.V on a specific branch of its Common Hybrid Agent Platform(CHAP).[1]

In the future, we intend to evaluate the field study that is currently ongoing. In addition, we have an interest for the evolution of communication among the personnel and, specifically, for informal communication networks and their influence on performance. When confronted with incidents people tend to rely on their social network. Supporting this could be an interesting way to enhance incident management.

Acknowledgment

The authors would like to thank Trigion, especially, Ron Knaap, Rick Fenne, Harry Visser, the team-leaders of the region of Amsterdam, the guards in the region of Amsterdam and the alarm service centre. Great appreciation also goes out to Alfons Salden and Marian Verhaegh. Furthermore, the authors would like to thank ICIS and the Ministry of Economic Affairs in The Netherlands for funding this research.

References

1. Boy, G.A.: Cognitive function analysis for human-centered automation of safety-critical systems. In: Proceedings of the SIGCHI conference on Human factors in computing systems (CHI 1998), pp. 265–272. ACM Press/Addison-Wesley Publishing Co., New York (1998)
2. Boy, G.A.: Theories of Human Cognition: To Better Understand the Co-Adaptation of People and Technology, in Knowledge Management, Organizational Intelligence and Learning, and Complexity. In: Kiel, L.D. (ed.) Encyclopedia of Life Support Systems (EOLSS), Developed under the Auspices of the UNESCO. Eolss Publishers, Oxford (2002)
3. Basilico, J., Hofmann, T.: Unifying collaborative and content-based filtering. In: Proceedings Twenty-first International Conference on Machine Learning (ICML 2004) (2004)

---

[1] See http://sourceforge.chap.net and http://www.groovyactors.com

4. Breese, J., Heckerman, D., Kadie, C.: Empirical analysis of predictive algorithms for collaborative filtering. In: Proceedings of the 14th Conference on Uncertainty in Artificial Intelligence, pp. 43–52 (1998)
5. Niemann, C., Eymann, T.: Beyond Automation: Hybrid Human-Computer Decision Support Systems in Hospitals. In: Fifth IEEE Workshop on Engineering of Autonomic and Autonomous Systems (Ease 2008), pp. 46–53 (2008)
6. Rocchio, J.: Relevance feedback in information retrieval. In: The SMART Retrieval System: Experiments in Automatic document processing, pp. 313–323. Prentice-Hall, Englewood Cliffs (1971)
7. Sarne, D., Kraus, S.: Time-Variant Distributed Agent Matching Applications. In: AAMAS 2004, pp. 168–175. IEEE Computer Society, Washington (2004)
8. Storms, P.: System of Systems Architecture. In: Proceedings of the First International Conference on Information Systems for Crisis Response and Management (ISCRAM 2004), Brussels, Belgium (May 2004)
9. Streefkerk, J.W., van Esch-Bussemakers, M.P., Neerincx, M.A.: Context-aware notification for mobile police officers. In: Harris, D. (ed.) HCII 2007 and EPCE 2007. LNCS (LNAI), vol. 4562, pp. 436–445. Springer, Heidelberg (2007)
10. Wettig, H., Lahtinen, J., Lepola, T., Myllyämki, P., Tirri, H.: Bayesian Analysis of Online Newspaper Log Data. In: Proceedings of the 2003 Symposium on Applications and the Internet Workshops (SAINT-W 2003), p. 282. IEEE Computer Society, Washington (2003)
11. Zografos, K.G., Androutsopoulos, K.N., Vasilakis, G.M.: A real-time decision support system for roadway network incident response logistics. Transportation Research Part C 10, 1–18 (2002)

Joint Equilibrium Policy Search
for Multi-Agent Scheduling Problems

Thomas Gabel and Martin Riedmiller

Neuroinformatics Group
Department of Mathematics and Computer Science
Institute of Cognitive Science
University of Osnabrück, 49069 Osnabrück, Germany
{thomas.gabel,martin.riedmiller}@uni-osnabrueck.de

Abstract. We propose joint equilibrium policy search as a multi-agent learning algorithm for decentralized Markov decision processes with changing action sets. In its basic form, it relies on stochastic agent-specific policies parameterized by probability distributions defined for every state as well as on a heuristic that tells whether a joint equilibrium could be obtained. We also suggest an extended version where each agent employs a global policy parameterization which renders the approach applicable to larger-scale problems. Joint-equilibrium policy search is well suited for production planning, traffic control, and other application problems. In support of this, we apply our algorithms to a number of challenging scheduling benchmark problems, finding that solutions of very high quality can be obtained.

1 Introduction

Establishing inter-agent coordination in multi-agent systems depicts a challenging task. Agents that are disallowed to exchange coordinative messages must both determine where equilibria are located in the joint state-action space and also find out which equilibria are strived for by other agents. In this paper, we consider teams of cooperative agents that all seek to optimize a global reward. We assume that there exists at least one sequence of joint actions that leads the collective to a joint equilibrium, i.e. to a final state reaching which means to collect maximal summed rewards for all agents. Our goal is to enable the agents to learn to reach a joint equilibrium with increasing frequency by allowing them to adjust their probabilities of executing actions appropriately.

On the one hand, we build upon the framework of decentralized Markov decision processes with changing action sets that we recently [7] proposed as a mean to model a subclass of general multi-agent problems that features provably lower complexity than solving general DEC-MDPs does. A key property of this class is that each action can be executed only once by each agent. On the other hand, we borrow from an equilibrium selection algorithm for single-stage games by Fulda [5] and extend it (a) towards scenarios with multiple states at which actions can be executed and (b) towards a compact and efficient representation of the agents'

R. Bergmann et al. (Eds.): MATES 2008, LNAI 5244, pp. 61–72, 2008.

policies. In so doing, we obtain substantial savings in terms of computation time and memory requirements.

Although our learning approach is applicable to various practical problems, such as network routing or railway traffic control, the paper at hand specifically targets an application from the realm of production planning: We focus on job-shop scheduling problems (JSSP) that can easily be posed as multi-agent problems and represent and interesting testbed for distributed learning algorithms. Problems of this type are well-known for their intricacy (NP-hardness) and, what makes them appealing for use as a testbed, there exist various established benchmark problem suites using which we can compare our algorithms to other approaches.

The remainder of this paper is structured as follows. In the next section, we describe the general problem setting, clarify necessary notation, and introduce joint equilibrium policy search as a distributed learning algorithm for independent agents with common interests. In Section 3 we propose and theoretically investigate a substantial extension of that algorithm towards the use of a global, instead of local (state-specific) policy parameterization which renders the approach better scalable to larger problems. Section 4 presents the application domain of job-shop scheduling, explains how scheduling problems can be cast as multi-agent learning problems, and evaluates empirically the usability of the algorithms proposed in this paper for several benchmark problems.

2   Joint Equilibrium Policy Search

Joint equilibrium policy search (JEPS) is a distributed purely policy-based algorithm. Before presenting its details, we start off by providing some necessary notation.

2.1   Basics

We embed the problem settings of our interest into the framework of decentralized Markov decision processes (DEC-MDP) [2].

Definition 1 (Factored m-Agent DEC-MDP). *A factored m-agent DEC-MDP M is defined by a tuple*

$$\langle Ag, S, A, P, R, \Omega, O \rangle$$

where $Ag = \{1, \ldots, m\}$ is a set of agents, S is the set of world states that can be factored into m components $S = S_1 \times \cdots \times S_m$ (S_i belong to one of the agents each, all local states are fully observable), $A = A_1 \times \ldots \times A_m$ is the set of joint actions to be performed by the agents ($a = (a_1, \ldots, a_m) \in A$ denotes a joint action that is made up of elementary actions a_i taken by agent i), P is the transition function with $P(s'|s, a)$ denoting the probability that the system arrives at state s' upon executing a in s, R is a reward function with $R(s, a, s')$ denoting the reward for executing a in s and transitioning to s'. Moreover, M is jointly fully observable, i.e. the current state is entirely determined by the amalgamation of all agents' state observations.

We refer to the agent-specific components $s_i \in S_i$ and $a_i \in A_i$ as the local state and action of agent i. Each agent has only its local view, i.e. gets no information about other agents' local states and actions. We assume that there are some regularities that determine the way local actions exert influence on other agents' states. First, we assume that the sets of local actions A_i change over time.

Definition 2 (DEC-MDP with Changing Action Sets). *A factored m-agent DEC-MDP is said to feature* changing action sets *if the local state of agent i is fully described by the set of actions currently selectable by i ($s_i = A_i$) and A_i is a subset of the set of all available local actions $\mathcal{A}_i = \{\alpha_{i1} \ldots \alpha_{ik}\}$, thus $S_i = \mathcal{P}(\mathcal{A}_i)$.*

Concerning state transition dependencies, one can distinguish between dependent and independent local actions. While the former influence an agent's local state only, the latter may additionally influence the state transitions of other agents. Our interest is in non-transition independent scenarios. In particular, we assume that an agent's local state can be affected by an arbitrary number of other agents, but that an agent's local action affects the local state of maximally one other agent (see [7] for a formalization). Also, there are no circular state transition influences which implies that each agent can execute each of its local actions only once.

The influence exerted on another agent always yields an extension of that agent's action set: If the execution of local action α by agent i influences the local state of agent j, and i takes local action α, and the execution of α has been finished, then α is added to $A_j(s_j)$, while it is removed from $A_i(s_i)$. Thus, the multi-agent system is guaranteed to reach a final state $s^f \in S$ at which all actions have been processed and it holds $s_i^f = \emptyset$ for all i.

2.2 Learning Joint Policies

JEPS is a purely policy-search based algorithm (i.e. no value functions are employed), where all agents' policies are stochastic and are dependent on state-specific probability vectors denoting the probabilities with which each action is executed.

Definition 3 (JEPS Policy with Local Parameterization). *Let $s_i \in \mathcal{P}(\mathcal{A}_i)$ be the current state of agent i, where $s_i = A_i(s_i) = \{\alpha_1, \ldots, \alpha_{|s_i|}\}$ corresponds to the set of actions agent i can currently execute. Let $P_L(s_i) = \{p(\alpha_1|s_i), \ldots, p(\alpha_{|s_i|}| s_i)\}$ be a probability distribution over all actions from s_i, thus $0 \leq p(\alpha_j|s_i) \leq 1$ and $\sum_j p(\alpha_j|s_i) = 1$. Then, for agent i's policy of action $\pi_i : S_i \to A_i$ it holds $s_i \mapsto \alpha$ where α is selected from s_i with probability $p(\alpha|s_i)$. Accordingly, the joint policy is defined as $\pi = \langle \pi_1, \ldots, \pi_m \rangle$.*

We assume that all action probability vectors are randomly initialized and that the set of agents repeatedly interacts with the DEC-MDP until the final state s^f has been reached (also called the processing of a single episode). Then, the global reward r is distributed to all agents and the system is reset to a starting state. JEPS borrows from [5] in that it employs a binary heuristic $H(r)$ that is capable of telling whether a joint equilibrium has been attained. If so, it returns true, otherwise false. In the remainder of this paper, we utilize a rather simplistic implementation of H that returns true only if the current global reward equals or exceeds the maximal reward r_{max} obtained so far, i.e. $H(r) = 1 \Leftrightarrow r \geq r_{max}$. This idea has been exploited in a different context already by the Rmax algorithm [3] and by optimistic assumption Q learning [8].

After having finished a single episode and only if having found that $H(r) = 1$, each agent starts updating its action probabilities for all states it has encountered during that episode. Here, the probabilities of all actions that were executed (and thus contributed to reaching the joint equilibrium) are increased, while the probabilities for executing any of the actions despised is decreased (see Algorithm 1). Note, that this update scheme preserves that $\sum_j p(\alpha_j|s_i) = 1$ for all s_i. While the updates JEPS does to the action probabilities are calculated in a similar manner as in [5], the crucial difference is that JEPS is capable of distinguishing between multiple states s_i, and can thus handle more than single-stage games as it stores a single action probability vector for each local state.

Algorithm 1. JEPS Policy Updates by Agent i Using Local Action Parameters

Input: learning rate $\gamma \in (0, 1]$, state-action history of current episode
$\qquad h = [s_i(0), a_i(0), s_i(1), \ldots, s_i(T-1), a_i(T-1), s^f]$
$\qquad$ where $T = |\mathcal{A}_i|$ denotes the episode's length, global reward $r \in \mathbb{R}$
1: **if** $H(r) = 1$ **then**
2: $\quad$ **for** $t = 0$ to $t < T$ **do**
3: $\qquad$ **for all** $\alpha \in s_i(t)$ **do**
4: $\qquad\quad$ **if** $\alpha = a_i(t)$ **then** $p(\alpha|s_i(t)) \leftarrow p(\alpha|s_i(t)) + \gamma(1 - p(\alpha|s_i(t)))$
5: $\qquad\qquad$ **else** $p(\alpha|s_i(t)) \leftarrow (1 - \gamma)p(\alpha|s_i(t))$

2.3   Discussion

JEPS extends the mentioned learning approach for single-stage games in a purposive manner to problems with multiple states. Consequently, the policy update mechanism is guaranteed to converge[1] to a joint equilibrium as long as the heuristic H is correct in the sense that it tells a true joint equilibrium. This follows immediately from the convergence proof for single-stage games, since each of JEPS' states together with its belonging action probability vector can be regarded as an individual single-stage game considered by Fulda [5].

When intending to apply the version of JEPS presented to practical problems, two considerable problems arise. First, with a growing number of actions $|\mathcal{A}_i|$ available to the agents, the size of the state space grows exponentially, since states correspond to sets of available actions and, hence, in the worst case it holds $|S_i| = |\mathcal{P}(\mathcal{A}_i)| = 2^{|\mathcal{A}_i|}$. Accordingly, storing action probability vectors

---

[1] Here, convergence means that for all states s_i there is an $\alpha \in s_i$ such that $p(\alpha|s_i) \to 1$ in the course of learning.

for all states (separately for each of the agents) quickly becomes intractable as the problem size grows. Additionally, the large number of action probability vectors also increases the learning time needed until convergence to a nearly deterministic policy is achieved.

To tackle these problems, in the next section, we suggest a compact policy representation in combination with an alternative policy update mechanism that clearly reduces the computational complexity and memory requirements while still allowing for convergence to a joint equilibrium.

3   JEPS with Global Action Parameterization

Knowing the properties of DEC-MDPs with changing action sets (Definition 2) and given the problems mentioned in Section 2.3, a crucial observation is that each agent actually just has to be capable of learning a *total order* in which it executes all actions from $\mathcal{A}_i$.

3.1   Learning Total Orders of Action Execution

The basic idea for a version of JEPS that employs global action parameters (JEPS$_G$) is that, for each of the agents, we attach a single, or global, parameter to each action in $\mathcal{A}_i$ from which then its probability of execution is induced.

Definition 4 (JEPS with Global Action Parameterization). *Let $P_G = \{p_G(\alpha_k)|\alpha_k \in \mathcal{A}_i\}$ be a probability distribution over the set $\mathcal{A}_i$ of local actions agent i can execute, and let $s_i = A_i(s_i) = \{\alpha_1, \ldots, \alpha_{|s_i|}\} \in \mathcal{P}(\mathcal{A}_i)$ be its current state. Then, for agent i's policy of action $\pi_i : S_i \to \mathcal{A}_i$ it holds $s_i \mapsto \alpha$ where α is selected with probability*

$$p(\alpha|s_i) = \begin{cases} \frac{p_G(\alpha)}{\sum_{\alpha_k \in s_i} p_G(\alpha_k)} & \text{if } \alpha \in s_i \\ 0 & \text{else} \end{cases}, \tag{1}$$

and the joint policy π is the concatenation of local policies $\langle \pi_1, \ldots, \pi_m \rangle$.

Using this kind of policy representation each agent must store only $|\mathcal{A}_i|$ parameters which represents an enormous saving in terms of memory requirements compared to the JEPS version with local action probabilities.

Based on the policy representation with global parameters according to Definition 4, we suggest a learning algorithm that, for each agent, performs the parameter updates directly on the global parameter vector P_G. The distinguishing property of Algorithm 2 is that all positive updates, i.e. updates for actions taken when having reached a joint equilibrium (line 4), are performed relative to a state-specific baseline $\kappa_{s_i(t)}$ that is defined as

$$\kappa_{s_i(t)} := \sum_{\alpha_k \in s_i(t)} p_G(\alpha_k). \tag{2}$$

Algorithm 2. Policy Updates by JEPS Agent i Using Global Action Parameters

---

Input: learning rate $\gamma \in (0, 1]$, state-action history of current episode
$\qquad h = [s_i(0), a_i(0), s_i(1), \ldots, s_i(T-1), a_i(T-1), s^f]$
$\qquad$ where $T = |\mathcal{A}_i|$ denotes the episode's horizon, global reward $r \in \mathbb{R}$
1: **if** $H(r) = 1$ **then**
2: $\quad$ **for** $t = 0$ **to** $t < T$ **do**
3: $\qquad$ **forall** $\alpha \in s_i(t)$ **do**
4: $\qquad\quad$ **if** $\alpha = a_i(t)$ **then** $p_G(\alpha) \leftarrow p_G(\alpha) + \gamma(\sum_{\alpha_k \in s_i(t)} p_G(\alpha_k) - p_G(\alpha))$
5: $\qquad\quad$ **else** $p_G(\alpha) \leftarrow (1 - \gamma)p_G(\alpha)$

By this, it is possible to relate the local situation of agent i, i.e. its current local state, to the set of global action parameters, and it also ensured that P_G stays a proper probability distribution with $\sum_{\alpha_k \in s_i(t)} p_G(\alpha_k) = 1$.

For this algorithm, we can show that for every agent and each local state s_i the probability of executing an action $\alpha \in s_i$ that does *not* support yielding a joint equilibrium is declining if it exceeds some threshold.

Lemma 1. *Let $\alpha \in s_i$ and $p_G(\alpha) > \frac{\kappa_{s_i}}{2}$. If the execution of α in state s_i does not yield a joint equilibrium, then $\Delta p_G(\alpha) < 0$, where Δp_G represents the difference of $p_G(\alpha)$ after and prior to the call to Algorithm 2.*

Proof. If the current episode did not reach an equilibrium, no updates are performed. Consider the case when an equilibrium has been reached and focus on the smallest value of t for which it holds $\alpha \in s_i(t)$ for an arbitrary $\alpha \in \mathcal{A}_i$. Let $t + v$ $(v \geq 1)$ be the stage at which α has finally been selected for execution. Then, the value of $p_G(\alpha)$ will have been decremented v times according to line 5 (denote the result of this calculation as $p_G^-(\alpha)$) and been increased a single time at $s_i(t+v)$. Thus,

$$p_G'(\alpha) := p_G(\alpha) + \Delta p_G(\alpha) = p_G^-(\alpha) + \gamma(\kappa_{s_i(t+v)} - p_G^-(\alpha))$$
$$= (1 - \gamma)^{v+1} p_G(\alpha) + \gamma \sum_{\alpha_k \in s_i(t+v)} p_G^-(\alpha_k).$$

For the sum on the right-hand side there exist values $v_k \geq 0$ for all $\alpha_k \in s_i(t+v)$ such that $p_G^-(\alpha_k) = (1 - \gamma)^{v_k} p_G(\alpha_k)$. Since we are looking for the circumstances under which $p_G'(\alpha) < p_G(\alpha)$, i.e. $\Delta p_G(\alpha) < 0$, we finally arrive at

$$\Delta p_G(\alpha) < 0 \Leftrightarrow p_G(\alpha) > \frac{\gamma \sum_{\alpha_k \in s_i(t+v)} (1 - \gamma)^{v_k} p_G(\alpha_k)}{1 - (1 - \gamma)^{v+1}} =: \delta(\gamma).$$

The term $\delta(\gamma)$ attains its maximal value for $v = 1$ and $v_k = 0 \forall k$. Then, $\delta(\gamma) = \frac{1-\gamma}{2-\gamma} \sum_{\alpha_k \in s_i(t+v)} p_G(\alpha_k)$. Maximizing subject to γ ($\gamma \to 0$), we obtain $\delta = \frac{\kappa_{s_i(t+v)}}{2}$. And because by definition $\kappa_{s_i(t)} > \kappa_{s_i(t+v)}$ for all $v \geq 1$, we finally see that for $p_G(\alpha) > \frac{\kappa_{s_i(t)}}{2}$ it holds $\Delta p_G(\alpha) < 0$. $\qquad\square$

Lemma 1 shows that probability updates cannot enforce convergence to suboptimal action choices. Unfortunately, still there may be the case of two joint equilibria with identical global reward between which the agent may oscillate. However, we can show that for any state s_i there is a critical action probability value such that upon exceeding that value one joint equilibrium starts dominating another one.

Lemma 2. *If $\alpha \in s_i(t)$ is an action within a joint equilibrium episode, then there exists a value p^* such that, if $p_G(\alpha) > p^*$, then $p_G(\alpha)$ is more likely to increase over time than to decrease.*

Proof. The critical case of $p_G(\alpha)$ decreasing can occur, if there is a $\beta \in s_i(t)$ such that still a joint equilibrium can be obtained when β is executed in s_i. If α is executed, then $p_G(\alpha)$ is increased (line 4), whereas $p_G(\beta)$ is decreased (line 5) at least one time and later increased at a $t + v > t$ when β is finally executed. If β is selected in s_i, the situation is the other way round ($p_G(\alpha)$ decreased v times according to line 5, if it is selected v decision time points later). Consequently, with a probability of $\frac{p_G(\alpha)}{\kappa_{s_i(t)}}$ it holds

$$p_G^\alpha(\alpha) := p_G(\alpha) + \Delta p_G(\alpha) = p_G(\alpha) + \gamma(\kappa_{s_i(t)} - p_G(\alpha))$$

and with a probability of $\frac{p_G(\beta)}{\kappa_{s_(t)}}$ it holds

$$p_G^\beta(\alpha) := p_G^-(\alpha) + \gamma(\kappa_{s_i(t+v)} - p_G^-(\alpha))$$
$$= (1 - \gamma)^v p_G(\alpha) + \gamma(\kappa_{s_i(t+v)} - (1 - \gamma)^v p_G(\alpha)).$$

Since we look for the conditions under which $\Delta p_G(\alpha) = p_G'(\alpha) - p_G(\alpha) > 0$, we can express this inequation using a weighted average as

$$\frac{p_G(\alpha)p_G^\alpha(\alpha) + p_G(\beta)p_G^\beta(\alpha)}{\kappa_{s_i(t)}(p_G(\alpha) + p_G(\alpha))} - p_G(\alpha) > 0.$$

After a number of algebraic reformulations, this simplifies to

$$\frac{\kappa_{s_i(t)}}{p_G(\beta)} + \frac{\kappa_{s_i(t+v)}}{p_G(\alpha)} > \frac{1 + \gamma - (1 - \gamma^{v+1})}{\gamma}.$$

The right-hand side of this inequation attains its maximum for $v \to \infty$ which becomes $1 + \frac{1}{\gamma}$. For the left-hand side, we know that $\kappa_{s_i(t)} \geq p_G(\alpha) + p_G(\beta)$ and $\kappa_{s_i(t+v)} \geq p_G(\alpha)$. Assuming the worst case (both equalities) here, too, we arrive at

$$\frac{p_G(\alpha) + p_G\beta}{p_G(\beta)} + \frac{p_G(\alpha)}{p_G(\alpha)} > 1 + \frac{1}{\gamma} \text{ and thus } \frac{p_G(\alpha)}{p_G(\beta)} > \frac{1 - \gamma}{\gamma}.$$

Consequently, if for a state s_i one joint equilibrium action $\alpha \in s_i$ dominates all other actions by a share of at least $p^* := \frac{1 - \gamma}{\gamma}$, then $\Delta p_G(\alpha)$ tends to be positive. □

3.2 Discussion

If for some action α within an equilibrium episode the probability of execution exceeds some critical value, then $p_G(\alpha)$ tends to be increasing continually. Since updates are not just made for single actions, but for all actions taken during an equilibrial episode, this argument transfers to the remaining actions from $\mathcal{A}_i$ as well. With continued positive updates all $p_G(\alpha_k)$ converge such that for each s_i there is a $\alpha_{s_i}^*$ with $\frac{p_G(\alpha_{s_i}^*)}{\kappa_{s_i}} \to 1$, which means that the policy the agent pursues approaches a deterministic one.

Of course, the time required for convergence to occur may be high. Setting the learning rate γ to a higher value, learning can be speeded up. However, this comes at the cost of an increased probability, that learning converges prematurely to a non-equilibrium, because the heuristic H we use is imperfect with respect to the true joint equilibrium of the system. Insofar, adjusting γ represents a mean to trade off learning speed and the goal of obtaining a joint policy very close to a joint equilibrium.

Returning to the point of view of a total order of action execution that is represented by the vector of global action parameters P_G, we observe that JEPS$_G$ may drive the parameters $p_G(\alpha)$ and $p_G(\beta)$ for some actions α and β (in particular for actions whose execution is repeatedly postponed) to very small numerical values – while at the same time it may be required that the share of $p_G(\alpha)$ and $p_G(\beta)$ must be either very large or small. As a consequence, a limiting factor when implementing and using Algorithm 2 is given by the smallest real-valued number that can be represented on the respective hardware[2]. Accordingly, the convergence behavior of a practical implementation of JEPS$_G$ will be as follows:

a) Convergence to a joint equilibrium policy, as indicated by heuristic H in conjunction with r_{max}, occurring with a probability of nearly one may occur. This means, after λ learning episodes it holds for all agents i, for all states s_i, and for all $\alpha \in s_i$ that $\frac{p_G(\alpha)}{\kappa_{s_i}} > 1 - \epsilon$ for some small $\epsilon > 0$.
b) Numerical underflow problems arise[3], i.e. that there is an agent i and a state s_i where for a $\alpha \in s_i$ it holds $p_G(\alpha) < \epsilon_{min}$, where $\epsilon_{min} \in \mathbb{R}^+$ is the smallest floating number representable on the respective hardware platform.
c) The learning time allotted to the algorithm is exceeded, i.e. λ_{max} learning episodes have been processed without situation a) and b) having occurred.

Note that, although no convergence is achieved in cases b) and c), the algorithm does not diverge – in fact, it rather stops its learning process too early. At least, in these cases we can use the value of the presumed joint equilibrium found so far (r_{max}) as an indicator of the true equilibrium that eventually would have been discovered if λ_{max} was larger or ϵ_{min} smaller.

4   Empirical Evaluation

In this section, we use the class of DEC-MDPs with changing action sets to model job-shop scheduling problems (JSSP), and we evaluate the performance of JEPS and JEPS$_G$ in this context using various established scheduling benchmarks.

4.1   Application Domain: Job-Shop Scheduling

The goal of scheduling is to allocate a specified number of jobs to a limited number of resources (also called machines) such that some objective is optimized. In

---

[2] According to the IEEE standard for binary floating-point arithmetic (IEEE 754), when using 64 bit, the smallest number is approximately $2.2 \cdot 10^{-308}$ (*double* type).
[3] This case is more likely to occur, the larger $|P_G|$ is.

job-shop scheduling n jobs must be processed on m machines in a given order. Each job j consists of ν_j operations $o_{j,1} \ldots o_{j,\nu_j}$ that have to be handled on a certain resource for a specific duration. A job is finished after its last operation has been entirely processed (completion time f_j). In general, scheduling objectives to be optimized all relate to the completion time of the jobs. In this paper, we concentrate on the goal of minimizing maximum makespan ($C_{max} = max_j\{f_j\}$), which corresponds to finishing processing (and hence reaching the final state s^f) as quickly as possible, since most publications on results for job-shop scheduling benchmarks focus on that objective, too.

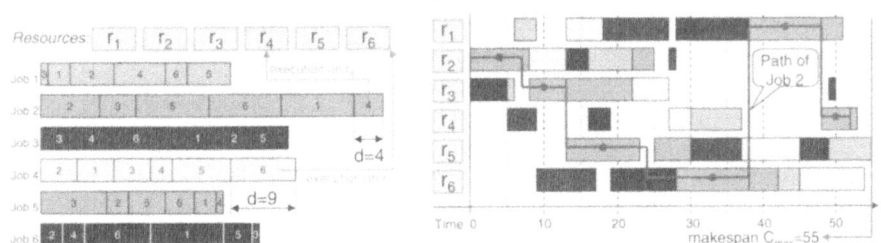

Fig. 1. Example Job-Shop Scheduling Problem FT6 (left) and Optimal Solution (right)

Solving JSSPs is well-known to be NP-hard. Over the years, numerous benchmark problem instances of varying sizes have been proposed and have been frequently used to compare different solution approaches. We revert to a collection of sample problems that is provided by the OR Library [1]. A common characteristic of those scheduling benchmarks is that usually no recirculation of jobs is allowed, i.e. that each job must be processed exactly once on each resource ($\nu_j = m$). Figure 1 shows an example of a small job-shop scheduling problem with six resource and six jobs consisting of six jobs each; also an optimal solution of that problem with respect to minimal makespan is illustrated using a Gantt chart. For more details on scheduling, the reader is referred to [10,4].

We model JSSPs as factored m-agent DEC-MDPs with changing action sets as follows. We attach to each of the resources one agent i whose local action is to decide which waiting job to process next. Agent i's local state of i can be fully described by the changing set of jobs currently waiting for further processing. Choosing and executing a job represents a local action ($\mathcal{A}_i$ is the set of jobs that must be processed on resource i), which is why it holds $S_i = \mathcal{P}(\mathcal{A}_i)$. After finishing the processing of a job's operation, this job is transferred to another resource, where the order of resources on which a job's operations must be processed is given a priori. In conjunction with the no recirculation property mentioned above, in fact, each job (one of its operations, respectively) has to be executed on each resource exactly once. As a consequence, for JEPS$_G$ is will be sufficient that each agent stores one action probability parameter for each job.

4.2   Benchmark Results

Given an instance of a JSSP, all agents process waiting jobs in a reactive manner, i.e. they select jobs with respect to the probability determined by their current policy parameters, and never remain idle, if there is at least one job waiting. When all jobs are finished and, hence, s^f has been reached, the global reward $r = -C_{max}$ is conveyed to the agents, the policy update algorithm (Algorithm 1/2) is called, and finally the system is reinitialized to the starting state where no jobs have been processed. We allow the agents to maximally process $\lambda_{max} = 250k$ episodes, however, in most cases convergence is achieved much faster. For consistency, during all experiments we set $\gamma = 0.1$, a value that ad hoc brought about good results and whose optimization should be subject to further studies.

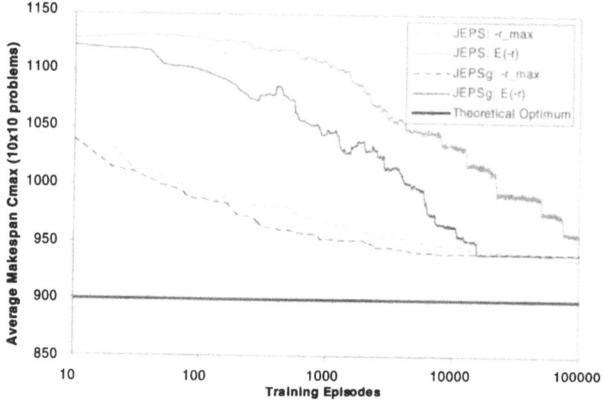

Fig. 2. Learning Progress for JEPS and JEPS$_G$

Figure 2 illustrates the learning progress averaged over 15 JSSP problems involving 10 jobs and 10 machines using JEPS as well as JEPS$_G$. The solid curves show the average expected performance (in terms of makespan C_{max}, i.e. negative reward) of the stochastic joint policies subject to the number of training episodes. Dashed curves indicate the development of the value of the supposed joint equilibrium $-r_{max}$, as utilized by the heuristic H.

Apparently the $-r_{max}$ and $E[-r]$ curves approach each other much faster for the JEPS$_G$ variant of the algorithm than for JEPS with local policy parameterization. For the 15 scenarios considered, JEPS$_G$ converges at the latest after about 11k episodes (note the log scale x-axis). By contrast, JEPS needs much longer to yield convergence, but achieves finding slightly superior values of r_{max}, i.e. on average the learnt joint policy comes closer to the true joint equilibrium (indicated by the average theoretical optimum for the scenarios considered).

The limitation of the basic form of JEPS becomes obvious when having a look at the sizes of the policies that must be kept in memory by the agents (see the rightmost columns in the of the JEPS and JEPS$_G$ part in Table 1, measured in bytes per policy). Since the number of policy parameters grows exponentially

Table 1. Learning results for scheduling benchmarks of varying size, opposed for *JEPS* and *JEPS$_g$*. All entries are averaged over *#Prbl*. *#a*, *#b*, and *#c* correspond to the convergence possibilities listed in Section 3.2. The last column in each part shows the average size of a policy measured in bytes. *Err.* columns denote the relative remaining error (%) of the makespan ($-r_{max}$) achieved by the joint policy compared to the theoretical optimum and, thus, indicate to what extent reaching the true joint equilibrium was missed. Indices *a*, *b*, *c* stand for problem sets provided by different authors.

Size $m \times n$	#Prbl	Theor. Optim.	JEPS #a	$-r_{max}$	$E[-r]$	Err.	Pol. Size	JEPS$_G$ #a	#b	#c	$-r_{max}$	$E[-r]$	Err.	Pol. Size
5×10	5	620.2	5	631.8	631.8	1.9%	1029k	4	0	1	635.4	644.2	2.5%	0.6k
5×15	5	917.6	5	917.6	917.6	0.0%	18M	5	0	0	917.6	917.6	0.0%	1.1k
5×20	6	1179.2	0	-	-	-	∞	5	1	0	1188.3	1196.5	0.8%	1.5k
$10 \times 10_a$	3	1035.7	3	1071.0	1071.0	3.4%	3.5M	3	1	0	1076.7	1076.7	3.9%	1.2k
$10 \times 10_b$	5	864.2	5	902.4	902.4	4.4%	973k	5	1	0	894.2	894.2	3.5%	1.1k
$10 \times 10_c$	9	898.2	8	935.3	937.9	4.1%	6.4M	8	1	0	952.4	953.6	6.0%	1.2k
10×15	5	983.4	0	-	-	-	∞	2	1	2	1032.4	1142.4	5.0%	2.1k
15×15	5	1263.2	0	-	-	-	∞	3	1	1	1341.2	1375.8	6.1%	3.0k
15×20	3	676.0	0	-	-	-	∞	0	0	3	732.0	819.7	8.3%	4.1k

with n, the application of JEPS for $m \times n$ problems with larger values of n is infeasible due to excessive memory requirements. On the contrary, the average policy sizes of JEPS$_G$ agents are negligible. Here, instead the underflow problem (cf. Section 3.2) may occur for larger values of n. However, using JEPS$_G$, policies of high quality can be learnt even for larger-sized problem instances.

The remaining error values achieved can well compete with alternative approaches that tackle the scheduling problem from a decentralized perspective (centralized algorithms mostly find the optimum). For example, dispatching priority rules are clearly outperformed (best rules are SPT, which chooses operations with shortest processing time, and AMCC [9], which is a heuristic to avoid the maximum current C_{max}, with an average error of 20.6% and 7.8% for the 46 problems mentioned in Table 1). OA-NFQ [6], a value-function based reinforcement learning approach to these problems, reaches an error of 4.2%.

We expect that, in future work, we will be able to further boost the performance of JEPS. In the version presented the reactive functioning of JEPS can generate schedules of the class $\mathbb{S}_n$ of *non-delay* schedules exclusively: If a resource has finished processing one operation and has at least one job waiting, the respective agent immediately continues processing by picking one of the waiting jobs. JEPS does not allow a resource to remain idle, if there is more work to be done. From scheduling theory, however, it is known that for certain scheduling problem instances the optimal schedule may be a delay schedule from the set of active schedules $\mathbb{S}_a \supsetneq \mathbb{S}_n$, i.e. a schedule where some resource has to remain idle for some time units in order to achieve minimal makespan. As a consequence, JEPS is currently able to produce near-optimal schedules from $\mathbb{S}_n$ and may miss the best schedule possible, though in several cases the true joint equilibrium is indeed found. Yet, an extension of JEPS towards behaving not purely reactively depicts an important and promising issue for future work.

5   Conclusion

We have presented a multi-agent policy search method, JEPS, that is effective in learning joint equilibria, or near-optimal approximations thereof, for decentralized Markov decision processes with changing action sets. Using a variant of the algorithm that employs a highly compacted policy representation, it is possible to apply JEPS to even larger problem instances without impairing performance.

A limiting factor of the approach is the necessity for a heuristic that indicates whether a joint equilibrium has been reached by the ensemble of agents. In future work, we will investigate more sophisticated versions of this heuristic and, moreover, we will explore state of the art mechanisms, such as policy-gradient descent methods, for updating the policy parameters, which we expect to significantly speed up the learning process.

Acknowledgements. This research has been supported by the German Research Foundation (DFG) under grant number Ri 923/2-3.

References

1. Beasley, J.: Or-library (2005),
   http://people.brunel.ac.uk/~mastjjb/jeb/info.html
2. Bernstein, D., Givan, D., Immerman, N., Zilberstein, S.: The Complexity of Decentralized Control of Markov Decision Processes. Mathematics of Operations Research 27(4), 819–840 (2002)
3. Brafman, R., Tennenholtz, M.: Learning to Cooperate Efficiently: A Model-Based Approach. Journal of Artificial Intelligence Research 19, 11–23 (2003)
4. Brucker, P., Knust, S.: Complex Scheduling. Springer, Berlin (2006)
5. Fulda, N., Ventura, D.: Incremental Policy Learning: An Equilibrium Selection Algorithm for Reinforcement Learning Agents with Common Interests. In: Proceedings of the 2004 IEEE International Joint Conference on Neural Networks (IJCNN), Budapest, Hungary, pp. 1121–1125. IEEE Computer Society Press, Los Alamitos (2004)
6. Gabel, T., Riedmiller, M.: Adaptive Reactive Job-Shop Scheduling with Learning Agents. International Journal of Information Technology and Intelligent Computing 2(4) (2008)
7. Gabel, T., Riedmiller, M.: Reinforcement Learning for DEC-MDPs with Changing Action Sets and Partially Ordered Dependencies. In: Proceedings of the 7th International Conference on Autonomous Agents and Multi-Agent Systems (AAMAS 2008), Estoril, Portugal (to appear, 2008)
8. Lauer, M., Riedmiller, M.: An Algorithm for Distributed Reinforcement Learning in Cooperative Multi-Agent Systems. In: Proceedings of the International Conference on Machine Learning (ICML 2000), Stanford, USA, pp. 535–542. AAAI Press, Menlo Park (2000)
9. Mascis, A., Pacciarelli, D.: Job-Shop Scheduling with Blocking and No-Wait Constraints. European Journal of Operational Research 143, 498–517 (2002)
10. Pinedo, M.: Scheduling. Theory, Algorithms, and Systems. Prentice Hall, USA (2002)

Making Allocations Collectively: Iterative Group Decision Making under Uncertainty

Christian Guttmann*

Department of General Practice
Faculty of Medicine, Nursing and Health Sciences
Monash University, Melbourne, Australia
christian.guttmann@gmail.com

Abstract. A major challenge in the field of Multi-Agent Systems (MAS) is to enable autonomous agents to allocate tasks and resources efficiently. This paper studies an extended approach to a problem we refer to as the Collective Iterative Allocation (CIA) problem. This problem involves a group of agents that progressively refine allocations of teams to tasks. This paper considers the case where the performance of a team is variable and non-deterministic. This requires that each agent is able to maintain and update its probabilistic models using observations of each team's performance. A key result is that each agent needs the capacity to store only two or three observations of a team's performance to find near optimal allocations, and a further increase of this capacity will reduce the number of reallocations significantly.

1 Introduction

Efficient approaches to distributed allocation problems are required in a wide range of applications, such as network routing, crisis management, logistics, computational grids, and collaborative student support environments [1]. We consider a problem we refer to as the Collective Iterative Allocation (CIA) problem [2,3,4]. This problem involves a group of agents that endeavours to find an optimal allocation of a team to a task, and subsequent allocations are then refined as the true performance of a team becomes known.[1] Note that this paper describes allocations using the terms *tasks* and *teams*, but this terminology

---

* The author would like to thank Michael Georgeff, Iyad Rahwan and Ingrid Zukerman for their assistance related to this research. The author is also grateful for the insightful comments of the reviewers. Part of this work was done at the School of Computer Science and Software Engineering at the Faculty of Information Technology and at the Monash Institute of Health Services Research at the Faculty of Medicine, Nursing and Health Sciences, Monash University, Melbourne, Australia.

[1] In this paper, we assume that agents are collaborative and task-rational. That is, each agent proposes a team with the highest performance according to the agent's models. In [3], we investigated issues related to competitive agents that follow a strategy when making group decisions.

R. Bergmann et al. (Eds.): MATES 2008, LNAI 5244, pp. 73–85, 2008.

is specific to the domain of application. The Multi-Agent System (MAS) paradigm is useful to study the efficiency of algorithms to distributed coordination problems [5], and particularly to the CIA problem [2,3,4].

Many research frameworks on allocation problems make a simplistic assumption: the performance of a team is deterministic and invariant [1]. This paper extends our previous framework [3] that copes with agents that exhibit variable and non-deterministic performance in the CIA problem. In particular, in [3], we consider how each agent maintains a probabilistic model which represents a team's performance by a mean (average performance of team) and standard deviation (stability of performance). Each agent updates its model when new information of a team is available. The focus of this paper is on (a) identifying conditions that influence finding near-optimal solutions and the time it takes to find such solutions, and (b) developing methods that refine the process of selection under conditions of uncertainty. This paper extends our work in [2,3,4] as follows.

- *Framework Extensions:* We offer extensions of the modelling and reasoning abilities of agents. For example, each agent uses a shared observation memory that determines how many observations of all teams can be remembered by an agent for the refinement of models (in previous research [3], each agent stores an observation of each agent in a separate memory).
- *Empirical Study:* We offer a deeper empirical understanding of the efficiency of our algorithm, as we explore parameters additional to those used in [3]. For example, we vary the termination criteria (which indicates the stability of converging to a solution), and also the level of ignorance that each agent exhibits prior to running the algorithm.
- *Evaluation:* We analyse the efficiency of the algorithm using measures of solution quality (average task performance of a team) and in addition to previous research [3], we also evaluate the algorithm's computational requirement (the average number of iterations before a solution is found).

Section 2 offers a formal representation of our extended approach. Section 3 investigates the efficiency of this algorithm under the condition that the performance of teams is variable. Related research is discussed in Section 4. Section 5 summarises the insights and contributions offered by this research.

2 Framework Coping with Uncertainty

Section 2.1 defines the main components of the CIA problem and Section 2.2 defines and illustrates our algorithm.

2.1 Defining the Main Components

The CIA problem is represented by the following tuple.

$$CIA = < T, AT, A = \{a_1(M_{a_1}, RP_{a_1}), \ldots, a_q(M_{a_q}, RP_{a_q})\}, P >$$

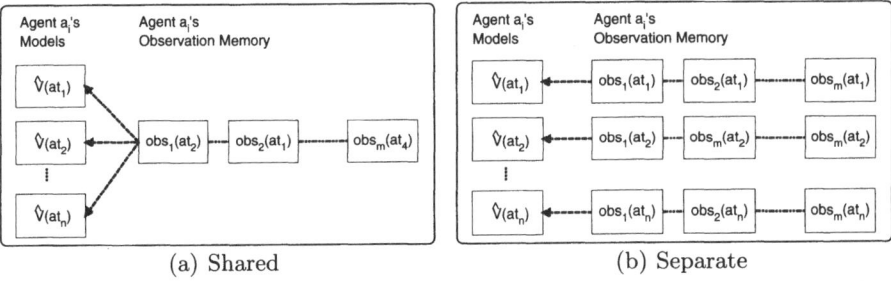

Fig. 1. Observation Memory

T is a set of Tasks, each can be assigned to an Agent Team ($\in$ AT). Each agent a_i in A maintains Models M and uses Reasoning Processes RP to make assignments collectively using a group decision Policy P. These elements are defined in the following paragraphs. Note that the models M_{a_i} and reasoning processes RP_{a_i} maintained by each agent a_i are substantially refined and extended compared to those offered in [3].

Definition 1. $T = \{t_1, \ldots, t_s\}$ *is a set of Tasks with* $s = |T|$.

Definition 2. $AT = \{at_1, \ldots, at_p\}$ *is a set of Agent Teams with* $p = |AT|$.

This paper assumes that a team's performance varies each time it performs a task. In particular, we assume that this varying performance is based on a normal distribution N_{at_j,t_k} with a mean μ_{at_j,t_k} (representing the average performance of a team), and a standard deviation σ_{at_j,t_k} (representing the stability of the performance), so that $N_{at_j,t_k}(\mu_{at_j,t_k}, \sigma_{at_j,t_k})$ for a given team at_j and task t_k. To be consistent with the notation used in previous research, we also refer to this distribution as $V(at_j, t_k)$ [4]. A set of distributions (that describe the true performance for several tasks) is called the *capability* of a team: $C(at_i)$.

We now define a group of agents that actively participates in assigning a team at_i to a task t_k.

Definition 3. $A = \{a_1, \ldots, a_q\}$ *is a set of Agents with* $q = |A|$.

The capability of a team $C(at_i)$ is *not* directly observable (as is the case for a team's deterministic performance [4]). Hence, each agent has a model consisting of a set of estimated distribution parameters (Definition 4). Each agent also executes reasoning processes that use these models (Definition 5).

Definition 4. M_{a_i} *are the* **Models** *maintained by agent* a_i: $M_{a_i} = \{M_{a_i}(at_1),$ $\ldots, M_{a_i}(at_p)\}$ *with* $p = |AT|$. *A specific model of a team* at_j *is defined by a set of estimations:* $M_{a_i}(at_j) = \{\hat{V}_{a_i}(at_j, t_1), \ldots, \hat{V}_{a_i}(at_j, t_s)\}$, *where* $\hat{V}_{a_i}(at_j) = \hat{N}_{a_i,at_j,t_k}(\hat{\mu}_{at_j,t_k}, \hat{\sigma}_{at_j,t_k})$ *for* $j = 1, \ldots, n$.

For example, for a given task, assume that lifesaver at_2's performance is represented by a normal distribution N_{at_2} with a mean $\mu_{at_2} = 0.4$ (representing the average rescue performance of at_2), and a standard deviation $\sigma_{at_2} = 0.1$ (representing its stability), such that $N_{at_2}(\mu_{at_2} = 0.4, \sigma_{at_2} = 0.1)$. Also, assume that a_1's model estimates the mean and stability of at_2's performance: $\hat{N}_{a_1, at_2}(\hat{\mu}_{at_2} = 0.5, \hat{\sigma}_{at_2} = 0.2)$. In this example, a_1 overestimates the mean of at_2's true performance as well as its variability when it performs the task.

Each agent in A executes reasoning processes that use the information stored in its models.

Definition 5. RP_{a_i} denote agent a_i's **Reasoning Processes.**

- *For agent a_i, $INITIALISE_{a_i}(M_{a_i}, t_k)$ returns a set of initial models.*
- *For agent a_i, $PROPOSE_{a_i}(M_{a_i}, t_k)$ returns a proposal specifying a_i's preference of a team that should perform a task: $proposal_{a_i} = \langle at_j, \hat{\mu}_{at_j} \rangle$. An agent is assumed to be task-rational and therefore proposes a team with the highest estimated value in its models (related studies investigate agents that make strategic proposals, e.g., [3]).*
- *For agent a_i, $UPDATE_{a_i}(M_{a_i}, observation(at_j))$ returns a set of updated models based on information of team at_j's performance. Let $observation(at_j)$ be a function that returns a measure of the performance of the team at_j for a given task. This value is drawn from a team's capability distribution ($observation(at_j) \sim V(at_j)$).*

The update process requires a memory to store these observations. We refer to this as *shared observation memory* (Figure 1(a)) and it works as follows. Each agent retains a window of the last k observations of the performance of all teams (each observation is tagged with the team that performed the task). The update process recalculates the estimated mean and standard deviation of the estimated distribution of a team each time an observation is made. When an agent updates its models of a team, the observations of this team are extracted from the shared observation memory using the corresponding tags. The results obtained by this process are moderated by the number of observations stored by each agent. That is, if an agent a_i has stored k observations of team at_k's performance, then the mean and standard deviation are calculated from k observations, such that $\hat{N}_{a_i, at_j}(\hat{\mu}_{at_j, k}, \hat{\sigma}_{at_j, k})$ for $j = 1, \ldots, n$.[2]

Definition 6. *A group decision Policy P is a function that selects a team based on the proposals submitted by agents A, such that*

$$at_{selected} := P(PROPOSALS_A), \text{ where}$$

- *agent $at_{selected}$ is one of the teams proposed by agents A, and*
- *$PROPOSALS_A$ is a set of proposals submitted by these agents.*

---

[2] Note that sharing memory to store observations (as opposed to separately storing the observations of each team as done in [3] and explained in Figure 1(b)) can significantly reduce the number of unused storage entries. As such, shared observation memory will be particularly efficient if we have a large number of teams and only few of them will perform a task.

TAP ASSIGNMENT ALGORITHM.
INPUT: Task $t_k \in T$, Agent Teams AT, Agents A, Policy P
OUTPUT: Assignment of $at_j \in AT$ to $t_k \in T$

- -

1. ANNOUNCE task $t_k \in T$
2. INITIALISE$_{a_i}(M_{a_i}, t_k)$ $(\forall a_i \in A)$
3. Repeat
    (a) $PROPOSALS_A = \bigcup_{a_i \in A} PROPOSE_{a_i}(M_{a_i}, t_k)$
    (b) $at_{selected} := P(PROPOSALS_A)$
    (c) UPDATE$_{a_i}(M_{a_i}, V(at_{selected}, t_k))$ $(\forall a_i \in A)$
4. Until a termination criterion is satisfied

Fig. 2. A task is repeatedly assigned to different teams until a criterion is satisfied (e.g., a team is believed to perform the task best)

2.2 Algorithm and Example

All agents in A follow the algorithm shown in Figure 2. This section illustrates how this algorithm interacts with the variable performance of lifesavers (this example is based on [2,3]). This example is illustrated using a surf rescue domain which consists of a group of lifesavers $AT = A = \{a_1, a_2, a_3\}$ which assign the task of rescuing a distressed person to each other. The values describing the capability distribution C of a_1, a_2 and a_3 of this task are

- $C(a_1) = \{V(a_1, rescue) = N_{a_1}(\mu_{a_1, rescue} = 0.5, \sigma_{a_1, rescue} = 0.4)\}$.
- $C(a_2) = \{V(a_2, rescue) = N_{a_2}(\mu_{a_2, rescue} = 0.8, \sigma_{a_2, rescue} = 0.3)\}$.
- $C(a_3) = \{V(a_3, rescue) = N_{a_3}(\mu_{a_3, rescue} = 0.3, \sigma_{a_3, rescue} = 0.2)\}$.

That is, lifesaver a_1 has a medium performance and is unstable, lifesaver a_2 has a high performance and is more stable, and lifesaver a_3 has a low performance and is the most stable. These distributions are learnt by the agents to find an optimal lifesaver.

For clarity of exposition, we assume the following settings in this example.

- Only agents a_1 and a_2 can propose lifesavers for a rescue and each agent learns from their performance. These two agents (which are both observers and lifesavers) maintain models of lifesavers a_1, a_2 and a_3 ($M_{a_1}(a_1), M_{a_1}(a_2)$ and $M_{a_1}(a_3)$, and $M_{a_2}(a_1), M_{a_2}(a_2)$ and $M_{a_2}(a_3)$), and generate proposals involving these lifesavers.
- In this example, a_1 stores up to eight observations of the performance of the lifesavers in its shared observation memory, as does a_2.
- The majority policy is applied for selecting a lifesaver for a rescue. This policy selects the lifesaver backed by most agents (in the event of a tie, the top agent in an ordered list of lifesavers is selected – the order is based on the index of the lifesaver).

Table 1 illustrates the assignment of lifesavers to rescues under the majority policy (values obtained after each rescue are boldfaced).

Table 1. Sample run of the assignment algorithm (explained in Section 2.2)

1	2	3	4	5	6	7	8	9	10	11	12	13	14	15
	Observer agent	Proposed lifesaver	Selected lifesaver	Shared Observation Capacity of Performance a_1, a_2, a_3								Models $M(a_1)$ $M(a_2)$ $M(a_3)$		
				1	2	3	4	5	6	7	8	$M(a_1)$	$M(a_2)$	$M(a_3)$
	a_1											0.3	0.4	0.5
	a_2											0.6	0.5	0.7
r_1	a_1	a_3	$P_{maj}=a_3$	0.5_{a_3}	0.4_{a_3}							0.3	0.4	**0.45**
	a_2	a_3		0.7_{a_3}	0.4_{a_3}							0.6	0.5	**0.55**
r_2	a_1	a_3	$P_{maj}=a_1$	0.5	0.4	0.3_{a_1}	0.3_{a_1}					0.3	0.4	0.45
	a_2	a_1		0.7	0.4	0.6_{a_1}	0.3_{a_1}					0.45	0.5	0.55
r_3	a_1	a_3	$P_{maj}=a_3$	0.5_{a_3}	0.4_{a_3}	0.3	0.3	0.2_{a_3}				0.3	0.4	**0.37**
	a_2	a_3		0.7_{a_3}	0.4_{a_3}	0.6	0.3	0.2_{a_3}				0.45	0.5	**0.43**
r_4	a_1	a_2	$P_{maj}=a_2$	0.5	0.4	0.3	0.3	0.2	0.4_{a_2}	0.8_{a_2}		0.3	**0.6**	0.37
	a_2	a_2		0.7	0.4	0.6	0.3	0.2	0.5_{a_2}	0.8_{a_2}		0.45	**0.65**	0.43
r_5	a_1	a_2	$P_{maj}=a_2$	0.5	0.4	0.3	0.3	0.2	0.4_{a_2}	0.8_{a_2}	0.7_{a_2}	0.3	**0.63**	0.37
	a_2	a_2		0.7	0.4	0.6	0.3	0.2	0.5_{a_2}	0.8_{a_2}	0.7_{a_2}	0.45	**0.67**	0.43
r_6	a_1	a_2	$P_{maj}=a_2$	0.9_{a_2}	0.4	0.3	0.3	0.2	0.4_{a_2}	0.8_{a_2}	0.7_{a_2}	0.3	**0.7**	0.37
	a_2	a_2		0.9_{a_2}	0.4	0.6	0.3	0.2	0.5_{a_2}	0.8_{a_2}	0.7_{a_2}	0.45	**0.68**	0.43

- Column 1 indicates the allocation round.
- Column 2 shows the observer agents.
- Column 3 shows the lifesaver proposed by each observer agent.
- Column 4 shows the lifesaver selected by the majority selection policy.
- Columns 5–12 contain values of the observed performance of the lifesavers.
- Columns 13–15 show the mean of the updated models.

The first two rows in Table 1 (before the first round r_1) contain values representing initial conditions: columns 5-12 show that no observations have been stored yet, and columns 13-15 contain the initial values of the models maintained by a_1 and a_2 for the rescue performance of a_1, a_2 and a_3. These initial values, which are *not* consistent with the true performance of the agents in question, are also recorded as the first "observed" performance of a_1, a_2 and a_3. This is to model a behaviour whereby an agent's initial "opinion" of lifesavers can be influenced, but not immediately replaced, by observations of the lifesavers' performance.

According to the models maintained by a_1 and a_2, the lifesaver a_3 has the best rescue performance. Hence, a_3 is selected by both a_1 and a_2 when a rescue is announced in round r_1. However, the true performance of a_3 (0.4 at round r_1, column 6) is lower than that anticipated by the observer agents. Both agents observe this performance, and update their models accordingly (column 15).

Now, when a new rescue must be performed (in round r_2), agent a_1 proposes a_3, as a_3 is still the best according to its models, but agent a_2 proposes a_1. As indicated above, according to our tie-breaking rule, the first agent in the ordered list of agents is selected. This is a_1, as it appears in the list before a_3. However, a_1 does not perform well in the rescue (0.3 in round r_2, column 5), which significantly lowers $M_{a_2}(a_1)$ to 0.45 (column 8). As a result, lifesaver a_3 is once more the top choice of both observer agents for the next rescue (in rescue r_3). But a_3 performs quite low (0.2 at round r_3, column 7), thereby further lowering its expected performance according to the models maintained by the observers (column 10).

At this stage, the low performance of both a_1 and a_3 yields models with low mean values for these lifesavers. Hence, for the next rescue (in round r_4), a_2 is proposed by both observer agents. This is a high-performing lifesaver that has initially been underestimated by both observers. As it performs the rescue well (0.8 in round r_4, column 6), it raises the estimated value in the models maintained by both observers (column 9). Agent a_2 is now clearly preferred by both observers and selected for the rescue in round r_5. Again, lifesaver a_2 offers a good performance (0.7 in round r_5, column 6).

At this point, the models maintained by the observer agents are closer to the capabilities of the lifesavers than the initial models. Since both observer agents have a shared observation memory of eight observations, the next time a rescue is performed, the initial value representing the performance of lifesaver a_3 will be dropped, which will further increase the accuracy of the models. In round r_6, a_2 is selected again and performs the rescue with 0.9. Both agents use this value to replace the initial observation of a_3 (0.5 and 0.7, respectively). The algorithm is terminated if we have an indication that one lifesaver is repeatedly selected over other lifesavers. In this example, the algorithm provides as solution a_2, because it has been selected three times in this run (more often than other lifesavers, which is an indication of a lifesaver's selection being reliable).

3   Experiment: Impact of Variable Performance

This experiment evaluates the framework extensions under the condition that the performance of lifesavers is variable and non-deterministic. Our simulation is illustrated by the Surf Rescue (SR) domain introduced in Section 2.2.

3.1   Experimental Parameters

We evaluated five experimental parameters which are varied as follows.

- **Capability Deviation (CD)** – We define lifesaver groups with different degrees of stability: *Invariant, Stable, Medium, Unstable* and *Mixed.* That is, the deviation σ of each lifesaver's performance distribution is drawn from one of the following distributions.
    - *Invariant* lifesavers exhibit the same performance in all rescues.
    - *Stable* lifesavers: low performance variability, $N(\mu = 0.25, \sigma = 0.1)$.
    - *Medium* lifesavers: medium performance variability, $N(\mu = 0.5, \sigma = 0.1)$.
    - *Unstable* lifesavers: highly unstable performance, $N(\mu = 0.75, \sigma = 0.1)$.
    - *Mixed* lifesavers represent a mixture of stable, medium and unstable agents, $N(\mu = 0.5, \sigma = 0.25)$.
- **Observation Capacity (OC)** – The OC of each agent is varied between 1 and 30 concurrently.[3] When OC=i, each agent retains the last i observations

---

[3] The results did not change significantly when agents had a capacity of storing more than 30 observations. Hence, values greater than 30 are not assigned to the OC parameter. Note also, that another way of setting the value for observation capacity for each agent is to draw this value from a normal distribution to simulate a more heterogonous distribution of observation capacity.

made, and when OC=1, their observation capacity is as for previous studies that assume deterministic performance [3,4]. This parameter specifies how many observations of the performance of lifesavers can be stored by an agent in its memory. When this limit is exceeded, the observer agent retains a window of the last k observations ("forgetting" the initial ones).

- **Stability Indicator (SI)** – The algorithm is terminated after a lifesaver is selected *SI=25, 50, 75* and *100* for a rescue. A greater SI value indicates that the solution is more reliable, because one lifesaver is selected more often than others. Note that the algorithm terminates if a lifesaver is selected SI times for a rescue during the entire simulation run (but not necessarily in SI consecutive rounds).

- **Policy (P)** defines two types of group decision policies: *maximum* and *majority*. We have chosen these two group decision policies for the experimental studies because under given theoretical conditions, they are guaranteed to find optimal solutions [4].

  - The *maximum* policy P_{max} selects a lifesaver with the highest proposed performance of all lifesavers proposed.
  - The *majority* policy P_{maj} selects a lifesaver proposed by a majority of agents.

- **Group Size (GS)** defines the number of agents (lifesavers) in a surf rescue domain: *5, 10, 20, 40* and *50*. These values are expected to show a representative trend of our results for a range of populations of agents.

We run one simulation for each combination of the experimental parameters (CD $\times$ OC $\times$ SI $\times$ GS $\times$ P $= 5 \times 30 \times 4 \times 5 \times 2 = 6000$), plus one simulation for each of two benchmark settings, EXHAUSTIVE and RANDOM. In short, both benchmark settings do not execute the TAP algorithm. Instead, an exhaustive setting assigns an optimal lifesaver, but requires that each lifesaver is assigned several times to better know the performance of each lifesaver (in this experiment, we assign each lifesaver GS multiplied by SI, as this assigns an optimal lifesaver with high certainty). A random setting assigns a random lifesaver and does not require any testing or remembering of the performance of lifesavers.

3.2   Efficiency Metrics

Solution Quality (SQ). The measure of SQ for a run is the mean of the capability distribution for the lifesaver on which the algorithm eventually converges. For instance, in the example in Table 1, the solution consists of lifesaver a_2, whose $C(a_2) = \{V(a_2, rescue)\}$ has a mean of $\hat{\mu}_{jk} = 0.8$ (in this example, SI=3, which means that lifesaver a_2 has been selected in three rounds). This measure reflects the final outcome of the combination of the parameters of the simulation run in question.[4]

---

[4] Another way to measure solution quality is to average the performance of a lifesaver that has been selected (one or more times) during a simulation run. However, this does not enable us to compare the results of the true capabilities of teams.

Computational Requirement (CR). The measure of the CR of the EX-HAUSTIVE setting is GS multiplied by SI (as this enables us to assign an optimal lifesaver with high certainty). For example, if we have a group of GS=10 life-savers and a stability indicator SI=50, then the CR is 500 assignment rounds (each lifesaver is assigned 50 times to a rescue). The CR of the procedure in the RANDOM setting is 0.

Averaging and Normalising SQ and CR. Results for each setting are aver-aged over 10000 trials (we selected this number of runs because it yields statis-tically significant results according to a 95% confidence interval). We normalise the SQ and CR of these 10000 trials as this enables a better comparison with the optimal and worst results of a particular setting. SQ and CR (which have been averaged over 10000 runs) is transformed into a range of 0 and 1. In par-ticular, 0 represents the average mean performance of the worst lifesavers SQ_{min} and 1 represents the average performance of an optimal lifesaver SQ_{max}. These value assignments are reversed for CR (0 is optimal and 1 is as poor as for the EXHAUSTIVE setting).

3.3   Initialising a Simulation Run of a Setting

At the beginning of each run, each lifesaver's capability mean μ_{at_j} is initialised using a truncated normal distribution with a mean of $\mu_{all} = 0.5$ and standard deviation of $\sigma_{all} = 0.25$ (truncation is required to keep performance values within a 0 to 1 interval).

Agents are "partially knowledgeable" of the true performance of each life-saver's performance. We have chosen the following method to initialise the esti-mated mean of each agent's model. For a given lifesaver at_j, the estimated mean is drawn from a normal distribution with a mean $\hat{\mu}_{at_j}$. The value $\hat{\mu}_{at_j}$ is an average of the mean μ_{at_j} (i.e., the mean of the distribution of a specific team's capability) and the mean of the distribution that initialises the mean of all team estimates (i.e., 0.5).

The parameter Capability Deviations CD initialises the performance stability of each lifesaver (e.g., Stable or Unstable, Section 3.1). As defined by the pa-rameter Observation Capacity (OC), each agent is endowed with the capacity to store 1 to 30 observations. For instance, if OC=8, then each agent is able to store 8 observations of the performance of different lifesavers (Section 2.2). The values for the capability distribution of each lifesaver remain constant through-out a run, while the mean of each agent's models is updated after a rescue has been performed (Section 2.2). Each run consists of the assignment of a rescue task that is repeated until a lifesaver has been selected SI times.

3.4   Results and Analysis

The results of our experiment are shown in Figure 3, which depicts (averaged and normalised) SQ and CR as a function of OC for our five types of lifesaver's capability deviations – Invariant, Stable, Medium, Unstable and Mixed, plus the two benchmark settings RANDOM and EXHAUSTIVE.

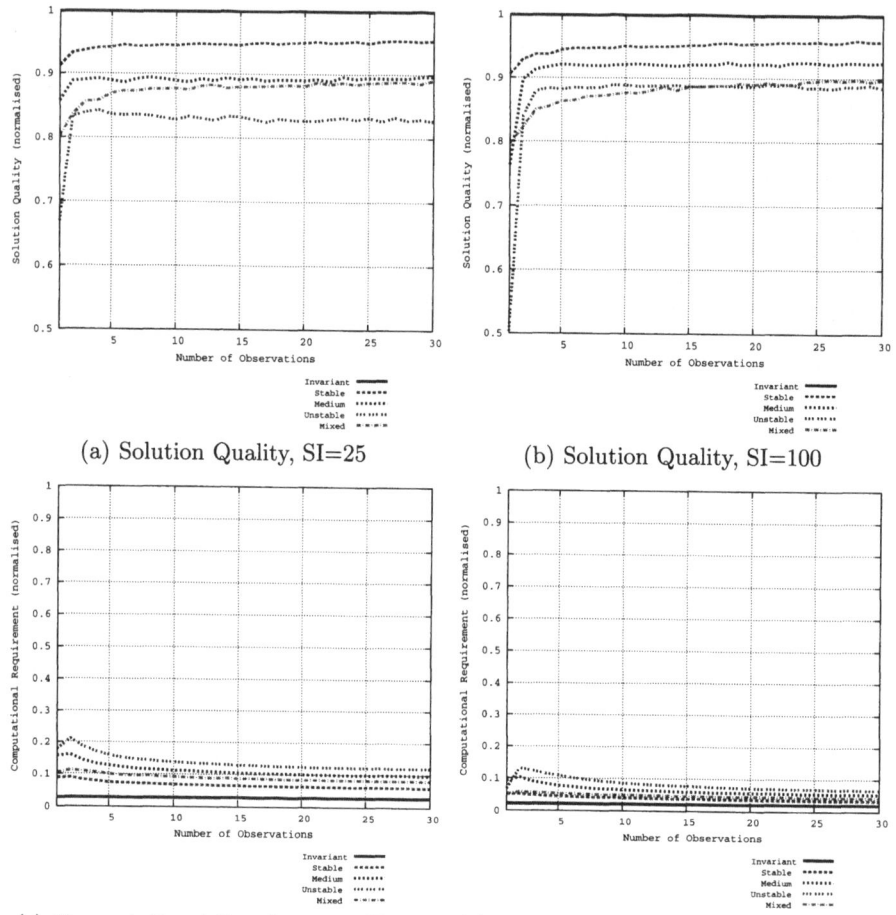

(a) Solution Quality, SI=25   (b) Solution Quality, SI=100

(c) Computational Requirement, SI=25   (d) Computational Requirement, SI=100

Fig. 3. Policy = $Pmax$, Group Size=50

Results of Benchmark Settings are as expected. The results for the RAN-DOM and EXHAUSTIVE settings correspond to the worst and best performance respectively, and are used as a benchmark for comparison with the other settings. The solution quality for the Invariant setting is slightly lower than that for the EXHAUSTIVE setting. These results are consistent with the results obtained for the RANDOM, EXHAUSTIVE and INVARIANT settings in previous experiments [3,4]. This is due to the fact that the algorithm with Invariant lifesavers sometimes converge to a suboptimal solution. For example, this result is reached when each agent underestimates the performance of optimal lifesavers [4].

The higher CD the worse SQ. As seen in Figures 3(a) and 3(b), the average performance obtained for the Stable, Medium, Unstable and Mixed settings is on average worse than that obtained for the Invariant setting. This is due to the higher variability in rescue performance. The more unstable the performance of lifesavers is (i.e., the higher the CD), the worse the solution quality becomes.

We posit that the main reason for this outcome is that the observer agents are unable to build reliable models when lifesavers exhibit unstable performance.

As SI increases, SQ increases (for Unstable lifesavers). Figures 3(a) and 3(b) also show how solution quality increases for unstable lifesavers as the SI increases. This benefit comes with a significantly higher computational requirement (as seen in Figures 3(c) and 3(d)). The reason is that agents have the opportunity to assess more observations and are able to build more accurate models.

SQ improves dramatically with increasing OC across all GS, CD and P. Average solution quality improves for all settings of CD, population sizes GS and policies P when agents are able to store more than one observation of the performance of lifesavers. The greatest improvement of solution quality is achieved when each agent stores 1-3 observations (when OC>3, solution quality still improves, but at a lesser rate). The reason for this dramatic improvement of solution quality is that the models updated by each agent capture much of the previous performance of the lifesaver, despite keeping only a small window of 1-3 observations. It is unnecessary to store a large number of observations to build accurate models. The main difference of the two policies is that the maximum policy offers better results on average than the majority policy (this has been explored in [4]).

CR becomes worse up to OC=2 and then gradually improves. Figures 3(c) and 3(d) show that the computational requirement is worst when OC=2. However, CR improves significantly when more than 2 observations are stored – the largest improvement is observed for $OC = 2, \ldots, 15$. This is due to the additional storage of observations that compensates for testing lifesavers in additional rounds required to build accurate models.

4 Related Research

Previous theoretical and empirical studies assume that the performance of a team is deterministic and invariant [4,1]. If the performance of a team is invariant, it can be adequately represented by one value. However, as a domain becomes more complex, predicting the performance of a team becomes more difficult due to the influence of factors that are not known. Such factors cannot be modelled explicitly and an accurate prediction of a team's future performance is not possible using a deterministic "one-value" representation. For example, human performance varies from task to task due to the complex nature of human behaviour. Hence, a prediction of human performance will not be accurate using a deterministic representation of human behaviour [6,7]. To deal with uncertainty, many research projects have successfully applied the theory of probability [8]. For example, an agent interacts more efficiently with human users if it predicts their behaviour using a probabilistic model [6,7]. Following this research, our extended framework enables agents to maintain probabilistic models to predict variable and non-deterministic performance of teams in the CIA problem.

Our work differs from existing research on Multi-Agent Reinforcement Learning (MARL) [9] and agent modelling [10]. Most work on MARL focuses on multiple agents that execute tasks individually and use Reinforcement Learning (RL) to coordinate their actions, taking into account various configurations (e.g., if agents can observe each others' actions). Perhaps the best-known agent modelling technique to coordinate agents uses a decision-theoretic approach whereby each agent makes decisions to maximise its own payoff by recursively estimating the payoff of collaborators [10]. A key difference is that agents described in [10] and [9] is that our agents make group decisions which that guide how the entire multi-agent system learns.

5   Conclusion

This paper offers extensions to our approach to the Collective Iterative Allocation (CIA) problem and evaluates an algorithm that is designed to cope with uncertain conditions regarding the performance of teams (i.e., the performance of a team varies each time it performs a task). In particular, agents are endowed with the ability to model the performance of a team by its average performance and its stability. Given different levels of stability (invariant, stable, medium, unstable and mixed), our experiment evaluated an algorithm by varying each agent's capacity to store observations (which are required for the refinement of its models). This paper offers the following insights.

1. Our results show that variable performance has a large impact on the efficiency of the algorithm. As the performance variability of teams increases, agents find it difficult to build accurate models of teams, which in turn results in lower solution quality and higher computational requirements.
2. The solution quality of the algorithm will improve dramatically if at least two or three past observations of a team's performance are used by each agent to refine its models (for any type of performance variability, group size and policy). The use of probabilistic models is particularly effective when the performance of lifesaver is highly variable. However, the benefit on solution quality by using more than two or three observations is small.
3. This initial improvement of solution quality extends to the computational requirement of the algorithm if more than two observations are made. That is, the computational requirement of the algorithm is greatest when agents store only two observations, but it decreases steadily as agents store more than 2 observations.

We now have a starting point to address many future challenges based on the uncertain nature of allocation domains. For example, the results stated in 2. and 3. are obtained with a self-contained group of agents (i.e., as many agents as we have teams, $A = AT$). We plan to analyse how many observations are required when the number of agents is different to the number of teams. Further, we plan to extend this framework such that each agent will also submit its confidence value of a lifesaver's performance (based on the estimated standard deviation).

These confidence values can be used to make risk-averse group decisions where greater weight is assigned to a proposal of an agent that is confident about a medium performing lifesaver (and vice versa for risk-tolerant policy). Further extensions are required to deal with uncertainties present in communication and observation, such as information specified in a proposal may change due to interference introduced during a transmission.

References

1. Chevaleyre, Y., Dunne, P.E., Endriss, U., Lang, J., Lemaître, M., Maudet, N., Padget, J., Phelps, S., Rodríguez-Aguilar, J.A., Sousa, P.: Issues in multiagent resource allocation. Informatica 30, 3–31 (2006)
2. Guttmann, C., Zukerman, I.: Towards models of incomplete and uncertain knowledge of collaborators' internal resources. In: Denzinger, J., Lindemann, G., Timm, I.J., Unland, R. (eds.) MATES 2004. LNCS (LNAI), vol. 3187, pp. 58–72. Springer, Heidelberg (2004)
3. Guttmann, C., Zukerman, I.: Agents with limited modeling abilities: Implications on collaborative problem solving. Journal of Computer Science and Software Engineering (CSSE) 21(3), 183–196 (2006)
4. Guttmann, C., Rahwan, I., Georgeff, M.: An approach to the collective iterative task allocation problem. In: Proc. of the International Conference of Intelligent Agent Technology (IAT), USA, pp. 363–369. IEEE Press, Los Alamitos (2007)
5. Bond, A.H., Gasser, L.: An analysis of problems and research in DAI. In: Bond, A.H., Gasser, L. (eds.) Readings in Distributed Artificial Intelligence (1988)
6. Billsus, D., Pazzani, M.: Learning probabilistic user models. In: Proc. of the Workshop on Machine Learning for User Modeling, Chia Laguna, Italy (1997)
7. Horvitz, E., Breese, J., Heckerman, D., Hovel, D., Rommelse, K.: The lumiere project: Bayesian user modeling for inferring the goals and needs of software users. In: Proc. of the fourteenth Conference on Uncertainty in Artificial Intelligence, Madison, Wisconsin, United Stated of America USA, pp. 256–265 (July 1998)
8. Pearl, J.: Probabilistic reasoning in intelligent systems: Networks of plausible inference. Morgan Kaufmann publishers Inc., San Francisco (1988)
9. Sandholm, T.: Perspectives on Multiagent Learning. Artificial Intelligence (Special Issue on Multiagent Learning) 171, 382–391 (2007)
10. Gmytrasiewicz, P.J., Durfee, E.H.: Rational communication in multi-agent environments. Autonomous Agents and Multi-Agent Systems 4(3), 233–272 (2001)

Compiling GOAL Agent Programs into Jazzyk Behavioural State Machines

Koen Hindriks[1] and Peter Novák[2]

[1] EEMCS, Delft University of Technology, The Netherlands
k.v.hindriks@tudelft.nl
[2] Department of Informatics, Clausthal University of Technology, Germany
peter.novak@tu-clausthal.de

Abstract. A variety of agent-oriented programming languages based on concepts such as beliefs and goals has been proposed in the literature. Even though most of these languages now come with interpreters implemented in e.g. Java and can be used to write software agents, there is little work reporting how to implement such languages or to identify a core instruction set that would facilitate such implementation. In this paper we introduce a compiler for the language *GOAL* into the framework of *Jazzyk Behavioural State Machines*. The result is a translation of key agent concepts such as beliefs and goals into *Jazzyk* which lacks these notions, thus providing some evidence that it may provide a sufficient instruction set for implementing agent programs. Moreover, arguably, the implementation strategy used can be applied also to other agent programming languages.

1 Introduction

Relatively little has been reported in the literature on implementing high-level agent programming languages [1]. An exception is the work of Dennis et al. [6], which aims at providing a common basis for a variety of such languages. As of yet, however, there is no equivalent of the *Warren Abstract Machine* [13] available - which provides such a basis for *Prolog* - that would facilitate implementation of these agent languages. In part this is due to the diversity of the proposed languages, ranging from extensions of Java with high-level agent concepts to completely new proposals for high-level agent-oriented programming languages. The effort needed, however, to implement the latter class of agent languages from scratch, in for example Java, is large, non-trivial and error-prone. Moreover a disadvantage of such an effort is that it is difficult to ascertain that such an implementation is a faithful implementation of the semantics. It therefore would be useful to have an *intermediate language that provides a core instruction set* of more high-level programming constructs than e.g. Java provides, and that could be used to compile agent programs into. As we will show, it turns out that the *Jazzyk* agent programming framework [8,9] provides an interesting option for compiling agent programs. *Jazzyk* agents are *Behavioural State Machines* (*Jazzyk BSM*) that exactly provide the behavioural layer on top of a knowledge representational layer that is needed to implement agent languages. The main contribution of the paper is a formal proof that shows it is relatively easy to compile *GOAL* agents [5,7] into *Jazzyk BSM*, demonstrating the usefulness of *Jazzyk* as a target language of an agent program compiler.

R. Bergmann et al. (Eds.): MATES 2008, LNAI 5244, pp. 86–98, 2008.

Besides showing that *Jazzyk* can be used as a target language of a compiler for such agents, our result provides some additional insights. One of the more important corollaries of the proof given is that it shows that the *GOAL* agent language is not committed to any particular knowledge representation (KR) technology. *GOAL* agents may use *Prolog* [12], but there is nothing specific about *GOAL* enforcing such a choice. One of the motivations behind the *Jazzyk* language has been to allow the use and combination of heterogeneous KR technologies in a single agent. A consequence of our result is that the choice of the KR technology used by *GOAL* agents can be seen as a parameter to be instantiated when these agents are written. In fact, our result shows in a formally precise sense that an agent language such as *GOAL* can be viewed as an action selection mechanism put on top of an arbitrary knowledge representation technology. Finally, by showing that *GOAL* agents can be compiled into *Jazzyk*, some evidence is provided that *Jazzyk* supports the core functionality needed for implementing agent-oriented programming.

Since a key ingredient of agent languages are the KR technology(ies) used, for our purpose, we need to clarify in detail what we mean by a KR technology.

Definition 1 (KR Technology). *A KR technology is a triple $\langle \mathcal{L}, \mathcal{Q}, \mathcal{U} \rangle$, where:*

- *$\mathcal{L}$ is some logical language, with a typical element $\phi \in \mathcal{L}$,*
- *$\mathcal{Q}$ is a set of query operators $\models \in \mathcal{Q}$ such that $\models \subseteq 2^{\mathcal{L}} \times \mathcal{L}$,*
- *$\mathcal{U}$ is a set of update operators $\oslash \in \mathcal{U}$ of type $: 2^{\mathcal{L}} \times \mathcal{L} \to 2^{\mathcal{L}}$.*

Our definition of a KR technology is quite abstract and only specifies the types of operators which are associated with a knowledge representation language. This makes our result general, since it allows for a wide range of KR technologies that fit the KR schema introduced, such as *Prolog*, *Answer Set Programming*, *SQL*, etc. The only assumption made is that a special symbol $\perp$ is part of the KR language $\mathcal{L}$, which is intuitively interpreted as *falsum*; when $\perp$ can be derived from a set of sentences this set is said to be *inconsistent*. Our definition is inspired by [4] and explained in more detail in [3]. Apart from minor differences, it corresponds to the notion of a KR module in [8].

2 GOAL

The agent programming language *GOAL*, for Goal-Oriented Agent Language, is a language that incorporates declarative notions of beliefs and goals, and a mechanism for action selection based on these notions. That is, *GOAL* agents derive their choice of action from their beliefs and goals. A *GOAL* agent consists of four sections: (1) a set of beliefs, collectively called the *belief base*, typically denoted by Σ, (2) a set of goals, called the *goal base*, typically denoted by Γ, (3) a *program section* which consists of a set of *action rules*, typically denoted by Π, and (4) an *action specification section* that consists of a specification of the pre- and postconditions of actions of the agent, typically denoted by A. A *GOAL* agent $\mathcal{A}$ thus can be represented as a tuple $\mathcal{A} = \langle \Sigma, \Gamma, \Pi, A \rangle$. See Figure 1 below for a simplified *GOAL* agent that manipulates blocks on a table; for other examples and a more extensive discussion of *GOAL* we refer the reader to [5,7].

Beliefs and Goals. The beliefs and goals of a *GOAL* agent are drawn from a *KR language* such as *Prolog* [12]. As mentioned, one of the contributions will be to show that *GOAL* agents are not married to *Prolog*. To this end, we abstract here from particulars of a specific KR language (similar to the abstraction presented in e.g. [5]). Instead, we use the abstract definition of a KR technology provided in Definition 1. For the purpose of introducing *GOAL* agents below and to simplify the technical presentation, without loss of generality, we introduce a slightly more specific instance of a KR Technology $\mathcal{K}_0 = \langle \mathcal{L}, \{\models\}, \{\oplus, \ominus\}\rangle$ where $\models$ is an entailment relation on $\mathcal{L}$, $\oplus$ is a revision operator and $\ominus$ is a contraction operator. In the remainder of this paper we will use the label $\mathcal{K}_0$ to refer to arbitrary KR technologies of this form *used by GOAL agents*. The notation used for the operators has been chosen to suggest the usual meaning associated with these symbols: $\models$ is used to verify that a sentence follows from a particular set of sentences; $\oplus$ is used to (consistently) add to a given set of sentences a new sentence; and $\ominus$ is used to remove (contracts) a sentence from a given set of sentences. Both $\oplus$ and $\ominus$ are assumed to yield consistent sets of sentences, i.e. $T \oplus \phi \not\models \bot$ and $T \ominus \phi \not\models \bot$.

The belief base Σ and the goal base Γ of a *GOAL* agent are defined as subsets of sentences from the KR language $\mathcal{L}$. Together the belief and the goal base make up a *mental state m* of a GOAL agent, i.e. $m = \langle \Sigma, \Gamma \rangle$. Belief bases Σ and individual goals $\gamma \in \Gamma$ are required to be consistent, i.e. $\Sigma \not\models \bot$ and $\{\gamma\} \not\models \bot$. Additionally, an agent does not believe it achieved its goals, i.e. for all $\gamma \in \Gamma$ we have $\Sigma \not\models \gamma$.

Action Selection and Specification. A *GOAL* agent chooses an action by means of a rule-based action selection mechanism. A program section in a *GOAL* agent consists of *action rules* of the form if ψ then a. These action rules define a mapping from states to actions, together specifying a non-deterministic policy or course of action. The condition of an action rule, typically denoted by ψ, is called a *mental state condition*. It determines the states in which the action a may be executed. Mental state conditions are Boolean combinations of basic formulae **bel**(ϕ) or **goal**(ϕ) with $\phi \in \mathcal{L}$. For example, $\neg$**bel**$(\phi_0) \wedge$ **goal**$(\phi_0 \wedge \phi_1)$ is a mental state condition.

Definition 2 (Mental State Condition Semantics). *The semantics of a mental state condition, given a mental state $m = \langle \Sigma, \Gamma \rangle$, is defined by the following four clauses:*

$$
\begin{array}{lll}
m \models_g \mathbf{bel}(\phi) & \textit{iff} & \Sigma \models \phi, \\
m \models_g \mathbf{goal}(\phi) & \textit{iff} & \textit{there is a } \gamma \in \Gamma \textit{ s.t. } \{\gamma\} \models \phi, \\
m \models_g \neg\psi & \textit{iff} & m \not\models_g \psi, \\
m \models_g \psi_1 \wedge \psi_2 & \textit{iff} & m \models_g \psi_1 \textit{ and } m \models_g \psi_2.
\end{array}
$$

Actions are specified in *GOAL* using a STRIPS-like specification. The action specification section in a *GOAL* agent consists of specifications of the form:

$$\mathbf{action}\{\ \mathbf{:pre}\{\phi\}\ \ \mathbf{:post}\{\phi'\}\ \}$$

Such a specification of action **action** consists of a precondition ϕ and a postcondition ϕ'. An action is *enabled* whenever the agent believes the precondition to be true. Upon its execution the agent updates its beliefs (and, indirectly, possibly also its goals) with the postcondition ϕ'. In line with STRIPS-style action specifications we assume that the postcondition ϕ' of an action consists of two parts $\phi' = \phi_d \wedge \phi_a$ with ϕ_d a list of negative literals (negated facts) also called the *delete list* and ϕ_a a conjunction of positive literals (facts) also called the *add list*.[1] It is assumed here that each action matches with exactly one corresponding action specification.

Semantics of a GOAL Agent. To specify what it means to execute a *GOAL* agent we use a transition style semantics [11]. For our purposes, it is sufficient to present the semantics for executing a single action by a *GOAL* agent. In Section 4 we show how this semantics can be *implemented* by means of a *Jazzyk BSM*.

Definition 3 (Action Semantics). *Let* $m = \langle \Sigma, \Gamma \rangle$ *be a mental state,* **if** ψ **then a** *be an action rule, and a* $\{:\mathbf{pre}\{\phi\} \ :\mathbf{post}\{\phi_a \wedge \phi_d\} \}$ *be a corresponding action specification of a GOAL agent. The following semantic rule can be used to derive that action* a *can be executed:*

$$\frac{m \models \psi, \Sigma \models \phi}{m \xrightarrow{\ \mathbf{a}\ } m'}$$

where $\Sigma' = (\Sigma \ominus \phi_d) \oplus \phi_a$ *and* $m' = \langle \Sigma', \Gamma \setminus \{\gamma \in \Gamma | \Sigma' \models \gamma\}\rangle$.

Besides user specified actions, *GOAL* has two built-in actions **adopt** and **drop** to modify an agent's goal base. The following axioms define the semantics of these actions:

$$\langle \Sigma, \Gamma \rangle \xrightarrow{\ \mathbf{adopt}(\phi)\ } \langle \Sigma, \Gamma \cup \{\phi\}\rangle$$

$$\langle \Sigma, \Gamma \rangle \xrightarrow{\ \mathbf{drop}(\phi)\ } \langle \Sigma, \Gamma \setminus \{\gamma \in \Gamma \mid \{\gamma\} \models \phi\}\rangle.$$

3   Jazzyk Behavioural State Machines

The programming language *Jazzyk* introduced in [8,9] elegantly combines concepts for programming *agent behaviour* with concepts for *knowledge representation*. *Jazzyk* agents can be seen as concrete instantiations of *Gurevich's Abstract State Machines* (*ASM*) [2] , named *Jazzyk Behavioural State Machines*, or alternatively *Jazzyk agents*. *Jazzyk* defines a new and unique agent-oriented programming language due to the clear distinction it makes between the *knowledge representation* and *behavioural* layers within an agent. It thus provides a programming framework that clearly separates the programming concerns of *how to represent an agent's knowledge* about, for example, its environment and *how to encode its behaviours*.

Mental states of *Jazzyk BSM* agents, different from those in *GOAL*, are collections of one or more so-called *knowledge representation modules*, typically denoted by $\mathcal{M}$, each of which represents part of the agent's knowledge base. Transitions between such states result from applying so-called *mental state transformers* (*mst*), typically denoted by τ. The various types of *mst* determine the behaviour that an agent can generate. A *Jazzyk BSM agent* $\mathcal{B}$ consists of a set of KR modules $\mathcal{M}_1, \ldots, \mathcal{M}_n$ and a mental state transformer τ, i.e. $\mathcal{B} = (\mathcal{M}_1, \ldots, \mathcal{M}_n, \tau)$; the *mst* τ is also called an *agent program*.

---

[1] We could also have used e.g. ADL specifications [10], but for reasons of simplicity we use a STRIPS-like specification, which also nicely matches the KR technology $\mathcal{K}_0$ with two update operators: the operator $\oplus$ to add facts, and the operator $\ominus$ to delete facts.

A KR module of a *Jazzyk BSM* can be seen as a database of statements drawn from a specific KR language. KR modules may be used to represent and maintain various attitudes of an agent such as its knowledge about its environment, or its goals, intentions, obligations, etc. *Jazzyk* allows agents to have any number of such KR modules and does not enforce any particular view on these modules. Unlike *GOAL*, *Jazzyk* abstracts from a particular purpose a KR module can be made to serve. Formally, a KR module $\langle D, \mathcal{L}, \mathcal{Q}, \mathcal{U} \rangle$ is a KR technology $\langle \mathcal{L}, \mathcal{Q}, \mathcal{U} \rangle$ (cf. Definition 1) extended with a state (knowledge base) $D \subseteq \mathcal{L}$. A KR module is a self-encapsulated computational entity providing two sets of interfaces: *query* operators for querying the knowledge base and *update* operators to modify it. In a *Jazzyk BSM* $(\mathcal{M}_1, \ldots, \mathcal{M}_n, \tau)$ we additionally require that the set of query and update operators of any two modules are disjoint, i.e. $\mathcal{Q}_i \cap \mathcal{Q}_j = \emptyset$ and $\mathcal{U}_i \cap \mathcal{U}_j = \emptyset$.

Syntax of Queries and Mental State Transformers. Queries, typically denoted by φ, are operators constructed from the set of available query operators $\mathcal{Q}$ that are available in a KR technology. A primitive query $\varphi = (\models \phi)$ consists of a query operator $\models \in \mathcal{Q}$ and a formula $\phi \in \mathcal{L}$ of the same KR technology. Arbitrary queries can be composed again by means of conjunction $\wedge$, disjunction $\vee$ and negation $\neg$. Mental state transformers enable transitions from one state to another. A primitive *mst* $\oslash \phi$, typically denoted by ρ and constructed from an update operator $\oslash \in \mathcal{U}$ and a formula $\phi \in \mathcal{L}$, is an update on the state of the corresponding KR module of a mental state. Conditional *mst* are of the form $\varphi \longrightarrow \tau$, where φ is a query and τ is a *mst*. Such a conditional *mst* allows to make the application of *mst* τ conditional on the evaluation of query φ. *Mst*s can be combined by means of the choice $|$ and the sequence $\circ$ syntactic constructs.

Definition 4 (Jazzyk Mental State Transformer). *Let* $\mathcal{M}_1, \ldots, \mathcal{M}_n$ *be KR modules of the form* $\langle D_i, \mathcal{L}_i, \mathcal{Q}_i, \mathcal{U}_i \rangle$. *The set of* mental state transformers *is defined as:*

1. **skip** *is a primitive mst,*
2. *if* $\oslash \in \mathcal{U}_i$ *and* $\phi \in \mathcal{L}_i$, *then* $\oslash \phi$ *is a primitive mst,*
3. *if* φ *is a query, and* τ *is a mst, then* $\varphi \longrightarrow \tau$ *is a conditional mst,*
4. *if* τ *and* τ' *are mst's, then* $\tau | \tau'$ *is an mst (choice) and* $\tau \circ \tau'$ *is an mst (sequence).*

Figure 1 provides an example of a *Jazzyk BSM* agent. To improve readability, we use a mix of concrete *Jazzyk* syntax and the formal syntax introduced above. For a more extensive example of a *Jazzyk BSM* program see [9].

Jazzyk BSM Semantics. The semantics of *Jazzyk BSM* is defined using a semantic calculus similar to that used for *ASM* [2]. This formalism provides a *functional* rather than an operational view on *Jazzyk* mental state transformers. The *yields* calculus, introduced below, specifies an update associated with executing an *mst*. It formally defines the meaning of the state transformation induced by executing an *mst* in a state.

   Formally, a mental state s of a *Jazzyk BSM* $(\mathcal{M}_1, \ldots, \mathcal{M}_n, \tau)$ consists of the corresponding states $\langle D_1, \ldots, D_n \rangle$ of its KR modules. To specify the semantics of a *Jazzyk BSM*, first we need to define how queries are evaluated and how a state is modified by applying updates to it. A primitive query $\models \phi$ in a *Jazzyk BSM* state $s = \langle D_1, \ldots, D_n \rangle$ evaluates the formula $\phi \in \mathcal{L}_i$ using the query operator $\models \in \mathcal{Q}_i$ in the current state

$D_i \subseteq \mathcal{L}_i$ of the corresponding KR module $\langle D_i, \mathcal{L}_i, \mathcal{Q}_i, \mathcal{U}_i \rangle$. That is, $s \models_j (\models \phi)$ holds in a mental state s iff $D_i \models \phi$, otherwise we have $s \not\models_j (\models \phi)$. Given the usual meaning of Boolean operators, it is straightforward to extend the query evaluation to compound query formulae. Note that a query $\models \phi$ does not change the mental state s.

The semantics of a mental state transformer is a set of (possibly sequences of) *updates* (update set). The same notation $\oslash\phi$ is used to denote a simple update as well as the corresponding primitive *mst*. It should be clear from the context which of the two is intended. Sequential application of updates is denoted by $\bullet$, i.e. $\rho_1 \bullet \rho_2$ is an update resulting from applying ρ_1 first and then applying ρ_2.

Definition 5 (Applying an Update). *The result of applying an update* $\rho = \oslash\phi$ *to a state* $s = \langle D_1, \ldots, D_n \rangle$ *of a BSM* $\mathcal{B} = (\mathcal{M}_1, \ldots, \mathcal{M}_n, \tau)$, *denoted by* $s \bigoplus \rho$, *is a new state* $s' = \langle D_1, \ldots, D_i', \ldots, D_n \rangle$ *where* $D_i' = D_i\rho = D_i \oslash \phi$ *and* $D_i, \oslash,$ *and* ϕ *correspond to one and the same* $\mathcal{M}_i$ *of* $\mathcal{B}$. *Applying the special update* $\emptyset$ *to a state* s *results in the same mental state* $s = s \bigoplus \emptyset$.

We write $D_i \bigoplus (\rho_1 \bullet \ldots \bullet \rho_k)$ *for* $(\ldots(D_i \bigoplus \rho_1) \bigoplus \ldots \bigoplus \rho_k)$ *where all* ρ_i *correspond to* D_i. *The result of applying an update of the form* $\rho_1 \bullet \rho_2$ *to a state* s, *i.e.* $s \bigoplus (\rho_1 \bullet \rho_2)$, *is the new state* $(s \bigoplus \rho_1) \bigoplus \rho_2$.

The meaning of a mental state transformer in state s, formally defined by the *yields* predicate below, is the update it yields in that state. We introduce a version of the *yields* calculus adapted from [9].

Definition 6 (Yields Calculus). *A mental state transformer* τ *yields an update* ρ *in a state* s, *iff* $yields(\tau, s, \rho)$ *is derivable in the following calculus:*

$$\frac{\top}{yields(\mathbf{skip}, s, \emptyset)} \qquad\qquad \frac{\top}{yields(\oslash\phi, s, \oslash\phi)} \qquad (\textit{yields of a primitive } \mathrm{mst})$$

$$\frac{yields(\tau, s, \rho),\ s \models_j \phi}{yields(\phi \longrightarrow \tau, s, \rho)} \qquad \frac{yields(\tau, s, \rho),\ s \not\models_j \phi}{yields(\phi \longrightarrow \tau, s, \emptyset)} \qquad (\textit{yields of a conditional } \mathrm{mst})$$

$$\frac{yields(\tau_1, s, \rho_1),\ yields(\tau_2, s, \rho_2)}{yields(\tau_1 | \tau_2, s, \rho_1)} \quad \frac{yields(\tau_1, s, \rho_1),\ yields(\tau_2, s, \rho_2)}{yields(\tau_1 | \tau_2, s, \rho_2)} \quad (\textit{yields of a choice } \mathrm{mst})$$

$$\frac{yields(\tau_1, s, \rho_1),\ yields(\tau_2, s \bigoplus \rho_1, \rho_2)}{yields(\tau_1 \circ \tau_2, s, \rho_1 \bullet \rho_2)} \qquad (\textit{yields of a sequential } \mathrm{mst})$$

The *mst* **skip** yields the update $\emptyset$. Similarly, a primitive update *mst* yields the corresponding update. In case the condition of a conditional *mst* $\varphi \longrightarrow \tau$ is satisfied in the current mental state, the calculus yields one of the updates corresponding to the right hand side *mst* τ, otherwise the $\emptyset$ update is yielded. A non-deterministic choice *mst* yields an update corresponding to either of its members and finally a sequential *mst* yields a sequence of updates corresponding to the first *mst* of the sequence and an update yielded by the second member of the sequence in a state resulting from application of the first update to the current mental state.

4   Compiling a GOAL Agent into a Jazzyk BSM

In this Section we show that *GOAL* agents can be implemented as, or compiled into, *Jazzyk BSM*. The compiler is abstractly represented here by a function $\mathfrak{C}$ that translates (compiles) *GOAL* agents into *Jazzyk Behavioural State Machines*. The main result is a proof that for every *GOAL* agent $\mathcal{A} = \langle \Sigma, \Gamma, \Pi, \mathcal{A} \rangle$ there is a *Jazzyk BSM* $\mathfrak{C}(\mathcal{A}) = (\mathcal{M}_1, \dots, \mathcal{M}_n, \tau)$ that implements that *GOAL* agent. In fact, we will show that a *Jazzyk BSM* $\mathfrak{C}(\mathcal{A}) = (\mathcal{M}_\Sigma, \mathcal{M}_\Gamma, \tau)$ with precisely two KR modules is sufficient, where module $\mathcal{M}_\Sigma$ corresponds to the belief base Σ and module $\mathcal{M}_\Gamma$ corresponds to the goal base Γ. We proceed as follows. First, we define the KR modules $\mathcal{M}_\Sigma$ and $\mathcal{M}_\Gamma$ of the *Jazzyk BSM*, using the KR technology employed by *GOAL* agents as a starting point. Second, we show how to obtain a *Jazzyk BSM* agent program τ that implements the action rules in the program section Π and action specifications A of the *GOAL* agent. Finally, the equivalence of the *GOAL* agent with its *Jazzyk BSM* counterpart $\mathfrak{C}(\mathcal{A})$ is proven by showing that both are able to generate the same mental states.

Translation. It is important to repeat that throughout this paper we have assumed that a *GOAL* agent uses a KR technology of the form $\mathcal{K}_0 = \langle \mathcal{L}, \{\models\}, \{\oplus, \ominus\} \rangle$ (see Section 2). Given this, it is straightforward to map a *GOAL* belief base onto a *Jazzyk BSM* KR module that is able to implement (i) the evaluation of a mental state condition $\mathbf{bel}(\phi)$ on a belief base as well as (ii) the execution of updates associated with performing an action. We simply map the *GOAL* belief base Σ onto the *Jazzyk BSM* module

$$\mathcal{M}_\Sigma = \mathfrak{C}_{\mathbf{bb}}(\Sigma) = \langle \Sigma, \mathcal{L}, \{\models\}, \{\oplus, \ominus\} \rangle \tag{1}$$

Whereas the underlying KR technology is implicitly assumed in a *GOAL* agent, this assumption is made explicit in the corresponding *Jazzyk BSM* KR module.

The translation of the goal base of a *GOAL* agent into a *Jazzyk BSM* module is less straightforward. A *Jazzyk BSM* module that implements the goal base needs to be able to implement (i) the evaluation of a mental state condition $\mathbf{goal}(\phi)$ on a goal base as well as (ii) the execution of updates on a goal base as a result of performing **adopt** or **drop** actions and the removal of goals that have been achieved. Because the **goal** operator has a somewhat non-standard semantics (see Definition 2), we need to define a non-standard KR technology associated with the *Jazzyk BSM* module implementing the goal base. Mapping a goal base Γ onto the module $\mathcal{M}_\Gamma$ provides what we need:

$$\mathcal{M}_\Gamma = \mathfrak{C}_{\mathbf{gb}}(\Gamma) = \langle \Gamma, \mathcal{L}, \{\models_{\mathbf{goal}}\}, \{\oplus_{\mathbf{adopt}}, \ominus_{\mathbf{drop}}, \ominus_{\mathbf{achieved}}\} \rangle \tag{2}$$

where:

- $\Gamma \models_{\mathbf{goal}} \phi$ iff there is a $\gamma \in \Gamma$ such that $\{\gamma\} \models \phi$.
- $\Gamma \oplus_{\mathbf{adopt}} \phi = \Gamma \cup \{\phi\}$.
- $\Gamma \ominus_{\mathbf{drop}} \phi = \Gamma \setminus \{\gamma \in \Gamma \mid \{\gamma\} \models \phi\}$.
- $\Gamma \ominus_{\mathbf{achieved}} \phi = \Gamma \setminus \{\phi\}$.

$\models_{\mathbf{goal}}$ is used to implement $\mathbf{goal}(\phi)$, $\oplus_{\mathbf{adopt}}$ implements **adopt**, $\ominus_{\mathbf{drop}}$ is used to implement **drop**, and finally $\ominus_{\mathbf{achieved}}$ implements the goal update mechanism to remove achieved goals. Note that the goal update mechanism of GOAL (cf. Definition 2) requires a simple set operator to remove a formula from the goal base such as $\ominus_{\mathbf{achieved}}$ and we cannot use $\ominus_{\mathbf{drop}}$ for this purpose.

Using the translations defined above it is now possible to translate mental state conditions ψ used in *GOAL* action rules of the form **if** ψ **then** a. As noted above,

$\mathfrak{C}(\mathbf{bel}(\phi))$ can be mapped onto the *Jazzyk BSM* query $\models \phi$; similarly, we can define $\mathfrak{C}(\mathbf{goal}(\phi)) = (\models_{\mathbf{goal}} \phi)$. Boolean combinations of mental state conditions are translated into Boolean combinations of *Jazzyk BSM* queries.

The translation of an action a, the second part of an action rule of a *GOAL* agent, into *Jazzyk BSM msts* is straightforward when a is either **adopt** or **drop** action. Since both **adopt**(ϕ) and **drop**(ϕ) are always enabled, we can map these actions simply onto their corresponding primitive update operators:

$$\mathfrak{C}(\mathbf{adopt}(\phi)) \quad = \quad \oplus_{\mathbf{adopt}} \phi \tag{3}$$

$$\mathfrak{C}(\mathbf{drop}(\phi)) \quad = \quad \ominus_{\mathbf{drop}} \phi \tag{4}$$

The compilation of user defined actions, i.e. actions specified in the action specification section A, into *Jazzyk BSM* depends on the action specification A of the compiled *GOAL* agent. Such actions are mapped onto conditional *msts* of the form $\varphi \longrightarrow \tau$. The preconditions of an action are mapped onto the query part φ of the *mst*; the effects of that action, expressed by a postcondition in *GOAL*, are translated into a sequential *mst* τ. Assuming that a is a *GOAL* action with the corresponding action specification a $\{:\mathbf{pre}\{\phi\} :\mathbf{post}\{\phi_d \wedge \phi_a\}$, we define:

$$\mathfrak{C}(\mathsf{a}) \quad = \quad (\models \phi \longrightarrow \ominus \phi_d \circ \oplus \phi_a) \tag{5}$$

Note that the *Jazzyk BSM* operators $\models$, $\oplus$, and $\ominus$ are associated with the KR module $\mathcal{M}_\Sigma$ that implements the belief base of the *GOAL* agent, which ensures that the precondition ϕ is evaluated on the belief base of the agent and in line with Definition 3, the postcondition $\phi_d \wedge \phi_a$ is used to update that belief base.

Combining the translations of mental state conditions and actions yields a translation of action rules in the program section of a *GOAL* agent. It is also convenient to introduce a translation of a complete program section, i.e. a set Π of such rules. Note that the order of translation is unimportant.

$$\mathfrak{C}(\mathbf{if}\ \psi\ \mathbf{then}\ \mathsf{a}) = \mathfrak{C}(\psi) \longrightarrow \mathfrak{C}(\mathsf{a}) \tag{6}$$

$$\mathfrak{C}(\emptyset) = \mathbf{skip} \tag{7}$$

$$\mathfrak{C}(\Pi) = \mathfrak{C}(r) \mid \mathfrak{C}(\Pi \setminus \{r\})\,, \text{if } r \in \Pi \tag{8}$$

The definitions above already allow us to define a compilation of a *GOAL* agent into a *Jazzyk BSM*, but it is convenient to first introduce the notion of a *possibly adopted goal*. A goal ϕ is said to be a *possibly adopted goal* whenever it is possible that the agent may come to adopt ϕ as a goal, i.e. whenever it is already present in the goal base or there is an action rule of the form **if** ψ **then adopt**(ϕ) in Π. The set of possibly adopted goals $\mathcal{P}_A$ of a *GOAL* agent $\mathcal{A} = \langle \Sigma, \Gamma, \Pi, A \rangle$ thus can be defined by $\mathcal{P}_A = \Gamma \cup \{\phi \mid \mathbf{if}\ \psi\ \mathbf{then\ adopt}(\phi) \in \Pi\}$. The notion introduced is useful since in the *Jazzyk BSM* translation we need to also implement the blind commitment strategy of *GOAL*, i.e. the removal of goals whenever these are completely achieved. A *Jazzyk BSM mst* that consists of a sequence of conditional *msts* is introduced to implement the goal update mechanism of *GOAL*. Each of these corresponds to a single possibly adopted goal. The corresponding query evaluates whether $\phi \in \mathcal{P}_A$ is (believed to be) achieved, whereupon ϕ is removed from the goal base:

```
:main: blocksWorld
{
    //*** Initializations omitted ***/
    :beliefs{...}
    :goals{...}

    :program{
        if bel(on_table([B|S]), clear(B),
               block(C), clear(C)) ,
           goal(on_table([C,B|S]))
        then move(C,B).
        if goal(on(B,A)),
           bel(on_table([C|S]),
               clear(C), member(B,S))
        then move(C,table).
    }

    :actionspec{
        move(X,Y) {
            :pre{ clear(X), clear(Y), on(X,Z), not(on(X,Y)) }
            :post{ not(on(X,Z)), on(X,Y) }
        }
    }
}
```

```
/*** Modules initialization omitted ***/
{ // ******** C(Π) ********
    when ⊨ [{on_table([B|S]), clear(B), block(C), clear(C)}]
    and ⊨goal [{on_table([C,B|S])}]
    then {
        when ⊨ [{clear(C), clear(B), on(C,Z), not(on(C,B))}]
        then ⊕ [{not(on(C,Z)), on(C,B)}]
    } ;
    when ⊨goal [{on(B,A)}] and
         ⊨ [{on_table([C|S]), clear(C), member(B,S)}]
    then {
        when ⊨ [{clear(C), clear(table),
                  on(C,Z), not(on(C,table))}]
        then ⊕ [{not(on(C,Z)), on(C,table)}]
    }
} ,
{ // ******** Cdrop(Gl(A)) ********
    when ⊨ [{on(b,a), on(a,table)}]
    then ⊖goal [{on(b,a), on(a, table)}] ,
    when ⊨ [{on_table([a,b])}]
    then ⊖goal [{on_table([a,b])}] ,
    when ⊨ [{on_table([b])}]
    then ⊖goal [{on_table([b])}]
}
```

Fig. 1. Example of a translation of a simple *GOAL* agent moving blocks on a table into *Jazzyk BSM* pseudocode. **when** ... **then** ... encodes a conditional *mst*, ; and , stand for | and ∘ respectively.

$$\mathfrak{C}_{\mathbf{bcs}}(\emptyset) = \mathbf{skip} \tag{9}$$

$$\mathfrak{C}_{\mathbf{bcs}}(\mathcal{P}_{\mathcal{A}}) = (\models \phi \longrightarrow \ominus_{\mathbf{achieved}}\phi) \circ \mathfrak{C}_{\mathbf{bcs}}(\mathcal{P}_{\mathcal{A}} \setminus \{\phi\}) \,, \text{if } \phi \in \mathcal{P}_{\mathcal{A}} \tag{10}$$

The compilation of a *GOAL* agent $\langle \Sigma, \Gamma, \Pi, A \rangle$ into a *Jazzyk BSM* is defined as:

$$\mathfrak{C}(\langle \Sigma, \Gamma, \Pi, A \rangle) = (\mathcal{M}_{\Sigma}, \mathcal{M}_{\Gamma}, \mathfrak{C}(\Pi) \circ \mathfrak{C}_{\mathbf{bcs}}(\mathcal{P}_{\mathcal{A}})) \tag{11}$$

Correctness of the Translation Function $\mathfrak{C}$. The main effort in proving that the compilation of a *GOAL* agent $\mathcal{A} = \langle \Sigma, \Gamma, \Pi, A \rangle$ into a *Jazzyk BSM* $\mathfrak{C}(\mathcal{A}) = (\mathcal{M}_{\Sigma}, \mathcal{M}_{\Gamma}, \mathfrak{C}(\Pi) \circ \mathfrak{C}_{\mathbf{bcs}}(\mathcal{P}_{\mathcal{A}}))$ is correct consists of showing that the action rules Π of the *GOAL* agent generate the same mental states as the mental state transformer $\mathfrak{C}(\Pi) \circ \mathfrak{C}_{\mathbf{bcs}}(\mathcal{P}_{\mathcal{A}})$. In order to prove this we first prove some useful properties of $\mathfrak{C}_{\mathbf{bcs}}(\mathcal{P}_{\mathcal{A}})$ that implements the goal update mechanism of *GOAL* (Lemma 1), the relation of *GOAL* mental states resulting from action execution to the application of updates to *Jazzyk BSM* mental states (Lemma 2), and the evaluation of mental state conditions in *GOAL* to the evaluation of their translations in *Jazzyk* (Lemma 3). Due to space limitations we omit the detailed proofs for these lemmas.

Lemma 1 shows that a *Jazzyk BSM* state, which does not need to be a *GOAL* state, nevertheless is a *GOAL* mental state after removing goals that are believed to be achieved, and that the mst $\mathfrak{C}_{\mathbf{bcs}}(\mathcal{P}_{\mathcal{A}})$ implements this goal update mechanism.

Lemma 1. *Let* $m = \langle \Sigma, \Gamma \rangle$ *be a Jazzyk BSM state such that* $\Sigma \not\models \bot$ *and* $\Gamma \subseteq \mathcal{P}_{\mathcal{A}}$, *and* ρ *be an update* $\ominus_{\mathbf{achieved}}\gamma_1 \bullet \ldots \bullet \ominus_{\mathbf{achieved}}\gamma_n$. *Then* $yields(\mathfrak{C}_{\mathbf{bcs}}(\mathcal{P}_{\mathcal{A}}), m, \rho)$ *iff*

(i) $\langle \Sigma, \Gamma \oplus \rho \rangle$ is a GOAL mental state, and

(ii) there is no $\Gamma': \Gamma \oplus \rho \subset \Gamma' \subseteq \Gamma$ such that $\langle \Sigma, \Gamma' \rangle$ is a GOAL mental state.

Lemma 2 proves that the *GOAL* states resulting from executing an action can also be obtained by applying updates of a particular structure, which is useful to relate *GOAL* actions to *Jazzyk BSM* updates. The fact that the *Jazzyk BSM* mst τ that is the *Jazzyk BSM* translation of a *GOAL* agent also yields updates with the same structure is useful to relate *Jazzyk BSM* updates to *GOAL* actions again.

Lemma 2. *Let* $\mathcal{A} = \langle \Sigma, \Gamma, \Pi, A \rangle$ *be a* GOAL *agent and* $\mathfrak{C}(\mathcal{A}) = (\mathcal{M}_{\Sigma}, \mathcal{M}_{\Gamma}, \tau)$ *its Jazzyk BSM compilation. Also let* a *be a user defined action of* GOAL *agent* $\mathcal{A}$, *with action specification* a $\{:\mathbf{pre}\{\phi\} \ :\mathbf{post}\{\phi_a \wedge \phi_d\}\}$. *Then*

(i) $m \xrightarrow{\ \mathsf{a}\ } m'$ *iff* $\exists n \geq 0 : m' = m \bigoplus (\ominus\phi_d \bullet \oplus\phi_a \bullet \ominus_{\mathbf{achieved}}\gamma_1 \bullet \cdots \bullet \ominus_{\mathbf{achieved}}\gamma_n)$.

(ii) $m \xrightarrow{\ \mathbf{drop}(\phi)\ } m'$ *iff* $m' = m \bigoplus (\ominus_{\mathbf{drop}}\phi)$.

(iii) $m \xrightarrow{\ \mathbf{adopt}(\phi)\ } m'$ *iff* $m' = m \bigoplus (\oplus_{\mathbf{adopt}}\phi)$.

(iv) *If* $yields(\tau, m, \rho)$, *then* ρ *is of the form* $\ominus\phi_d \bullet \oplus\phi_a \bullet \ominus_{\mathbf{achieved}}\gamma_1 \bullet \cdots \bullet \ominus_{\mathbf{achieved}}\gamma_n$ *for some* $n \geq 0$, *or of the form* $\ominus_{\mathbf{drop}}\phi$ *or* $\ominus_{\mathbf{adopt}}\phi$.

Lemma 3 relates the evaluation of *GOAL* mental state conditions to the evaluation of their *Jazzyk BSM* translation in the same state.

Lemma 3. *Let* ψ *be a mental state condition. It holds that*

$$m \models_g \psi \ \textit{iff} \ m \models_j \mathfrak{C}(\psi)$$

Finally, Theorem 1 shows that the updates generated by the *Jazzyk* translation of a *GOAL* agent produce the same mental states as the execution of actions by that *GOAL* agent, which shows that the *Jazzyk BSM* implements the *GOAL* agent.

Theorem 1 (Correctness of GOAL-2-BSM Compilation). *Let* $\mathcal{A} = \langle \Sigma, \Gamma, \Pi, A \rangle$ *be a* GOAL *agent with mental state* $m = \langle \Sigma, \Gamma \rangle$ *and* $\mathfrak{C}(\mathcal{A}) = (\mathcal{M}_{\Sigma}, \mathcal{M}_{\Gamma}, \tau)$ *its corresponding* Jazzyk BSM *translation. Then for all* ρ:

$$\exists \mathsf{a} : m \xrightarrow{\ \mathsf{a}\ } m \bigoplus \rho \quad \textit{iff} \quad yields(\tau, m, \rho).$$

Proof. Informally, to show the left to right direction ($\Longrightarrow$), we have to show that if a *GOAL* action a is enabled in a mental state m, there exists an update ρ such that (a) the state resulting from performing a is $m \bigoplus \rho$ and (b) ρ is yielded by τ in this state. Note that even though an update operator ρ occurs on the left hand side the expression on the left hand side denotes a *GOAL* transition. From Lemma 2 we know that such a ρ exists and is of the form (i) $\rho = \ominus\phi_d \bullet \oplus\phi_a \bullet \ominus_{\mathbf{achieved}}\gamma_1 \bullet \cdots \bullet \ominus_{\mathbf{achieved}}\gamma_n$ for user specified actions a, (ii) $\rho = \ominus_{\mathbf{drop}}\phi$ if a = $\mathbf{drop}(\phi)$ and (iii) $\rho = \oplus_{\mathbf{adopt}}\phi$ if a = $\mathbf{adopt}(\phi)$.

So suppose that $m \xrightarrow{\ \mathsf{a}\ } m \bigoplus \rho$ and a is a user defined action (the other cases dealing with a = $\mathbf{drop}(\phi)$ and a = $\mathbf{adopt}(\phi)$ are similar). This means there is an action rule if ψ then a, and precondition ϕ and postcondition $\phi_d \wedge \phi_a$ associated with action a such that $m \models_g \psi$ and $\Sigma \models \phi$. It remains to show that update ρ is also yielded by τ. By construction, we must have that

$$\tau = (...|(\mathfrak{C}(\psi) \longrightarrow (\models \phi \longrightarrow \ominus\phi_d \circ \oplus\phi_a))|...) \circ \mathfrak{C}_{\mathbf{bcs}}(\mathcal{P}_\mathcal{A})$$

Since we have $m \models_g \psi$ and $\Sigma \models \phi$, using Lemma 3 it is immediate that we have $yields(\mathfrak{C}(\psi) \longrightarrow (\models \phi \longrightarrow \ominus\phi_d \circ \oplus\phi_a), m, \ominus\phi_d \bullet \oplus\phi_a)$. Finally, from Lemma 1, we have that $yields(\mathfrak{C}_{\mathbf{bcs}}(\mathcal{P}_\mathcal{A}), m \bigoplus(\ominus\phi_d \bullet \oplus\phi_a), \{\ominus_{\mathbf{achieved}}\gamma_1 \bullet \ldots \bullet \ominus_{\mathbf{achieved}}\gamma_n)$ and by applying sequential composition on the resulting updates we are done.

($\Longleftarrow$) In the other direction, we have to prove that the updates performed by $\mathfrak{C}(\mathcal{A})$ correspond to enabled actions of the *GOAL* agent $\mathcal{A}$. So suppose that $yields(\tau, m, \rho)$, and ρ is of the form $\ominus\phi_d \bullet \oplus\phi_a \bullet \ominus_{\mathbf{achieved}}\gamma_1 \bullet \ldots \bullet \ominus_{\mathbf{achieved}}\gamma_n$ (using Lemma 2(iv); the other cases with $\rho = \ominus_{\mathbf{drop}}\phi$ and $\rho = \oplus_{\mathbf{adopt}}\phi$ are again similar). From the construction of $\mathfrak{C}$ it follows that we must have $yields(\mathfrak{C}(\psi) \longrightarrow (\models \phi \longrightarrow \ominus\phi_d \circ \oplus\phi_a) \circ \mathfrak{C}_{\mathbf{bcs}}(\mathcal{P}_\mathcal{A}), m, \rho)$. From the rule for conditional *mst* in the yields calculus (Definition 6) follows that $m \models_j \mathfrak{C}(\psi)$ and $m \models_j (\models \phi)$. By Lemma 3 we then have $m \models_g \psi$ and $\Sigma \models \phi$. We must also have an action rule if ψ then a with action specification a $\{:\mathbf{pre}\{\phi\} \ :\mathbf{post}\{\phi_a \wedge \phi_d\}$ such that $m \xrightarrow{a} m \bigoplus(\ominus\phi_d \bullet \oplus\phi_a \bullet \ominus_{\mathbf{achieved}}\gamma'_1 \bullet \ldots \bullet \ominus_{\mathbf{achieved}}\gamma'_m)$ (cf. Lemma 2(i)). It remains to be shown that $\ominus_{\mathbf{achieved}}\gamma_1 \bullet \ldots \bullet \ominus_{\mathbf{achieved}}\gamma_n$ is equal to $\ominus_{\mathbf{achieved}}\gamma'_1 \bullet \ldots \bullet \ominus_{\mathbf{achieved}}\gamma'_m$; this follows immediately from Lemma 1.

5 Discussion and Conclusion

We showed that any *GOAL* agent can be compiled into a *Jazzyk Behavioural State Machine*. More precisely, it was shown that every possible computation step of a *GOAL* agent can be emulated by the *Jazzyk BSM* that is the result of compiling the *GOAL* agent into *Jazzyk BSM*. The compilation procedure is *compositional* in the sense that any modifications or extensions of the belief base, goal base or program and action specification sections of the *GOAL* agent only *locally* affect, respectively, the compiled belief base module, the compiled goal base module, or the mental state transformer that is the result of compiling the program and action specification sections.

The compilation function introduced provides a means to translate *GOAL* agents into *Jazzyk BSM*, but not vice versa. Abstracting from a number of details a *Jazzyk BSM* could be viewed as a *GOAL* agent that does not use its goal base and associated goal update mechanism. As mentioned above, *Jazzyk* does not commit to any particular view on the KR modules of a *Jazzyk BSM*. This flexibility allowed us to implement the goal base of a *GOAL* agent by means of explicit emulation of the goal update mechanism.

As already noted in the introduction, there is not much related work aimed at providing an effective strategy or tools for implementing a variety of rule-based agent programming languages such as those described in [1]. To the best of our knowledge, only [6] has presented a framework to this end. The resulting framework, however, is based on the idea to incorporate each and every semantic feature of a variety of available high-level agent languages in order to be able to cover every type of agent. It thus does not provide an implementation strategy as the one promoted and illustrated in this paper, which is based on the idea to provide a concise set of simple high-level concepts (a common core) facilitating compilation of a variety of agent programs into this core instruction set. This strategy is explicitly aimed at *reducing* a set of high-level agent programming concepts to a *simpler*, more basic set of concepts.

The implementation strategy used to identify specific semantic features of the *GOAL* language and to emulate these explicitly in *Jazzyk* also raises the question whether features of other agent programming languages can be compiled in a similar way. Although we do not have room to extensively argue for this, we believe that a similar approach can also be applied to other rule-based agent programming languages. In particular, the following implementation strategy could be applied to compile agent programs into *Jazzyk BSM*: (i) compile the underlying knowledge base(s) into equivalent *Jazzyk BSM* KR module(s), (ii) compile the (action, planning, ...) rules of the agent program into *Jazzyk BSM* mental state transformers using the operators of the KR module(s), and finally (iii) implement any specific semantic features of the language by a *Jazzyk BSM* *mst* and "append" it to the one constructed in the previous step. Moreover, since *Jazzyk BSM* also features a much simpler conceptual scheme than higher level agent languages, we believe that it provides a promising basis for an intermediate language into which agent programs can be compiled and interpreted.

Our result shows that *GOAL* does not commit to any particular KR technology such as Prolog. Another issue that remains is whether it would be possible to allow *GOAL* agents to use multiple KR technologies. The compilation into *Jazzyk BSM* provides some evidence that this is possible since *Jazzyk BSM* enables the use of many different KR technologies. However, the use of multiple KR technologies within a single agent will add expressive power only when certain key issues related to the "interoperability" of different KRs have been solved (for a discussion see also [3]).

References

1. Bordini, R.H., Dastani, M., Dix, J., El Fallah Seghrouchni, A.: Multi-Agent Programming Languages, Platforms and Applications. Kluwer Academic Publishers, Dordrecht (2005)
2. Börger, E., Stärk, R.F.: Abstract State Machines. A Method for High-Level System Design and Analysis. Springer, Heidelberg (2003)
3. Dastani, M., Hindriks, K.V., Novák, P., Tinnemeier, N.A.M.: Combining multiple knowledge representation technologies into agent programming languages. In: Proc. of the Intl. Workshop on Declarative Agent Languages and Technologies (DALT 2008) (2008)
4. Davis, R., Shrobe, H.E., Szolovits, P.: What Is a Knowledge Representation? AI 14(1), 17–33 (1993)
5. de Boer, F., Hindriks, K., van der Hoek, W., Meyer, J.-J.C.: A Verification Framework for Agent Programming with Declarative Goals. Journal of Applied Logic 5(2), 277–302 (2007)
6. Dennis, L.A., Bordini, R.H., Farwer, B., Fisher, M., Wooldridge, M.: A common semantic basis for BDI languages. In: Dastani, M., El Fallah Seghrouchni, A., Ricci, A., Winikoff, M. (eds.) ProMAS 2007. LNCS (LNAI), vol. 4908. Springer, Heidelberg (2008)
7. Hindriks, K.: Modules as Policy-Based Intentions. In: Dastani, M., El Fallah Seghrouchni, A., Ricci, A., Winikoff, M. (eds.) ProMAS 2007. LNCS (LNAI), vol. 4908. Springer, Heidelberg (2008)
8. Novák, P.: Behavioural State Machines: programming modular agents. In: AAAI 2008 Spring Symposium: Architectures for Intelligent Theory-Based Agents (AITA 2008) (2008)

9. Novák, P.: Jazzyk: A programming language for hybrid agents with heterogeneous knowledge representations. In: Proc. of the 6th Intl. Workshop on Programming Multi-Agent Systems (ProMAS 2008) (2008)
10. Pednault, E.: ADL: exploring the middle ground between STRIPS and the situation calculus. In: Proc. of the Int. Conf. on Principles of Knowledge Representation and Reasoning (1989)
11. Plotkin, G.D.: A Structural Approach to Operational Semantics. Technical Report DAIMI FN-19, University of Aarhus (1981)
12. Sterling, L., Shapiro, E.: The Art of Prolog. MIT Press, Cambridge (1986)
13. Warren, D.H.D.: An Abstract Prolog Instruction Set. Technical Report 309, AI Center, SRI International, 333 Ravenswood Ave., Menlo Park, CA 94025 (1983)

Knowledge and Strategic Ability for Model Checking: A Refined Approach

Wojciech Jamroga

Department of Informatics, Clausthal University of Technology, Germany
wjamroga@in.tu-clausthal.de

Abstract. We present a translation that reduces epistemic operators to strategic operators in the context of model checking. The translation is a refinement of the one from [4], and it improves on the previous scheme in two ways. First, it does not suffer any blowup in the length of formulae (the one from [4] did). Second, the new translation is defined in a more general setting: additional constraints can be imposed on strategy profiles that agents can execute. We show the applicability of such a general translation on the case of strategic abilities under imperfect information.

1 Introduction

Modal logics of multi-agent systems usually combine several dimensions. Knowledge, time, actions, strategic abilities, norms/obligations, intentions, desires etc. can all be involved in a description of an agent system. This way, modal logic can support sufficiently realistic descriptions of agents. But there is a price to pay: such multi-modal logics are usually harder to handle semantically as well as algorithmically. Thus, a designer is usually faced with the task of finding a good tradeoff between a "clean" logic with few modalities (and clear overall semantics) and a "realistic" language with many modalities (where it is not immediately visible how parts of the semantics interfere). A reduction method that allows to express one modality with the others offers two kinds of advantage. In terms of theory, it allows to make the logic "cleaner", and study its theoretical properties (semantics, computational complexity) in a simpler environment. On the practical side, we can reuse the advances in, say, model checking of one sort of modality to improve the techniques used for dealing with the other dimensions.

In [4], we proposed how epistemic modalities can be equivalently expressed by strategic operators of alternating-time temporal logic ATL [1] in the context of model checking. The reduction was polynomial in *almost* every respect. Unfortunately, the length of formulae could suffer exponential blowup (although the number of *different* subformulae in the formula increased only linearly). We argued that, for most model checking algorithms, it would not increase the verification time. Still, it was a flaw that made using the reduction awkward, at least for theoretical purposes. The aim of this paper is to propose a refinement of the reduction that does not suffer from the blowup any more. Moreover, we point out that the reduction can be used even if we impose some "behavioral

R. Bergmann et al. (Eds.): MATES 2008, LNAI 5244, pp. 99–110, 2008.

constraints" on the strategies that can be played by agents. Thus, the method can be used also for variants of ATL where one assumes that the agents can only play in a uniform [7], socially acceptable [11], or rational way [6].

Our presentation here is based on some material from [4]. It should be also mentioned that the original reduction was inspired by [9], and shared some similarities with [13] (although the reduction proposed in the latter paper had a more limited scope). Similar translations of modal logics include [8,3]. Our presentation of strategic constraints is based on the approach of [6].

2   Preliminaries

2.1   ATL: Abilities in Perfect Information Games

ATL [1] generalizes the branching time logic CTL [2] by replacing path quantifiers with so called *cooperation modalities*. The formula $\langle\!\langle A \rangle\!\rangle \varphi$ expresses that group of agents A have a collective strategy to enforce φ. ATL formulae include temporal operators: "$\bigcirc$" ("in the next state"), $\square$ ("always from now on") and $\mathcal{U}$ ("until"). Operator $\Diamond$ ("now or sometime in the future") can be defined as $\Diamond\varphi \equiv \top \mathcal{U} \varphi$. Formally, the recursive definition of ATL formulae is:

$$\varphi ::= p \mid \neg\varphi \mid \varphi \wedge \varphi \mid \langle\!\langle A \rangle\!\rangle \bigcirc \varphi \mid \langle\!\langle A \rangle\!\rangle \square \varphi \mid \langle\!\langle A \rangle\!\rangle \varphi \mathcal{U} \varphi.$$

A *concurrent game structure* (CGS) is a tuple $M = \langle \text{Agt}, St, \Pi, \pi, Act, d, o \rangle$ which includes a nonempty finite set of all agents $\text{Agt} = \{1, \ldots, k\}$, a nonempty set of states St, a set of atomic propositions Π, a valuation of propositions $\pi : St \rightarrow 2^{\Pi}$, and a set of (atomic) actions Act. Function $d : \text{Agt} \times St \rightarrow (2^{Act} \setminus \emptyset)$ defines nonempty sets of actions available to agents at each state, and o is a transition function that assigns the outcome state $q' = o(q, \alpha_1, \ldots, \alpha_k)$ to state q and a tuple of actions $\langle \alpha_1, \ldots, \alpha_k \rangle$, $\alpha_i \in d(i, q)$, that can be executed by Agt in q.

A (memoryless) *strategy* s_a of agent a is a conditional plan that specifies what a is going to do for every possible situation: $s_a : St \rightarrow Act$ such that $s_a(q) \in d(a, q)$. We denote the set of such functions by Σ_a. A *collective strategy* s_A for a group of agents A is a tuple of strategies, one per agent from A; the set of A's collective strategies is given by $\Sigma_A = \prod_{a \in A} \Sigma_a$. The set of all *strategy profiles* is given by $\Sigma = \Sigma_{\text{Agt}}$.

A *path* λ in model M is an infinite sequence of states that can be effected by subsequent transitions, and refers to a possible course of action (or a possible computation) that may occur in the system; by $\lambda[i]$, we denote the ith position on path λ. The set of all paths starting from state q is given by $\Lambda(q)$. Function $out(q, s_A)$ returns the set of all paths that may result from agents A executing strategy s_A from state q onward.

Formally, the semantics of cooperation modalities can be given via the following clauses:

$M, q \models \langle\!\langle A \rangle\!\rangle \bigcirc \varphi$ iff there is a collective strategy s_A such that, for every $\lambda \in out(q, s_A)$, we have $M, \lambda[1] \models \varphi$;

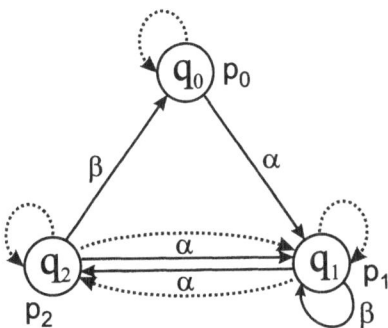

Fig. 1. Simple concurrent epistemic game structure M_1. Nodes represent states of the system, solid arrows depict transitions (labeled by the agent's actions), and dotted arrows show indistinguishability of states.

$M, q \models \langle\!\langle A \rangle\!\rangle \Box \varphi$ iff there exists s_A such that, for every $\lambda \in out(q, s_A)$, we have $M, \lambda[i] \models \varphi$ for every $i \geq 0$;

$M, q \models \langle\!\langle A \rangle\!\rangle \varphi \mathcal{U} \psi$ iff there exists s_A such that for every $\lambda \in out(q, s_A)$ there is an $i \geq 0$, for which $M, \lambda[i] \models \psi$, and $M, \lambda[j] \models \varphi$ for every $0 \leq j < i$.

2.2 Epistemic Logic: Knowledge and Imperfect Information

Epistemic logic uses operators $K_a\varphi$ ("agent a knows that φ"). Additional operators $E_A\varphi$, $C_A\varphi$, and $D_A\varphi$, where A is a set of agents, refer to *mutual knowledge* ("everybody knows"), *common knowledge*, and *distributed knowledge* among the agents from A. On the semantic side, uncertainty of agents is modeled by indistinguishability relations $\sim_1, \ldots, \sim_k \subseteq St \times St$ (one per agent). The semantics of K_a is defined as: $M, q \models K_a\varphi$ iff $M, q' \models \varphi$ for every q' such that $q \sim_a q'$.

Relations $\sim_A^E$, $\sim_A^C$ and $\sim_A^D$, used to model group epistemics, are derived from the individual relations of agents from A. First, $\sim_A^E$ is the union of relations $\sim_a$, $a \in A$. Next, $\sim_A^C$ is defined as the transitive closure of $\sim_A^E$. Finally, $\sim_A^D$ is the intersection of all the $\sim_a$, $a \in A$. Then, for $\mathcal{K} = C, E, D$, we define: $M, q \models \mathcal{K}_A\varphi$ iff $M, q' \models \varphi$ for every q' such that $q \sim_A^{\mathcal{K}} q'$.

A straightforward combination of ATL and epistemic logic, called ATEL was introduced in [12]. The language of ATEL allows to express knowledge about agents' (perfect information) abilities. Models of ATEL are called *concurrent epistemic game structures* (CEGS). A simple CEGS (with only one agent a) is depicted in Figure 1. For that model, we have for instance that $M_1, q_1 \models K_a\langle\!\langle a \rangle\!\rangle \Diamond p_0$.

3   Restricting Strategies of Agents

In many cases, it seems appropriate to put some constraints on the "good" (allowed, legal etc.) behaviors. We define a class of such *strategic constraints* in this section. Our constraints are based on the idea of plausibility sets [6], and generalize the behavioral constraints from the framework of social laws [11].

3.1 Strategic Constraints

A behavioral constraint in [11] is a function $\beta : \text{Agt} \times St \to 2^{Act}$ that specifies which actions can be "legally" played by agents. More specifically, $\beta(a, q)$ is the set of actions that a is allowed to play at state q. Naturally, $\beta(a, q) \subseteq d(a, q)$, and the inclusion can be strict. $\beta(a, q)$ is assumed to implement a social norm: agent a (when in state q) may be forbidden to play some actions in his repertoire; if he decides to play them, he will violate the norm.

Note that using constraints of this type implies that norms only apply to actions of individual agents (independently). It is therefore not possible to specify e.g. that one is allowed to shoot in self-defense, i.e., *right at the moment* when another person is trying to harm him. Likewise, norms of that type specify legal actions independently for each state. Thus, if we do not accept lying, then making a false statement will be always forbidden, even if it is just a joke, and the speaker is going to disclose the truth in the very next moment.

Here, we are looking for a model that enables to cope with such interrelationships between the allowed actions of different agents at different states, too. Another rationale for this comes from game theory. Unlike in normative systems, we are interested in "rational" rather than "moral" behavior there, but the general pattern is the same. That is, some strategy profiles of agents (e.g., those in Nash equilibrium) are deemed "rational", while the others are rejected as "irrational". Note that, especially for Nash equilibrium, the rationality of an action does depend on what the agent is going to do at other states; moreover, it depends on what *the other agents* are going to do at this and other states. Thus, our requirements with respect to agents' behavior will be modeled as *sets of strategy profiles*.

When defining agents' behavior via strategy sets, one assumes implicitly that agents actually *play strategies*. In our case, it would for instance imply that each agent does the same action every time the system comes back again to one of the previous states (as memoryless strategies are used in our semantics of ATL). This is a very strong assumption, and we do not always want to make it with respect to *all* agents. Thus, our strategic constraints will also include the set of agents to whom the constraint should apply.

Definition 1. *A strategic constraint is a pair* $\eta = \langle \Upsilon, A \rangle$, *where* $\Upsilon \subseteq \Sigma$ *is a non-empty set of strategy profiles and* $A \subseteq \text{Agt}$ *is a set of agents.*

Definition 2 (Substrategy). *Let* $A, B \subseteq \text{Agt}$, *and let* s_A *be a collective strategy for* A. *We use* $s_A[B]$ *to denote the substrategy of* s_A *for agents from* B *only, i.e., strategy* $t_{A \cap B}$ *such that* $t^a_{A \cap B} = s^a_A$ *for every* $a \in A \cap B$. *We extend the notation to sets in a natural way: for a set of collective strategies* $\Upsilon_A \subseteq \Sigma_A$, *we define* $\Upsilon_A[B] = \{ t \in \Sigma_{A \cap B} \mid \exists s_A \in \Upsilon_A. t = s_A[B] \}$.

Definition 3 (Consistency with a constraint). *Let* s_A *be a collective strategy of* $A \subseteq \text{Agt}$, *and* $\eta = \langle \Upsilon, B \rangle$ *be a strategic constraint. Strategy* s_A *is consistent with constraint* η *iff the part of* s_A *to which the constraint should apply occurs in* Υ, *i.e.,* $s_A[B] \in \Upsilon[A \cap B]$.

Definition 4 (Outcome under constraint). *Let M be a* CGS, *and q a state in M. Furthermore, let s_A be a collective strategy, and $\eta = \langle \Upsilon, B \rangle$ be a strategic constraint. The outcome of s_A from q under constraint η contains all paths which may result from agents A executing s_A from q on, when the opponents are only allowed to play strategies which complement s_A in a way that complies with η. Formally, the set is defined as:*

$$out(q, s_A, \eta) = \{\lambda \in \Lambda(q) \mid \text{ there is } t \in \Sigma_{A \cup B}, \text{ consistent with } \eta, \text{ such that}$$
$$t[A] = s_A \text{ and for every } i = 1, 2, \ldots \text{ there exists a tuple of agents' decisions}$$
$$\langle \alpha_1, \ldots, \alpha_k \rangle \text{ for which: } \alpha_a = t^a(\lambda[i-1]) \text{ for } a \in A \cup B, \; \alpha_a \in d(a, \lambda[i-1])$$
$$\text{for } a \notin A \cup B, \text{ and } o(\lambda[i-1], \alpha_1, \ldots, \alpha_k) = \lambda[i]\}.$$

3.2 Abilities Under Strategic Constraints: Semantics

The intuition behind strategic constraints is rather simple: for a constraint $\eta = \langle \Upsilon, B \rangle$ we assume that the actual collective strategy of agents B must occur somewhere in Υ. Note that the agents from B do not have to be all in the same coalition – B can collect both "proponents" and "opponents". The formal semantics of ATL formulae in the presence of strategic constraints is given by the clauses below.

$M, q, \eta \models p$ iff $p \in \pi(q)$ (for $p \in \Pi$);

$M, q, \eta \models \neg\varphi$ iff $M, q, \eta \not\models \varphi$;

$M, q, \eta \models \varphi \land \psi$ iff $M, q, \eta \models \varphi$ and $M, q, \eta \models \psi$;

$M, q, \eta \models \langle\!\langle A \rangle\!\rangle \bigcirc \varphi$ iff there is a collective strategy s_A, consistent with η, such that for every $\lambda \in out(q, s_A, \eta)$ we have $M, \lambda[1], \eta \models \varphi$;

$M, q, \eta \models \langle\!\langle A \rangle\!\rangle \Box \varphi$ iff there exists s_A consistent with η, such that for every $\lambda \in out(q, s_A, \eta)$ we have $M, \lambda[i], \eta \models \varphi$ for every $i \geq 0$;

$M, q, \eta \models \langle\!\langle A \rangle\!\rangle \varphi \mathcal{U} \psi$ iff there exists s_A consistent with η, such that for every $\lambda \in out(q, s_A, \eta)$ there is an $i \geq 0$, for which $M, \lambda[i], \eta \models \psi$, and $M, \lambda[j], \eta \models \varphi$ for every $0 \leq j < i$.

The semantics of knowledge under strategic constraints is defined in a straightforward way: agents know that φ under η iff φ holds under η in every indistinguishable state.

$M, q, \eta \models K_a \varphi$ iff $M, q', \eta \models \varphi$ for every q' such that $q \sim_a q'$.

$M, q, \eta \models \mathcal{K}_A \varphi$ iff $M, q', \eta \models \varphi$ for every q' such that $q \sim_A^{\mathcal{K}} q'$ (where $\mathcal{K} = C, E, D$).

A useful example of strategic constraints are so called *uniform strategies*, i.e., strategies that can be feasibly executed by an agent under imperfect information. We say that s_a is uniform iff, for every q, q', $q \sim_a q'$ implies that $s_a(q) = s_a(q')$; that is, agent a must specify same choices in states that look the same to him. A collective strategy s_A is uniform iff it consists only of uniform individual strategies. Let Σ_a^u denote the set of uniform strategies of agent a. Then $\Sigma_A^u = \prod_{a \in A} \Sigma_a^u$ is the set of collective uniform strategies of A, and $\Sigma^u = \Sigma_{Agt}^u$ is the set of uniform strategy profiles. Now, the requirement that agents from A should only use uniform strategies can be captured by the strategic constraint $\eta = \langle \Sigma^u, A \rangle$.

Consider CEGS M_1 from Figure 1. For that model, the requirement that the only agent sticks to executable (i.e., uniform) strategies can be captured by the constraint $\eta = \langle \{[q_0 \mapsto \alpha, q_1 \mapsto \alpha, q_2 \mapsto \alpha], [q_0 \mapsto \alpha, q_1 \mapsto \beta, q_2 \mapsto \beta]\}, \{a\} \rangle$. Then, we have for instance that $M_1, q_1, \eta \models K_a \neg \langle\langle a \rangle\rangle \Diamond \mathsf{p}_0$: no uniform strategy can guarantee that a gets from q_1 to q_0, and the agent knows about it.

4 Translating Knowledge to Strategic Ability

In this section, we show a satisfaction-preserving interpretation of ATEL formulae and models into ATL. The interpretation is an update of that proposed in [4]. Two things are changed. First, we slightly change the transformation of models so that, after visiting an "epistemic" state, the system *always* returns immediately to its corresponding "action" state. In consequence, it is possible to define the translation of formulae without exponential blowup in their length. Second, we show that the translation is also correct when we add constraints on the behavior of agents.

4.1 Idea of the Translation

ATEL consists of two orthogonal layers. The first one, inherited from ATL, refers to what agents can achieve in temporal perspective, and is underpinned by the structure defined via transition function o. The other layer is the epistemic component, reflected by epistemic indistinguishability relations. Our idea of the translation is to leave the original temporal structure intact, while extending it with additional transitions to "simulate" epistemic links. The simulation is achieved through adding new "epistemic" agents who can enforce transitions to special "epistemic" copies of "action" states (i.e., the states inherited from the original model). The "action" and "epistemic" states form separate strata in the resulting model, and are labeled accordingly to distinguish transitions that implement different modalities.

The interpretation consists of two independent parts: a transformation of models and a translation of formulae. First, we propose a construction that transforms every concurrent epistemic game structure M for a set of agents $\{1, ..., k\}$, into a (pure) concurrent game structure M' over a set of agents $\{1, ..., k, e_1, ..., e_k\}$. Agents $1, ..., k$ are the original agents from M (we will call them "real agents"). Agents $e_1, ..., e_k$ are "epistemic doubles" of the real agents: the role of e_i is to "point out" the states that were epistemically indistinguishable from the current state for agent i in M. In order to distinguish transitions referring to different modalities, we introduce additional states in model M'. States $q_1^{\mathsf{e}_i}, ..., q_n^{\mathsf{e}_i}$ satisfy new proposition e_i added to enable identifying moves of epistemic agent e_i. Moreover, epistemic state q^{e_i} has the same "epistemic" transitions as q (leading to epistemic copies of states indistinguishable from q), plus one outgoing transition leading to the corresponding action state q. The original states $q_1, ..., q_n$ are still in M' to represent targets of "action" moves of the real agents $1, ..., k$. We will use a new proposition act to label these states. Now, the type of a transition can be recognized by the label of its target state. The structure of the transformation can be seen in Figure 2.

Defining the transition function o so that both epistemic and "action" transitions can occur is the trickiest part of the construction. We achieve this by giving priority to the epistemic agents' decisions. Every epistemic agent can choose to be "passive" and let the others decide upon the next move, or may try to effect an epistemic move. The resulting transition leads to the state selected by the *first* non-passive epistemic agent. If all the epistemic agents have decided to be passive, the action transition chosen by the real agents follows. Epistemic states are given special treatment, as we assume that the real agents are always passive there. Thus, if all the epistemic agents decide to be passive at an epistemic state, the system proceeds to the corresponding action state.

With the above construction in mind, ATEL formulae can be translated to ATL according to the following scheme:

- $K_i\varphi$ can be rephrased as $\neg\langle\langle e_1, ..., e_i\rangle\rangle \bigcirc (\mathsf{e_i} \wedge \langle\langle e_1, ..., e_k\rangle\rangle \bigcirc (\mathsf{act} \wedge \neg\varphi))$: the epistemic moves to agent e_i's epistemic states do not lead to a state where φ fails (more precisely: where φ fails in the corresponding "action" state). Note that player e_i can select a state of his if, and only if, players $e_1, ..., e_{i-1}$ are passive (hence their presence in the cooperation modality).
- $\langle\langle A\rangle\rangle \bigcirc \varphi$ becomes $\langle\langle A \cup \{e_1, ..., e_k\}\rangle\rangle \bigcirc (\mathsf{act} \wedge \varphi)$ in a similar way.
- Translation of the other temporal operators is now more straightforward than in [4]: $\langle\langle A\rangle\rangle \square \varphi$ can be rephrased as $\langle\langle A \cup \{e_1, ..., e_k\}\rangle\rangle \square (\mathsf{act} \wedge \varphi)$, and $\langle\langle A\rangle\rangle \varphi \mathcal{U} \psi$ becomes $\langle\langle A \cup \{e_1, ..., e_k\}\rangle\rangle (\mathsf{act} \wedge \varphi) \mathcal{U} (\mathsf{act} \wedge \psi)$. This is possible because the construction of epistemic states (and the translation of K_a) ensures that strategic (sub)formulae will be always evaluated in "action" states. We observe that the new translation of $\square$ and $\mathcal{U}$ does not involve exponential increase in the length of formulae (contrary to the construction from [4]).
- Translation of mutual knowledge (E_A) is analogous to the individual knowledge case. Translation of common knowledge refers to the definition of relation $\sim_A^C$ as the transitive closure of relations $\sim_i$ for $i \in A$: $C_A\varphi$ means that all the (finite) sequences of appropriate epistemic transitions must end up in a state where φ is true.

The only operator that does not seem to lend itself to a translation according to the above scheme is the distributed knowledge operator D_A, for which we seem to need more "auxiliary" agents. Thus, we will begin with presenting details of our interpretation for ATEL_{CE} – a reduced version of ATEL that includes only common knowledge and "everybody knows" operators for group epistemics. Section 4.3 shows how to modify the translation to include distributed knowledge as well.

4.2   Interpreting Models and Formulae of ATEL$_{CE}$ into ATL

Transforming Models. Given a concurrent epistemic game structure $M = \langle \text{Agt}, St, \Pi, \pi, Act, d, o, \sim_1, ..., \sim_k \rangle$, we construct a new concurrent game structure $M' = \langle \text{Agt}', St', \Pi', \pi', Act', d', o' \rangle$ as follows:

- $\text{Agt}' = \text{Agt} \cup \text{Agt}^e$, where $\text{Agt}^e = \{e_1, ..., e_k\}$ is the set of epistemic agents;
- $St' = St \cup St^{e_1} \cup ... \cup St^{e_k}$, where $St^{e_i} = \{q^{e_i} \mid q \in St\}$.
- $\Pi' = \Pi \cup \{\text{act}, e_1, ..., e_k\}$;
- $\pi'(p) = \pi(p)$ for every proposition $p \in \Pi$. Moreover, $\pi'(\text{act}) = St$ and $\pi'(e_i) = St^{e_i}$;
- $Act' = Act \cup St \cup \{pass\}$: the new model M' contains the original actions from M, plus epistemic actions (pointing indistinguishable states), and the "do nothing" action $pass$;
- $d'_a(q) = d_a(q)$ for $a \in \text{Agt}$, $q \in St$; $d'_a(q) = \{pass\}$ for $a \in \text{Agt}$, $q \in St' \setminus St$; $d'_{e_i}(q) = \text{img}(q, \sim_i) \cup \{pass\}$ for $q \in St'$;
- the new transition function is defined as follows:

$$o'(q, \alpha_1, ..., \alpha_k, \alpha_{e_1}, ..., \alpha_{e_k}) = \begin{cases} o(q, \alpha_1, ..., \alpha_k) & \text{if } q \in St \text{ and} \\ & \alpha_{e_1} = ... = \alpha_{e_k} = pass \\[1em] q_0 & \text{if } q = q_0^{e_i} \in St^{e_i} \text{and} \\ & \alpha_{e_1} = ... = \alpha_{e_k} = pass \\[1em] (\alpha_{e_i})^{e_i} & \text{if } e_i \text{ is the first active} \\ & \text{epistemic agent.} \end{cases}$$

We assume that all the epistemic agents from Agt^e, states from $St^{e_1} \cup ... \cup St^{e_k}$, and propositions from $\{\text{act}, e_1, ..., e_k\}$, are new and were absent in the original model M.

The transformation of the simple CEGS from Figure 1 is shown in Figure 2.

Translation of Formulae. Now, we define a translation of formulae from ATEL$_{CE}$ to ATL corresponding to the above transformation of models:

$$tr(p) = p, \quad \text{for } p \in \Pi$$
$$tr(\neg \varphi) = \neg tr(\varphi)$$
$$tr(\varphi \wedge \psi) = tr(\varphi) \wedge tr(\psi)$$
$$tr(\langle\!\langle A \rangle\!\rangle \bigcirc \varphi) = \langle\!\langle A \cup \text{Agt}^e \rangle\!\rangle \bigcirc (\text{act} \wedge tr(\varphi))$$
$$tr(\langle\!\langle A \rangle\!\rangle \square \varphi) = \langle\!\langle A \cup \text{Agt}^e \rangle\!\rangle \square (\text{act} \wedge tr(\varphi))$$
$$tr(\langle\!\langle A \rangle\!\rangle \varphi \mathcal{U} \psi) = \langle\!\langle A \cup \text{Agt}^e \rangle\!\rangle (\text{act} \wedge tr(\varphi)) \mathcal{U} (\text{act} \wedge tr(\psi))$$
$$tr(K_i \varphi) = \neg \langle\!\langle e_1, ..., e_i \rangle\!\rangle \bigcirc (e_i \wedge \langle\!\langle \text{Agt}^e \rangle\!\rangle \bigcirc (\text{act} \wedge \neg tr(\varphi)))$$
$$tr(E_A \varphi) = \neg \langle\!\langle \text{Agt}^e \rangle\!\rangle \bigcirc ((\bigvee_{a_i \in A} e_i) \wedge \langle\!\langle \text{Agt}^e \rangle\!\rangle \bigcirc (\text{act} \wedge \neg tr(\varphi)))$$
$$tr(C_A \varphi) = \neg \langle\!\langle \text{Agt}^e \rangle\!\rangle \bigcirc \langle\!\langle \text{Agt}^e \rangle\!\rangle$$
$$(\bigvee_{a_i \in A} e_i) \mathcal{U} ((\bigvee_{a_i \in A} e_i) \wedge \langle\!\langle \text{Agt}^e \rangle\!\rangle \bigcirc (\text{act} \wedge \neg tr(\varphi))).$$

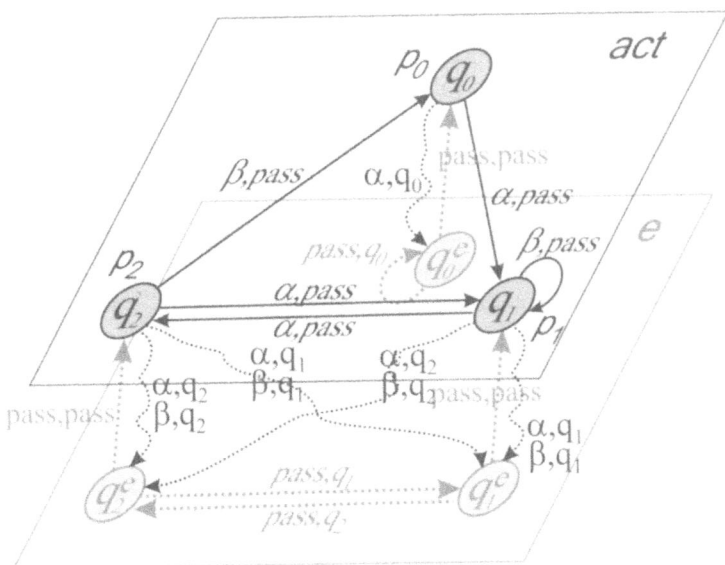

Fig. 2. Reconstruction for the concurrent epistemic game structure from Figure 1

Extending Strategic Constraints. Given a strategic constraint $\eta = \langle \Upsilon, B \rangle$ in M, we must extend it to match the type of constraints in M' (because M' includes more agents than M, and in consequence the elements of Υ, which are full strategy profiles in M, are only partial profiles in M').[1] This can be done in many ways; here, we explicitly assume that the additional (epistemic) agents can use any strategies they like. The new constraint must apply to the agents from B, plus (possibly) to some of the new agents from Agt^e. That is, agents from B are constrained in the same way as before, agents from $\mathrm{Agt} \setminus B$ are unconstrained in the same way as before, and the new agents can be put under constraints or not – but even if they are, they can play any available strategy.[2]

Definition 5. *Let $\eta = \langle \Upsilon, B \rangle$ be a strategic constraint in concurrent epistemic game structure M, and let M' be the concurrent game structure obtained from M by the construction presented in Section 4.2. We say that constraint $\eta' = \langle \Upsilon', B' \rangle$ extends η in M' iff: (1) $\Upsilon' = \Upsilon \times \Sigma_{\mathrm{Agt}^e}$, and   (2) $B \subseteq B' \subseteq B \cup \mathrm{Agt}^e$.*

Soundness and Complexity of the Translation

Theorem 1. *Let φ be a formula of ATEL_{CE}, M be a CEGS, $q \in St$ a state in M, and M' the CGS resulting from the transformation. Furthermore, let η be a behavioral constraint in M, and let η' extend η in M'.*
Then, $M, q, \eta \models \varphi$ iff $M', q, \eta' \models tr(\varphi)$.

---

[1] Note that the old agents from Agt have no real choice in the new states ($St' \setminus St$), so extending the set of states is not a problem (for every $s_a : St \to Act$ there is a unique $s'_a : St' \to Act$ that extends s_a).

[2] We recall that the assumption that a player plays a memoryless strategy is itself a restriction on the agent's behavior.

A proof of the theorem can be found in the technical report [5].

Note that the construction used above has several nice complexity properties. In the following list, k denotes the number of agents, p the number of propositions, n the number of states, m the number of transitions, and $\overline{m}$ the number of epistemic links in the original CEGS M. Likewise, k', p', n', m' denote the number of agents, propositions, states and transitions in the resulting CGS M'.

- The vocabulary (set of propositions Π) and the set of agents only increase linearly: $p' = p + k + 1 = O(p + k)$ and $k' = 2k = O(k)$.
- The set of states in an ATEL-model grows linearly, too: $n' = (k+1)n = O(kn)$.
- We have $m' = m + k(\overline{m} + 1) = O(m + k\overline{m})$ transitions in M' (m "action" transitions and $\overline{m}$ epistemic transitions from "action" states, plus $\overline{m} + 1$ transitions from each "epistemic" state).
- The length of formulae also increases linearly: $l \leq l' \leq l(8 + 5k) = O(kl)$.

The transformation of models and formulae is straightforward, and in consequence its complexity is no worse than the complexity of the resulting structures.

4.3 Handling Distributed Knowledge

In order to interpret the full ATEL we modify the construction from Section 4.2 by introducing additional epistemic agents (and states) indexed with coalitions which occur with a distributed knowledge operator:

- $\mathrm{Agt}^e = \{e_i \mid i \in \mathrm{Agt}\} \cup \{e_A \mid D_A \in \varphi\}$;
- $St' = St \cup \bigcup_{i \in \mathrm{Agt}} St^{e_i} \cup \bigcup_{D_A \in \varphi} St^{e_A}$.

Accordingly, we extend the language with new propositions $\{e_i \mid i \in \mathrm{Agt}\}$ and $\{e_A \mid D_A \in \varphi\}$. The choices of collective epistemic agents e_A refer to the (epistemic copies of) states accessible via distributed knowledge relations:

- $d'_{e_A}(q) = \{pass\} \cup img(q, \sim_A^D)^{e_A}$.

The new transition function extends the one from Section 4.2 with choices of agents e_A (putting them in any predefined order, e.g. alphabetical order):

$$
o'(q, \alpha_1, ..., \alpha_k, \alpha_{e_1}, ..., \alpha_{e_k}, \\ ..., \alpha_{e_A}, ...) = \begin{cases} o(q, \alpha_1, ..., \alpha_k) & \text{if } q \in St \text{ and} \\ & \alpha_a = pass \text{ for all } a \in \mathrm{Agt}^e \\ \\ q_0 & \text{if } q = q_0^{e_i} \in St^{e_i} \text{and} \\ & \alpha_a = pass \text{ for all } a \in \mathrm{Agt}^e \\ \\ (\alpha_{e_a})^{e_a} & \text{if } e_a \text{ is the first active} \\ & \text{epistemic agent.} \end{cases}
$$

The translation of formulae for all operators of ATEL_{CE} remains the same as well, and the translation of D_A is:

$$
tr(D_A \varphi) = \neg \langle\!\langle \mathrm{Agt}^e \rangle\!\rangle \bigcirc \left(e_A \wedge \langle\!\langle \mathrm{Agt}^e \rangle\!\rangle \bigcirc (act \wedge \neg tr(\varphi))\right).
$$

Theorem 2. *Let φ be a formula of* ATEL, *M be a* CEGS, *and $q \in St$ an "action" state in M. Furthermore, let η be a behavioral constraint in M, and let η' extend η in M'. Then, $M, q, \eta \models \varphi$ iff $M', q, \eta' \models tr(\varphi)$.*

This construction, too, does not involve any substantial increase of complexity. Still, it has one disadvantage when compared to the construction from Section 4.2: there, models and formulae could be translated independently; here, the transformation of a model depends on the formula which will be model-checked. Thus, it is not possible any more to "pre-compile" a given CEGS in advance, and then model-check on the fly any formulae that will become relevant.

4.4 Reducing Knowledge to Strategic Ability: Example

Since the transformation of models and formulae involves only linear increase of their size, it can be used for an efficient reduction of model checking when we want to get rid of epistemic operators from formulae. Strategic constraints, on the other hand, enable realistic approach to the semantics of abilities. The idea behind indistinguishability relations is that they capture agents' uncertainty about the current state of the game, so our analysis of abilities should be in most cases restricted to uniform strategies.

Let $\langle\!\langle A \rangle\!\rangle_u$ be a "uniform" version of cooperation modality, similar to the operator $\langle\!\langle A \rangle\!\rangle_{ir}$ from [10]. The semantics of $\langle\!\langle A \rangle\!\rangle_u \gamma$ is the same as for $\langle\!\langle A \rangle\!\rangle \gamma$ except that only uniform strategies can be used by A. It is easy to see that $\langle\!\langle A \rangle\!\rangle_u$ can be rephrased as an ordinary cooperation modality with the strategic constraint that requires A's choices to be uniform: $M, q \models \langle\!\langle A \rangle\!\rangle_u \gamma$ iff $M, q, \langle \Sigma^u, A \rangle \models \langle\!\langle A \rangle\!\rangle \gamma$.

For example, we have that $M_1, q_1 \models K_a \neg \langle\!\langle a \rangle\!\rangle_u \Diamond p_0$ for the CEGS from Figure 1. This can be rephrased as $M_1, q_1, \langle \Sigma^u, \{a\} \rangle \models K_a \neg \langle\!\langle a \rangle\!\rangle_u \Diamond p_0$, which is by Theorem 1 equivalent to $M_1', q_1, \langle \Sigma^u, \{a\} \rangle \models \neg \langle\!\langle e_a \rangle\!\rangle \bigcirc (e_a \wedge \langle\!\langle e_a \rangle\!\rangle \bigcirc (\mathsf{act} \wedge \langle\!\langle a \rangle\!\rangle \Diamond p_0))$, where M_1' is the concurrent game structure from Figure 2. Thus, we have reduced the original property (and model) to ones that include no epistemic dimension.

Note that we can incorporate the uniformity constraints back into the cooperation modalities if we keep epistemic links in the reconstructed model. Let M_1'' be M_1' with epistemic links retained from the original model M_1 (plus reflective epistemic links added for the epistemic agent e_a to indicate that e_a has perfect information in every state). Then, $M_1, q_1 \models K_a \neg \langle\!\langle a \rangle\!\rangle_u \Diamond p_0$ iff $M_1'', q_1 \models \neg \langle\!\langle e_a \rangle\!\rangle_u \bigcirc (e_a \wedge \langle\!\langle e_a \rangle\!\rangle_u \bigcirc (\mathsf{act} \wedge \langle\!\langle a \rangle\!\rangle_u \Diamond p_0))$. On a more general level, Theorem 1 implies that adding explicit operators K_a for describing agents' knowledge does not increase the complexity of model checking agents' abilities also in the case of imperfect information strategies.

5 Conclusions

In this paper, we propose an update of the reduction scheme that was presented in [4]. The original reduction allowed to get rid of epistemic operators by translating them to cooperation modalities of ATL which made use of additional "epistemic" agents. The new version has two new features. First, we avoid the exponential blowup of formulae, which was to some extent present in the original reduction. Second, we show that the reduction is valid also if we specify *strategic constraints* which restrict collective strategies that some (or all) agents are allowed to use. Thus, the applicability of the new reduction scheme goes well beyond ATEL (i.e., perfect information ATL + knowledge operators). We can use the scheme to translate knowledge to strategic ability for agents playing under imperfect information (like in ATL_{ir} from [10]), acting in the presence of social norms [11], or choosing only rational play [6]. It seems that many other extensions of alternating-time logic should submit to the reduction, too.

References

1. Alur, R., Henzinger, T.A., Kupferman, O.: Alternating-time Temporal Logic. Journal of the ACM 49, 672–713 (2002)
2. Clarke, E.M., Emerson, E.A.: Design and synthesis of synchronization skeletons using branching time temporal logic. In: Kozen, D. (ed.) Logic of Programs 1981. LNCS, vol. 131, pp. 52–71. Springer, Heidelberg (1982)
3. Gerbrandy, J.: Bisimulations on Planet Kripke. PhD thesis, University of Amsterdam (1999)
4. Goranko, V., Jamroga, W.: Comparing semantics of logics for multi-agent systems. Synthese 139(2), 241–280 (2004)
5. Jamroga, W.: Reducing knowledge operators in the context of model checking. Technical Report IfI-07-09, Clausthal University of Technology (2007)
6. Jamroga, W., Bulling, N.: A framework for reasoning about rational agents. In: Proceedings of AAMAS 2007, pp. 592–594 (2007)
7. Jamroga, W., van der Hoek, W.: Agents that know how to play. Fundamenta Informaticae 63(2–3), 185–219 (2004)
8. Meyer, J.-J.C.: A different approach to deontic logic: Deontic logic viewed as a variant of dynamic logic. Notre Dame Journal of Formal Logic 29(1), 109–136 (1988)
9. Schild, K.: On the relationship between BDI logics and standard logics of concurrency. Autonomous Agents and Multi Agent Systems, 259–283 (2000)
10. Schobbens, P.Y.: Alternating-time logic with imperfect recall. Electronic Notes in Theoretical Computer Science 85(2) (2004)
11. van der Hoek, W., Roberts, M., Wooldridge, M.: Social laws in alternating time: Effectiveness, feasibility and synthesis. Synthese (2005)
12. van der Hoek, W., Wooldridge, M.: Cooperation, knowledge and time: Alternating-time Temporal Epistemic Logic and its applications. Studia Logica 75(1), 125–157 (2003)
13. van Otterloo, S., van der Hoek, W., Wooldridge, M.: Knowledge as strategic ability. Electronic Lecture Notes in Theoretical Computer Science 85(2) (2003)

Agent Learning Instead of Behavior Implementation for Simulations – A Case Study Using Classifier Systems

Franziska Klügl[1], Reinhard Hatko[1], and Martin V. Butz[2]

[1] Dep. of Artificial Intelligence and Applied Computer Science
University of Würzburg
Würzburg, Germany
{hatko,kluegl}@informatik.uni-wuerzburg.de
[2] Dep. of Psychology, Cognitive Psychology III
University of Würzburg
Würzburg, Germany
butz@psychologie.uni-wuerzburg.de

Abstract. Although multi-agent simulations are an intuitive way of conceptualizing systems that consist of autonomous actors, a major problem is the actual design of the agent behavior. In this contribution, we examine the potential of using agent-based learning for implementing the agent behavior. We enhanced SeSAm, a platform for agent-based simulation, by replacing the usual rule-based agent architecture by XCS, a well-known learning classifier system (LCS). The resulting model is tested using a simple evacuation scenario. The results show that on the one hand side plausible agent behavior could be learned. On the other hand side, though, the results are quite brittle concerning the frame of environmental feedback, perception and action modeling.

1 Introduction

Agent-based simulations pose very few restrictions on the model designer. Heterogeneous structures and behavior, adaptivity, multi-level relations, or complex local decision making are only a few features that give high potential to the agent-based simulation paradigm. However, a high degree of freedom in design means low guidance along the constraints that restrict what can be formalized. Since many details can be manipulated, it is hard to determine which functionalities should be added to a particular model. Which level of detail is necessary? How should all the parameters be handled? The general challenge is how to exactly formulate the agent behavior so that the correct overall high-level behavior emerges.

Answers to these questions vary for particular simulation studies and must be based on experience with modeling and simulation. Due to the missing link between local agent-behavior and overall aggregate measurements on the system level, systematic model design is hard and is destined to undergo many loops of trial and error. Thus, there is a current lack of rigorous modeling and automation principles in agent-based modeling—a general blue-print of building plausible, well-designed models is missing.

R. Bergmann et al. (Eds.): MATES 2008, LNAI 5244, pp. 111–122, 2008.

To reach a higher level of model design automation, one option is to give the agents increased learning and adaptation capabilities. The intention is to design agent environments in which the agents develop their own behavior. In this case, the modeler has "only" to specify the general agent capabilities concerning perception, action, feedback, and the environmental model. The expected advantage of such an approach is that setting the frame for agent behavior in form of agent-environment interfaces and environmental model should be easier than to generate complete agent behaviors.

A learning mechanism as a tool for agent design must fulfill some requirements for being a useful model design tool:

- *Applicability:* The learning mechanism should be able to cope with complex environmental models. Thus, it should usually not be necessary to simplify or even to completely reformulate the problem just for being able to apply the learning mechanism.
- *Interpretability:* The mechanism should produce behavior models that can be understood and interpreted by the human modeler—thus serving as a source of inspiration for the modeler as well as a source of explanation of the processes involved in the overall agent system.
- *Plausibility:* The mechanisms in the learning tool should be well-established and well-understood because it should be possible to plausibly explain the emergence of the overall individual and system behavior.

We identified Learning Classifier Systems (LCSs) [1,2] as a representative paradigm that may fulfill these requirements.

Using the LCS paradigm as our learning tool, we conducted experiments in a typical agent-based simulation scenario, namely crowd simulation. Elsewhere [3], we presented a real world application of a pedestrian simulation of a railway station. This project had shown to us that it can be very complicated to specify collision-free movements with individual destinations, speeds, perception radius, etc. using a rule-based approach. Therefore, we selected a reduced scenario, namely an evacuation scenario, as a testbed for the learning approach. The results show that while also learning agent modeling has its challenges, the potential for generating novel but plausible agent strategies are high.

In the next section, a short survey about agent learning paradigms that have been used in the context of simulation modeling is given. The survey is followed by a short introduction to XCS [4], which is the particular LCS we used for our experiments. Section 4 introduces SeSAmXCS, followed by the particular scenario modeling for our example in Section 5. In Section 6 first results are given and discussed. The paper ends with a discussion and conclusions.

2   Learning Agents for Behavior Implementation in Simulation Contexts

Research on agent and multi-agent learning has been one of the major focuses within distributed artificial intelligence since its very beginning [5], continuing up to now [6]. Many different forms of learning have shown to be successful in the context of agent systems: Especially different forms of reinforcement learning [7], learning automata [8], but also evolutionary and neural forms of learning can be found.

In the context of simulation, one may find all of them either as an optimization technique for parameter calibration [9] or as a means of simply programming agents in kid-level applications [10] and successors in the area of learning by demonstration and visual programming. Techniques inspired by biological evolution have been applied in the area of Artificial Life [11,12], where evolutionary elements can be found throughout the agent simulation approach. In this way, the evolutionary potential of an agent scenario can be tested. One of the earliest examples of a simulation of a concrete scenario is [13], in which simulated ant agents were controlled by a neural network that was actually designed by a genetic algorithm. An experiment that is similar to a general LCS approach can be found in [14] using a rule set modified by a genetic algorithm. The interesting point is that rule conditions are based on situation descriptions. Rules are than selected by a nearest-neighbour heuristic.

Learning Classifier Systems (LCSs) are also a well-known adaptive agent architecture that has been successfully applied in agent-based simulation contexts for many years, including application in minority game analysis, economic simulations [15], biological research, and others. In most cases, though, only resulting architectures and simulations were described, while hardly any modeling issues were discussed. We chose LCSs for supporting model design because it generally satisfies our three proposed learning system requirements: (1) LCSs are a general learning framework that have been shown to be applicable to a wide range of problems including classification, function approximation, and online generalizing reinforcement learning problems. (2) The knowledge in LCS is defined by a set of rules, which is generally easily interpretable. (3) The learning path to a final solution can be reconstructed. Thus, further support and information is available for and how the developed solution was constructed.

3 XCS

The accuracy-based learning classifier system XCS is an iterative online learning system [4]. As in most LCSs, knowledge in XCS is represented by a fixed-size *population* of condition-action-prediction classifiers. Each classifier predicts the consequences of executing the specified action given that the conditions are satisfied. In most cases, consequences are experienced reward values. In this paper, we focus on solving Markov decision processes in an MAS environment, for which XCS is designed to approximate the underlying Q-value function with a generalized representation.

XCS evolves rule condition structures by means of a genetic algorithm and it approximates prediction values by means of credit assignment mechanisms [1]. Credit assignment is strongly correlated with Q-learning principles [4,16]. Rule generation and evolution is done via a steady-state, niched genetic algorithm [17,18]. Rule

fitness in XCS is defined by the relative estimated accuracy of a classifier prediction. Due to this accuracy-based fitness approach, XCS learns not only the rules
(or classifiers) that denote the best classification possible, but rather a complete
situation-action-reward mapping. Learning in XCS is an iterative process, that is,
the system iteratively interacts with the problem at hand and evaluates and evolves
relevant classifiers on the fly. Thus, XCS is an online learning approach that strives
to learn a complete and maximally accurate model of the underlying Q-value function, where the model is represented by a set of maximally general rules.

To ensure successful learning with XCS, several conditions have to be satisfied. First, the underlying problem has to be approximately Markov, that is, the
current observations need to be sufficient to allow accurate reward predictions.
Second, the problem space has to be explored somewhat uniformly, although recent studies show that XCS can learn also rather robust in non-uniform datasets
[19]. For behavior learning problems, such as the MAS scenario investigated in
this paper, usually random exploration during learning suffices to ensure complete problem coverage. Third, the formation of long reward chains (more than
ten steps) should be avoided, since the online generalizing mechanism tends to
disrupt long chains [20].

These design principles are taken into account for the application example
given below. Before continuing with the example, we first describe how XCS
has been integrated into SeSAm (Shell for Simulated Multi-Agent Systems,
www.simsesam.de), a modeling and simulation environment for agent-based simulation models.

4   SeSAmXCS

In order to integrate new elements into the multiagent platform SeSAm, two
aspects have to be tackled: the model representation language and the visual programming and experimentation environment. SeSAm basically provides structures such as entity classes, which define agents and resources, and an explicit
world class as the active container for the environment. All classes consist of the
description of the state variables and parameters ("body") and—in the case of
the agents and the world—of an activity- and rule-based behavior description.
Instance descriptions form the configuration of start situations.

In SeSAmXCS, an additional agent class was implemented that consists of
the standard body description, which consists of a set of state variables and
individual parameters, and XCS, which replaces the behavior description. The
implementation of XCS used for this purpose is described elsewhere [21]. The
configuration of the XCS Agent is described on the class level. In a simulation
run, every instance of an agent possesses its own classifier system with individual
classifiers and adaptation processes.

The most interesting aspect of the XCS integration are the interfaces between
environment and agent that are very different from the previous agent architecture. Whereas in the usual agent behavior description activities explicitly trigger
access to the environment, the classifier system needs a perceptual input that

can be matched against the classifiers precondition string. The actually realized interface consists of two phases: In a first step, a particular perception category is defined, which is given a number of bits for specifying its basic range. A second step transfers the particular perception category to one particular bit code. An example for a perception category would be the perceivable distance to the exit, which could, for example, be coded by two bits where no exit perceivable → 00, exit perceivable between 50 and 100m → 11, between 10 and 50m → 10 and less than 10m → 01. Action codes are similarly modified. Whereas in the standard architecture, agent actions are primitive calls in activity scripts, for integrating the classifier architecture a finite action set has to be defined based on particular primitive calls. Figure 1 shows the integration into SeSAm's visual programming environment for simulated agents.

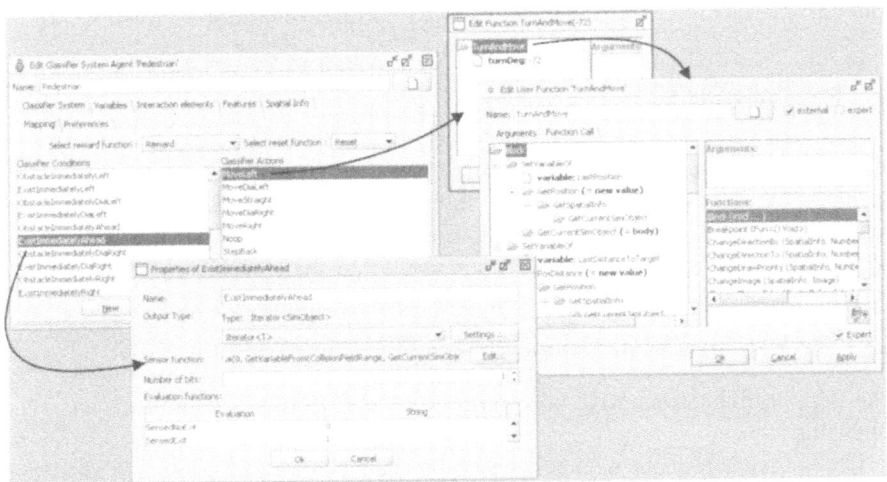

Fig. 1. Modeling environment for XCS agents in SeSAm

5   Learning to Find the Exit: Evacuation Scenario

We used a pedestrian simulation as a first testbed to demonstrate the basic SeSAmXCS capabilities. We chose this application for two reasons:

(1) Crowd simulation is a quite typical application domain for agent-based simulation. Albeit the employed scenario may by oversimplified, we expected that the relative simplicity of the scenario will enable us to evaluate the potentials of a successful XCS integration and meanwhile to easily deduce the involved challenges.

(2) The design of a proper rule base for crowd simulation scenarios is by no means a trivial task, as we had to realize ourselves in a previous rule-based approach in a more complex pedestrian simulation scenario [3].

Our pedestrian simulation testbed was an evacuation simulation where agents had to leave a room with six column-type obstacles (with a diameter of 1.75m) as fast as possible without hurting themselves during collisions. The room corresponded to a hall of $30 \times 20m$. We assumed that each pedestrian agent covers $50 \times 50cm$ and moves with a speed of $1.5m/sec$. One time-step in the discrete simulation corresponded to 0.5 sec. Space was continuous. At the beginning of a test-run, all agents were randomly positioned (avoiding any collision) in the upper half of the hall between the columns.

All experiments alternated between explore and exploit trials. During the explore trials, the agents evolved their rule sets by means of XCS, randomly executing an action and consequently evaluating and evolving the rule set given the experienced effects. In exploitation trials, the best action with the best predicted feedback was selected in each iteration. Every trial lasted 250 iterations. Every experiment lasted 150 000 iterations, that is, 300 explore-exploit cycles. The parameter of the XCS system are set to standard values as given in [21].

6   Experiments

In this rather simple scenario we made several experiments to test the performance of the agents in terms of their ability to learn effective evacuation behaviors. That is, we tested how fast the agents were able to head towards the exit while avoiding collisions with walls and other pedestrians.

6.1   Pedestrians with Orientation

The first configurations with successful agent and feedback definitions were the following:

The perception of the agents is based on their basic orientation. We identified 5 sectors in relation to the agents movement direction and divided the sectors into two areas with respect to the range. Figure 2 shows the different areas. For every area two binary perception categories were used. The first bit encoded whether the exit was perceivable in this area and the second bit encoded whether

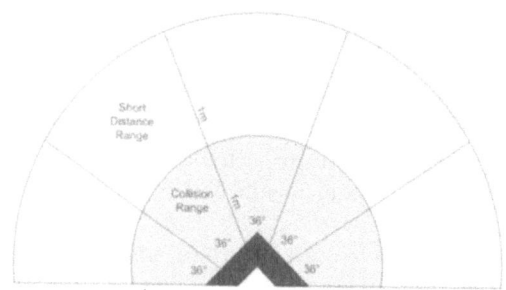

Fig. 2. Definition of perception areas of the classifier agents

an obstacle was present—where an obstacle includes everything with which a collision should be avoided: walls, columns and other pedestrians.

As in the perception definition, we assumed that the agents always know the direction towards the exit and integrated this knowledge into the different possible movements. The action set consisted of $A = \{move_{left}, move_{slightlyLeft}, move_{straight}, move_{slightlyRight}, move_{right}, noop, stepback\}$. After the execution of one of these actions, the agent re-orients itself towards the exit.

The purpose of this initial simulation was to generate a single step problem, in which action feedback is immediately available. Thus, the reward the agent a received after executing an action at time-step t was computed in the following way:

$$reward(a, t) = reward_{exit}(a, t) + reward_{dist}(a, t) + feedback_{collision}(a, t), \quad (1)$$

where $reward_{exit}(a, t) = 200$, if agent a has reached the exit in time t and 0 otherwise; $reward_{dist}(a, t) = \tau * (d_t(exit, a) - d_{t-1}(exit, a))$ with τ set to 5; $feedback_{collision}(a, t)$ was set to 100 if a collision free actual movement had been made, to 0 if no movement happened, and to -500 if a collision occurred. Together, the different components of the feedback function stress goal-directed collision-free movements.

6.2 Experiments with Different Numbers of Agents

Figure 3 shows a sequence of trajectories for an exemplary learning experiment with 40 pedestrians. One can notice an improvement in how clearly the movement is directed towards the exit and also that a decreasing number of collisions

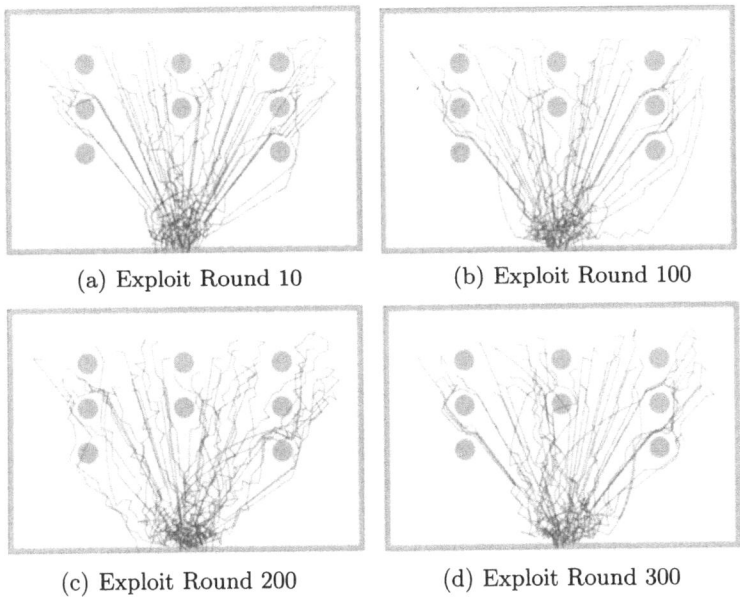

(a) Exploit Round 10   (b) Exploit Round 100

(c) Exploit Round 200   (d) Exploit Round 300

Fig. 3. Sample trajectories improve with increasing learning iterations

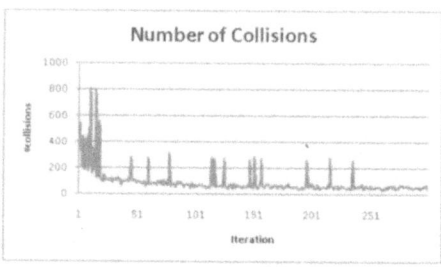

Fig. 4. Development of the number of collisions during an exemplary run with fourty agents

occur, which is particularly noticeable at the columns. The trajectories are less straight when the density increases near the exit, because more and more deviation actions have to be selected in this area.

These coarse observations are confirmed when looking at the development of the numbers of collisions and the duration until the last agent has left the hall. In Figure 4, the development of numbers of collisions during a learning experiment with 40 agents is shown. As the genetic algorithm is still active, the set of rules is not stable. Suboptimal rules may be inserted to the set, occasionally resulting in suboptimal behavior, that is, a temporarily increased number of collisions. Although we did not make sufficient runs for any statistical analysis, we noticed that there are only little variations in the overall outcome of the model.

We also tested to what extent performance depends on the number of agents. The following table reports the mean number of collisions during the last 500 exploit iterations are given.

Agent Numbers	10	20	30	40	50	70	100
Mean Number of Collisions	2.5	13.3	30.2	62.0	105.2	258.8	687.8

Clearly, more agents cause a larger number of collisions. The observed nonlinear relationship is not surprising because agents cannot only bump into columns but also into all other agents—especially when the crowd becomes really dense near the exit. A similar relationship can be noticed when depicting the time needed to fully evacuate the hall. Thus, behavior learning generally works well for all tested agent numbers and thus for all initial agent densities.

6.3   Alternative Settings

Instead of adapting the reward function—with obvious effects on the learning performance—we want to illustrate that coming to the given results is by no means trivial. In fact, the result is rather strongly dependent on the particular agent architecture configuration used.

To illustrate the brittleness of the modeling process, we present a "failure" configuration of agent architecture and involved feedback. Instead of the built-in orientation of movement towards the exit, we used 5 turn actions, one into each sector, one move straight ahead action in addition to the *noop* and the *stepback* action. Such an action set does not make sense without an enhanced range of perceptions because situations that require different actions must be distinguishable. Therefore, we added long-distance perceptions to the perception categories so that perception almost covers the complete hall. In addition to that, we added a perception category that tells the agent in which sector the exit is located. Figure 5 shows two snapshots from an example run for agents with the adapted action set and enhanced perception.

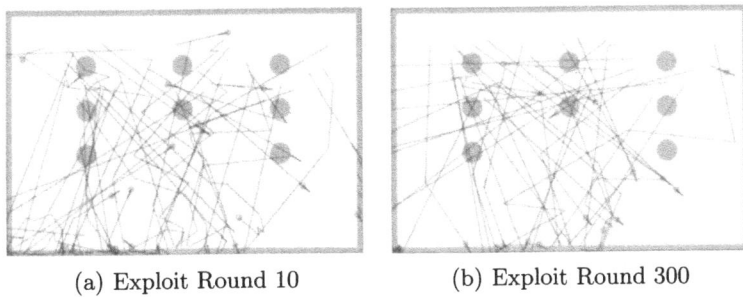

(a) Exploit Round 10   (b) Exploit Round 300

Fig. 5. Effect of alternative, less "guiding" action set and enhanced perception. Reward biases reaching the exit, less preventing collisions.

It is interesting to see that the movements are quite straight. This is basically an effect of the collision-free-movement reward: an agent that moves without a collision receives a positive reward, whereas staying at the same position results in zero reward. Experiments with even higher punishments resulted in similar outcomes.

One may also observe a slight increase in the tendency to move towards the exit. However, less than 18 agents managed to leave the hall after 300 trials on average. This is far less than the performance of the initially described set. Increasing the reward for going towards the exit hinders efficient learning of collision avoidance, but did not have the intended effect of driving the agents towards the exit. This is simply due to the fact that during exploration of the rule set, reaching the exit is highly improbable causing the overall problem to be a hard multi-step problem: Since the large payoff when receiving the exit is so delayed in time, distant places hardly ever experience the correlation that turning and moving towards the exit eventually leads to high reward.

The agents have the information where the exit is located and they learn that moving towards the exit will give positive reward, but coming near the exit in the exploit phase does not help as they did not learn how to react properly to the exit. On the other hand, occasional movements through the exit or even just coming near the exit door is more frequent in the oriented action set than in the other one where contiguous turn- and move actions are necessary to solve the individual evacuation task.

7   Discussion

When starting our investigations into automatic agent behavior programming using learning techniques, we expected that the feedback function is essential, but that the design of the agent perception and action set would be basically given by the environmental model. However, for a successful learning agent design, also the degrees of freedom in the agent perception/action design can have a large performance effect. Also, the parameters of the learner are not necessarily trivial to specify, although in our case standard settings did the trick.

Despite these challenges, we were able to present a solution that consisted of a particular set of perceptions and actions that produced the intended exit-oriented behavior. Due to the action orientedness towards the exit, the behavior repertoire got much more focused while still allowing avoidance behaviors. Other configurations with more turn and move actions, increased perceptions, and variations in the feedback function yielded results somewhat similar to the ones achieved in the presented alternative settings. Thus, sufficient prior knowledge had to be provided to enable successful learning.

This lesson is actually rather well-known in the machine learning community. Learning biases are not only inherent in learning system themselves but are also induced by the used representations. In the case of an evacuation scenario, the learner needs to have sufficient information to be able to deduce the task. Thus, feedback had to be sufficiently immediate and movement encodings had to be oriented towards the exit. As stated above, though, the general assumption that pedestrians know the exit location and furthermore know that movements towards the exit are usually efficient is plausible. Thus, it can also not really be expected that the employed learning mechanism learns about such facts from scratch when the learning purpose is to evolve particular exit strategies.

The aim of the model combination was to facilitate agent modeling. Using an LCS somewhat transferred the basic problem from direct behavior modeling to the challenge of designing the agent interface and the environment's reward computation. To do so successfully, a general understanding of problem difficulty and machine learning techniques is necessary. We framed the learning problem as a reinforcement learning (RL) problem, in which only reward-based feedback is provided. In such problem domains, two problem aspects are known to be particularly challenging: (1) Delayed reward enforces the formation of long reward chains, which strongly decreases learning speed and, furthermore, poses a strong learning challenge for online generalizing RL systems, such as LCSs [20]. (2) A fundamental problem difficulty in the RL domain is the Markov property [7]. Simply put, provided perceptions need to contain sufficient information to be able to learn the expectation of immediate and future possible reward accurately. For example, if the agent does not know its distance to the goal, it cannot know when it will reach it and consequently cannot know how far in the future the reaching-the-exit reward lies. Thus, the agent cannot know if it is currently useful to head towards the exit at all or rather to avoid collisions or look for an alternative route.

While our success in the first scenario is encouraging, there are admittedly many more challenging application scenarios than an evacuation scenario where all agents have the same goal, the behavior repertoire is quite restricted, and there is no direct communication between agents. In such advanced environments, the classifier and environment design will certainly pose additional challenges.

8   Conclusion and Future Work

In this paper we described the integration of an LCS architecture into a multi-agent simulation platform. In a small evacuation scenario, we showed that the employed system XCS can produce plausible behavior in an agent-based simulation. However, the coupling of XCS with the agent environment is by no means trivial. The environmental model, feedback function, perception, and action sets had to be defined appropriately. We also showed the effects of some unsuitable settings pointing-out that focused learning can be biased by proper representations and immediate feedback functions. Despite this initial encouraging results, we must admit that additional experiences have to be made until we can apply LCS-based approaches in a rigorous way.

Based on the full integration of the XCS architecture into SeSAm, we will pursue further self-modeling agent experiments, examining the classifier system-based approach more thoroughly and testing it in a middle-size real world scenario, such as an evacuation of a train with about 500 agents, complex geometry with exit signs and time pressure. This scenario is currently developed in a "traditional" way. After that, other scenarios in different domains will be tested to examine the successful integration of LCSs into agent-based simulation applications more systematically. Additionally, we intend to test alternative learning paradigms, such as pure evolutionary behavior programming or non-generalizing reinforcement learning, deducing the feasibility and challenges of an application to crowd simulations.

References

1. Holland, J.H., Reitman, J.S.: Cognitive systems based on adaptive algorithms. In: Waterman, D.A., Hayes-Roth, F. (eds.) Pattern directed inference systems, pp. 313–329. Academic Press, New York (1978)
2. Butz, M.V.: Combining gradient-basedwith evolutionary online learning: An introduction to learning classifier systems. In: 7th International Conference on Hybrid Intelligent Systems HIS 2007, pp. 12–17 (2007)
3. Klügl, F., Rindsfüser, G.: Large-scale agent-based pedestrian simulation. In: Petta, P., Müller, J.P., Klusch, M., Georgeff, M. (eds.) MATES 2007. LNCS (LNAI), vol. 4687, pp. 145–156. Springer, Heidelberg (2007)
4. Wilson, S.W.: Classifier fitness based on accuracy. Evolutionary Computation 3(2), 149–175 (1995)
5. Weiss, G.: Adaptation and learning in multiagent systems: Some remarks and a bibliography. In: Weiss, G., Sen, S. (eds.) Adaption and learning in multi-agent systems. Springer, Heidelberg (1996)

6. Klügl, F., Tuys, K., Sen, S. (eds.): ALAMAS&ALAg - Adaptive and Learning Agents and Multiagent Systems (workshop at AAMAS 2008) (2008)

7. Sutton, R.S., Barto, A.G.: Reinforcement Learning. MIT Press, Cambridge (1998)

8. Nowe, A., Verbeeck, K., Peeters, M.: Learning automata as a basis for multi agent reinforcement learning. In: Tuyls, K., 't Hoen, P.J., Verbeeck, K., Sen, S. (eds.) LAMAS 2005. LNCS (LNAI), vol. 3898, pp. 71–85. Springer, Heidelberg (2006)

9. Oechslein, C., Hörnlein, A., Klügl, F.: Evolutionary optimization of societies in simulated multi-agent systems. In: Jonker, C., Letia, A., Lindemann, G., Uthmann, T. (eds.) MASHO Workshop at ECAI 2000, Humboldt-Universität, Berlin, vol. 149 (2000)

10. Smith, D.C., Cypher, A., Spohrer, J.: Kidsim: Programming agents without a programming language. Communications of the ACM 37(7), 54–67 (1994)

11. Adami, C.: Introduction to Artificial Life. Springer, Heidelberg (1998)

12. Grefenstette, J.J.: The Evolution of Strategies for Multi-agent Environments. Adaptive Behavior 1, 65–89 (1992)

13. Collins, R.J., Jefferson, D.R.: Antfarm: Towards simulated evolution. In: Langton, C.G., Taylor, C., Farmer, J.D., Rasmussen, S. (eds.) Artificial Life II, pp. 579–601. Addison-Wesley, Redwood City (1992)

14. Denzinger, J., Fuchs, M.: Experiments in learning prototypical situations for variants of the pursuit game. In: Proc. of Int. Conf. on Multi-Agent Systems, 1996, Kyoto 1996, pp. 48–55 (1996)

15. Guessoum, Z., Rejeb, L., Durand, R.: Using adaptive multi-agent systems to simulate economic models. In: AAMAS 2004, pp. 68–75. IEEE Computer Society, Los Alamitos (2004)

16. Lanzi, P.L.: Learning classifier systems from a reinforcement learning perspective. Soft Computing: A Fusion of Foundations, Methodologies and Applications 6, 162–170 (2002)

17. Holland, J.H.: Adaptation in Natural and Artificial Systems, 2nd edn. (1992). University of Michigan Press (1975)

18. Goldberg, D.E.: Genetic Algorithms in Search, Optimization and Machine Learning. Addison-Wesley, Reading (1989)

19. Orriols-Puig, A., Bernadó-Mansilla, E.: Bounding XCS's parameters for unbalanced datasets. In: GECCO 2006: Genetic and Evolutionary Computation Conference, pp. 1561–1568 (2006)

20. Butz, M.V.: Rule-Based Evolutionary Online Learning Systems: A Principled Approach to LCS Analysis and Design. Springer, Berlin (2006)

21. Butz, M.V.: XCSJava 1.0: An implementation of the XCS classifier system in Java. IlliGAL report 2000027, Illinois Genetic Algorithms Laboratory, University of Illinois at Urbana-Champaign (2000)

Providing Integrated Development Environments for Multi-Agent Systems

Simon Lynch and Keerthi Rajendran

University of Teesside, Middlesbrough, United Kingdom
{s.c.lynch,k.rajendran}@tees.ac.uk

Abstract. The computing industry has yet to take up agent technology as a new approach to software development. While other paradigms are supported by various tools, including generic IDEs, these are not well developed for agent-ware. Many agent platforms provide some form of IDE but these are platform-specific and are typically so tightly coupled to their agent platforms that they offer little re-use. There has been too little discussion about which tools an IDE should contain and few attempts to produce a generic IDE. In this paper, we identify two levels of abstraction requiring IDE tool support and draw on current research to categorise a set of generic tools for each level. We describe the reasons why existing MAS IDEs are coupled to their platforms and present an extendible software architecture which avoids this coupling. We build an IDE using this architecture and demonstrate its decoupling and extensibility by experimentation.

Keywords: MAS, IDE, debugging, deployment, software architectures.

1 Introduction

Writing agent-based software requires a varied set of skills and imposes a level of complexity beyond that experienced with other approaches to software construction [5, 6, 12]. One reason for this is that agent-based code is reactive - agents respond to messages and changes in their environment. This can make debugging agents more complex than debugging traditional systems. Other problems are introduced by the distribution and concurrency which is present in systems containing multiple agents [12] where processing is spread across agents and performance is as much a result of agent-agent interaction as it is a result of the data manipulations from individual blocks of program code.

Research into Multiagent Systems (MAS) has produced a choice of methodologies, design tools and platforms for deploying agents, yet the development of MAS in industry is still limited to a few research-supported implementations like those conducted by Agentis Software [2]. While these industrial implementations have demonstrated some benefits in using agents they have also highlighted a need for appropriate programmer support. Currently, tool support for general MAS technology is not sufficient for widespread adoption [3, 5] and practitioners suggest that the consolidation of a suitable set of tools and technologies for Agent Oriented Software Engineering

R. Bergmann et al. (Eds.): MATES 2008, LNAI 5244, pp. 123–134, 2008.

(AOSE) is one of the most important challenges for transferring the results of agent-based research into industry [3, 5, 13]. A complete set of AOSE tools would include those used for deployment and monitoring as well as those used early in the design phases of agent-based solutions.

As with other paradigms (like object-orientation) an IDE for MAS development is an important tool [2] but, while there has been some publication of ideas [6, 10, 11] and different MAS platforms provide varying levels of support [9, 12, 15, 16], there has not been enough discussion within the research community about the features a MAS IDE should contain and IDEs have, to date, only been developed as adjuncts to existing MAS languages and platforms. This is understandable: the first priority for researchers is to build the run-time platform itself since there is little point in having an IDE without a platform. IDE development becomes important only after the platform is operational and often only once a user group becomes established. The result of this trend is that existing IDEs are so tightly coupled to their target agent-languages and/or agent-platforms that they offer little opportunity for re-use.

Our initial work in IDE construction followed this approach. Furthermore, many of the tools in our original IDE were aimed at programming and debugging individual agents rather than higher level tasks like system-wide debugging and deployment. Providing tools for individual agents is less demanding because these tools can often use technologies borrowed from other paradigms (like objects). We were not alone in this, the lack of tool support at the MAS system level, mainly for post-implementation activities, has been recognised [12, 5, 6] and we have more recently focused on this. We have also acknowledged the need, discussed by Bordini et al. [5], to decouple agent tools from any specific agent framework and language. For example, the JACK Development Environment (JDE) is used with the JACK agent platform (www.agent-software.com) while the JADE toolset is used with the JADE framework [1] and these cannot be interchanged. We have taken a different approach to IDE development and believe we have achieved cross-platform reuse by constructing our IDE as a MAS in its own right. In this paper we describe our approach by considering two questions that underpin this work:

(i)   are there common tools, across MAS platforms which can be included in a generic IDE and is it possible to classify these in any way?

(ii)   how is it possible to build a generic IDE for cross-platform use so it may be modified/extended to take account of other platform-specific features?

2 Classification of Tools

This section considers a means of classifying tools for MAS development and identifies tools/features important for inclusion in a MAS IDE. Some of these are generic across applications while others are agent paradigm specific.

There are a wide range of agent types and associated concepts of agency: some research communities are mostly concerned with web-based software components with communication ability, other communities concentrate on platforms like Jade [1] and Midas [8] which implement agents but have an open view of the nature of these agents, others focus on specific types of agents using languages/platforms like 3APL [7] and Jason [4] which support BDI agents. Typically, specialised agents are built on and supported by a more general agent-layer which provides facilities for message transmission, etc. (3APL and Jason are supported by Jade for example). The IDE presented in this paper integrates with platforms operating at the level of Jade but in doing so supports any languages/platforms deployed on top of them. As discussed in later sections, the IDE is itself developed as a MAS and the agents making up this MAS are also mid-level agents.

With respect to the reference model proposed by Modi *et al.* [17], the IDE will typically receive information from the framework layer but this information will describe activity within the agent layer. While we recognise the importance of the Reference Model, we are concerned with the *tasks* performed by agent developers rather than levels of agent implementation. This leads us to sub-divide activity in the Reference Model's agent layer since it involves both individual agents as well as interacting MAS. In this paper we consider a classification of tools from two different levels of abstraction: the system-level and the agent-level. Tools in each of these levels can be further classified into build-time or run-time tools according to their use,

(i)   the system-level considers the semantic content of agent-agent messages but represents the agents themselves as black box entities. It is concerned with building MAS as opposed to building individual agents. System level tasks are similar to the high level tasks in more traditional paradigms (system wide testing, interoperability, deployment, etc). This level also captures additional MAS concepts like emergent behaviour, groups and teamwork. At run time, during monitoring and debugging phases, activities at this level are concerned with the emergent properties of a MAS which include the nature of agent-agent interactions and messaging, the system's architecture, etc.;

(ii)   the agent-level, in contrast is concerned primarily with the functionality of individual agents and considers, for example, how they react to given messages. Internal workings of agents have focus and activities are those associated with building single agents. Agent-level tasks map on to the programming tasks performed in other paradigms (editing source files, testing individual classes, etc).

Our analysis reveals that system level tools are often generic while agent-level tools tend to match the agent language used and the type of agency involved. Categorising tools into these levels has allowed us to determine which tools can be provided by plugging in existing (programming language based) development and debugging environments (which operate at the agent-level) and which are the direct responsibility of a system-level IDE.

Previous research acknowledges that debugging agents is difficult and has recognised the need for tools like the Tracing method [12] but still debugging, especially at the system-level, has not received sufficient attention [9, 19] and needs further investigation. System-level debugging where individual agents are black boxes, involves activities like analysing scenarios of activity involving groups of agents and solving errors in the functioning of the system as a whole. Tools are also needed for system-level phases of deployment and post-implementation monitoring but many of these tasks are inadequately supported [3, 6].

Since system-level tools are often neglected, the term "MAS IDE" can be misleading with most current MAS IDEs only providing the kind of tools associated with object-oriented IDEs, i.e.: focusing on programming issues and serving primarily to *"automate tedious coding tasks"* [5]. In this paper we use the term MAS IDE to refer to a toolkit with provision for both the agent-level and the system-level.

2.1 Generic Systems Support

This section discusses generic tool requirements at the system level. They have been derived from MAS literature and through our experience with MAS development.

2.1.1 Representing MAS Structure

A simple MAS may be composed of a homogeneous collection of interacting agents in which all elements of the system can be presented as black box components with a messaging interface. With larger scale systems there may be benefits in viewing a MAS as a hierarchical organisation where collections of agents are grouped into higher level forms which can be viewed as single-entity black-boxes. Agents can be sensibly grouped for various reasons: because the agents they contain represent a single holon, because they are deployed on a single physical network, because they form well established societies or because the model of agency considers group relationships of some kind (the Aalaadin AGR model for example). Allowing users to expand and collapse agent collections into single entities allows them to view a MAS at different levels of abstraction. This aids system comprehension as well as tasks like debugging.

2.1.2 Messaging

MAS are conceptualised and designed as interacting entities; these interactions are a key aspect of the MAS workings. Developers of message oriented systems have traditionally used tools that aggregate all message transmissions for later examination. A survey of MAS IDEs shows that many do little more than this. Some of the more developed IDEs also provide useful functions like conversation tracking [10], verification of scenarios by matching messages against design [19] and the ability to restrict logs to messages relating to particular agents [1]. Some simply produce text files of data while others provide a more readable display.

Since analysing messages is so fundamental to MAS debugging, a general purpose MAS IDE should provide extensive and specialised support for viewing messages. We suggest the following as a minimal set of facilities:

- separation of agent messages from system messages (e.g.: error messages);
- collation of messages under different search criteria like the identities of sending/receiving agents, conversation id, time frames, physical distribution, etc;
- offline storage of all messages with flexible filtering mechanisms so that the user may inspect different subsets of messages by applying different filtering criteria;
- synchronisation with other functions like logging and playback (described next).

2.1.3 Logging and Playback

For analysis and debugging it is difficult to observe any system, including MAS, in real-time because system activity occurs too fast for human comprehension. Some traditional programming tools use features like breakpoints to pause execution so that current system states can be inspected. These facilities are important for troubleshooting but are impossible to use with distributed, concurrent systems. One solution is to capture MAS activity (e.g.: agents joining the MAS, messages and errors) and allow users to replay it at slower speeds and apply breakpoints on the replay mechanism. This can be supported by filtering mechanisms that allow the user to focus on particular agents, agent groups, parts of the agent network and interaction scenarios. These kinds of activity are currently not well supported although their importance has been highlighted for some time, for example Ndumu *et al.* [18] explain the importance of offline replay of MAS activity from different perspectives. In addition, offline playback allows developers some opportunity to visualise the emergent properties of a system as they occur since an IDE can show the changing system architecture, message transmissions, system errors, etc. slowing down and pausing the replay as necessary.

2.1.4 Testing

It is necessary to test either single agents or sets of agents without the presence of other agents that send or receive messages from them. This may be because related agents have not yet been developed or because the agent(s) are being developed as plug and play agents. An IDE that allows agent interactions to be driven manually (or through scripts) therefore offers some advantages. Some systems provide messaging agents for this (e.g.: JADE's "Dummy Agent", Mock Agents in Agile PASSI). These are useful for testing agents' internal response to messages, the interactions between agents and to identify emergent behaviour in an agent sub-group.

2.1.5 Deployment

MAS consist of independently executing entities and do not have a single starting point like other types of applications so launching them is more complex but this is only addressed by few platforms [6]. Toolkits that allow MAS launching information to be specified and also automate the launching process reduce the likelihood of errors and aid system reconfiguration. Information to support launching may include details such as agent instances (type and number of agents), locations of agent executable files, their dependencies (constraints on the order in which they are started up) and structure (hierarchical groupings).

There is also a need to remove agents or add new agents to a running MAS. Administrators may be required to monitor running MAS for conditions that need correction [6], this is more important for dynamic MAS whose composition and structure change frequently at runtime. Platforms produce messages indicating error and abnormal conditions. Some messages indicate failures that require agent repair or redundancy; others may indicate system-level conditions like high message traffic which may need correction by reconfiguring MAS structure. Administrators require facilities to change MAS structure at run-time by adding/removing agents or relocating agents to other parts of the MAS network. Support for these tasks is also required during the testing and debugging of MAS.

3   Decoupling and Reuse

Choosing to use MAS as a paradigm for development and selecting a platform comes with the constraints of the agent language, philosophy and toolset associated with the platform. Such a "platform package" will tend to have leanings towards certain types of applications and types of agency rather than be generic/tailorable. If a developer selects 3APL they commit to using BDI agents and the 3APL IDE/toolkit. If they need to build mobile agents on portable devices for some other work they will change agent languages but in doing so they will be forced to discard all those tools they used with 3APL including the IDE. IDEs used in object oriented development are no longer like this, they can be readily reconfigured for different languages and linked to specific tools for those languages. This is not only true for well featured packages like Eclipse but is also the case with tools that are little more than editors. WinEdit for example (www.winedit.com) can be configured to color program code according to simple syntax rules and link to specific compilers. This kind of cross-platform reuse is not offered by IDEs for MAS.

Bordini et al. [5] identify a number of priorities to enable wider development of agent based software. In relation to practical MAS construction they highlight the need to integrate MAS development environments with existing object oriented IDEs and imply that a key challenge is also to develop a MAS IDE that can integrate across different MAS platforms but acknowledge that this is difficult currently since there is "unavoidabl[ly] tight coupling of agent IDEs and agent platforms" [ibid. p.40].

3.1 The Causes of Coupling

There are various factors which tend to increase the levels of coupling between components in software systems. These affect agent based software in similar ways to other types of software. In considering those coupling dependencies which occur between an agent platform and an IDE we identify three issues. The first relates to the nature of communication and information exchange between agent platform and IDE. If they use some unique mechanism for interaction or pass data which is structured in complex ways then their relationship will exhibit close coupling. In the worse case, if they communicate through a series of method calls and share internal data structures, they will effectively be using some common API and it will only be possible to reuse the IDE (or replace it) with other software built on the same API.

A second factor is the extent to which the IDE provides specific support for features unique to the platform (or perhaps handled in a unique way by the platform). This can be overcome by restricting the IDE so that it only supports those generic features which form part of all agent platforms but this would be a poor solution since the IDE would then implement only the small subset of features and fail to provide many of the tools that developers need. When working with mobile agents, for example, it is highly desirable for an IDE to manage aspects of mobility yet mobility tools would probably not be included in a generic set of features. This apparently presents a conflict of interests since an IDE can only implement generic features if it is to offer cross-platform reuse and yet, if it is going to offer a comprehensive set of tools for developers, it must also provide platform specific tools.

Finally, a third factor which increases coupling dependency is the extent to which the design of the IDE is influenced by the design (or agent-paradigm) of any platform/agent language. This relates in part to the previous two factors (if the IDE shares an API with the platform or is influenced by platform specific features then coupling will be increased) but it may also be caused by less explicit dependencies. If, for example, it is assumed that agents are BDI and the IDE is built around this premise then the reporting of agent behavior may be in terms of "plans". This approach would limit reuse since the IDE would be less suitable for non-BDI agents.

3.2 Achieving Decoupling

The first requirement to limit coupling is that the IDE and the platform avoid communicating by uniquely defined method calls and avoid passing complex data structures which may not be appropriate for other platforms. It would be possible to achieve this with existing OO techniques (such as using a command pattern) but we also want an IDE which can be modified at run-time without a need for recompilation or rebuild (to provide enhanced reporting of agent mobility for example) and can be used, simultaneously, with multiple frameworks which may each provide different information (structure and content) to the IDE. After results of initial experimentation, in preference to using an OO approach, we have constructed the IDE in the form of its own, independent MAS. Communication to and from this *IDE-MAS* is sent textually in the form of inter-agent messages by following an agreed protocol for message structuring. In keeping with the principle that agents written in different languages, using different paradigms are able to communicate as long as they do so using some agreed protocol, an IDE deployed in the form of a MAS is less tightly coupled than one relying on some other means of communication. In this case the coupling is defined only in terms of the message protocol required by the IDE. Any platform wishing to use the IDE need only send the IDE messages about the platform's events (agents joining / leaving the system, agent-agent message passing, errors, etc).

This approach overcomes the first point discussed in the section above but does not address the paradox of how an IDE can provide platform-specific features and still be suitable for cross-platform reuse. We have addressed this by following the model used with object oriented IDEs which provide a generic set of OO tools but then allow specific language tools (compilers, etc) to be plugged in to them. In our case, since the MAS IDE is now in the form of its own MAS, these tools are plugged in by adding new agents to the *IDE-MAS*.

Initially then, the IDE provides only a generic set of tools independent of any agent and not specific to any particular notion of agency. Further tools are then freely added in the form of additional agents which are incorporated into the IDE. This approach is made possible by tightly encapsulating the IDE so that its internal architecture and agent composition is not visible externally and by using a flexible protocol for messaging between its agents.

3.3 Architecture and Message Protocol

The IDE is arranged as an organisation of agents who's internal structure is invisible to external systems and who's agents present a shared interface. In addition the internal agents are arranged so that all messages received from external systems are received by a single internal message-dispatch agent. In practice these externally generated messages are sent by some external MAS (or, more likely its supporting MAS platform) to report on events occurring in the external system. It is by virtue of these messages that the IDE is able to monitor the structures and behaviours occurring in the external system.

The IDE-internal message-dispatch agent forwards messages to other agents within the IDE according to the *message type* which is a facet of the IDE message protocol.

All agents inside the IDE register their interests with the message-dispatcher by telling it which types of message they wish to receive. For example: the internal agent which dynamically shows the architecture of an external system will register an interest in messages containing information about agents joining and leaving the external system. There are a number of advantages to using a dispatch agent:

(i)   it hides the internal agents to such an extent that, even though the composition of agents in the IDE may change, external agents remain unaffected by any changes. External agents are unaffected by changes even if the structure of the IDE changes at run-time, this allows IDE users to switch on/off agents while monitoring a live system;

(ii) new agents can be added to the IDE simply by registering them with the dispatcher and noting what types of messages they wish to be copied into. There is no requirement for further configuration;

(iii) it is possible to dispatch the same message to multiple intra-IDE agents.

The flexibility of the IDE is further improved by using an extendible message protocol which is only weakly specified. Developers will typically incorporate additional agents in the IDE to monitor or manipulate some specific feature of the external agent platform they are using. These additional IDE agents will often need different types of information from that required by those standardised, generic tools provided by the IDE by default. By implication they will need this additional information transmitted to them within the IDE messages.

The IDE message protocol is based on a simple slot-filler notation but allows extra information to be included in additional slots. The IDE recognises specific types of MAS event (agents joining/leaving the systems, messages sent between agents, etc) indicated by the use of tags in the message protocol. For example, a message indicating that an agent named "Sue" has joined the system will use a register-agent tag and appear something like...

```
((from   external-sender)
 (to     IDE-dispatch)
 (type   register-agent)
 (body   (name Sue))
```

The tags *from*, *to* and *type* identify the agents involved in the information transfer and the type of information sent. The *body* tag contains information specific to the message type. As outlined above IDE dispatcher routes this message to its internal registry agent on the basis of the message type.

The protocol allows extra slots to be included in any message. For example, one platform tested in this study allows agents to have a scope indicating their visibility. "Global" agents are visible across an entire MAS, "local" and "internal" agents have restricted visibility. Messages indicating agents have joined the system have an extra slot when used with this platform, e.g.:

```
((from   external-sender)
 (to     IDE-dispatch)
 (type   register-agent)
 (body   (name    Sue)
         (scope   global))
```

The IDE provides generic tools to monitor the architecture of an external MAS, its messages and report on any errors. The generic tool to monitor agent messaging is agnostic about the ACL used by the external system, it simply displays the content of external messages in a textual form. Alternative IDE agents, oriented to specific ACLs can be substituted, these will provide better information by making more effective use of the data contained in the body of IDE messages.

As well as introducing new tags to pre-existing message types, The IDE message protocol can be extended by introducing new message types. If the IDE is being used with a platform which supports mobility for example, the protocol could be extended to allow the following format of message which states that the agent mobile3 has moved from node7 to node11.

```
((from   external-sender)
 (to     IDE-dispatch)
 (type   mobile-relocate)
 (body   (name    mobile3)
         (source node7)
         (dest    node11))
```

No changes to the IDE or its existing agents are needed in order to accommodate this new message type. All that is required is that the external system generates a message of type *mobile-relocate* when appropriate and sends them to IDE-dispatch.

So far our discussions have focused on system level tools, these are provided by including generic tools in the IDE which can be added to and replaced by more specific tools as required. It is also necessary to supply agent level tools. However, the nature of tools at the agent level is different to those at the system level and the ways that they can be provided by the IDE are also different. There are a range of approaches to agent implementation provided by various platforms. Broadly we consider two different categories:

(i)   platforms where agents are based on extensions of existing languages (Java for example) and,

(ii)   those based on specialised agent definition languages.

In the first case neither system-level concepts nor many aspects of agency are explicitly visible in the program code. Agent-level activities like debugging and editing the code that defines an agent are similar to those carried out with code not involving agents and existing IDEs, editors, etc. provided for the base language are suitable. In the second case, where agents are defined in a specialised language, the language/framework has an obligation to its developer community to provide appropriate agent-level tools if it intends widespread use. Currently the tendency is either to plug-in to an existing IDE e.g.: The Living Systems Developer which uses Eclipse (www.eclipse.org) or to provide a specialised IDE (these typically follow the model set out by the object-oriented IDEs [5]).

Consequently, whether platform specific or not, agent-level tools can be provided in the form of a conventional IDE. The requirement for a platform-independent MAS-toolkit to provide agent-level tools is then only that it must allow a range of IDEs to be registered so agents of different types can be inspected, traced and edited using appropriate tools.

Building the IDE as a MAS makes it possible to link agent-level tools (editors, object-IDEs, etc) by simply adding an agent to the IDE-MAS which calls up the tool. Alteration to the internal structure of the IDE is invisible to any other sub-systems so does not require them to be modified.

4 Evaluation

Our primary interest is the extent to which the design approach of the IDE allows it to be decoupled from any particular agent platform thereby allowing it to be reused. To evaluate the design we have constructed an IDE based on the principles described above. We have examined two aspects in judging the level of decoupling achieved:

(i)   the decoupling of the IDE from any specific agent platform;
(ii) the decoupling from other components.

The first allows the IDE to be used with different platforms, the second allows further tools to be integrated with the IDE. The IDE is implemented as a MAS which defines a text-based message protocol and can link to any other software capable of socket-based communication. The IDE itself is not dependent on any platform for gathering system information. This suggests that the level of coupling is low but we have also demonstrated this experimentally in the following ways:

(i)   the IDE has been used successfully with a MAS platform supporting agents written in Java and in Lisp [14];
(ii) while Galaxy Communicator (http://communicator.sourceforge.net/) should perhaps not be considered a true MAS, the IDE has been successfully used with Galaxy;
(iii) the IDE has been successfully used as a link between a MAS framework and Galaxy (readily achieved since the IDE can communicate with both systems);
(iv) the IDE has been used with a virtual MAS – a shell masquerading as a running MAS which, through the use of scripts, generates agent architectures and messages which are passed to non-virtual agents.

Since the IDE is deployed in the form of a MAS, providing new MAS-level tools is readily achieved by adding new agents to the IDE. This has been verified experimentally. Similarly, we have demonstrated by experimentation that the IDE can integrate with agent-level tools. In practice this is achieved by allowing agents to be inspected by different object-IDEs, according to their type. This capability is provided in the same way that a general purpose editor can call up appropriate compilers for the programs it is editing.

The IDE has also been tested for usability by following small user-groups of students involved in MAS development. Observations confirmed the importance of MAS tools in general (also noted by other authors [11, 12, 16]) and supported our proposition that the two levels of development and debugging for MAS, the agent-level and the system-level, involve different types of activity, the first where the focus of attention relates more to issues concerning program code, the second where the focus is systems architecture and messaging. Users reported a perceived reduction in the learning curve associated with moving to a new MAS platform while retaining the same IDE and highlighted the benefit of adopting their own personal preference of agent-level tools (eg: Eclipse).

5 Conclusion

This paper acknowledges that the lack of a complete set of engineering tools is a contributing factor to the slow uptake of agent-based software development in industry. In particular we have focused on the provision of IDEs.

We have categorised suitable tools for MAS IDEs into two levels of abstraction the agent-level and the system-level. We suggest that tools for use at the agent-level are generally available but there is a greater problem in providing tools at the system-level. Furthermore, we note that for tools to be of general use they must be decoupled from any particular agent platform.

We have presented a generalised set of requirements for system wide tools irrespective of the agent platform used. This minimal set of tools comprises facilities to inspect, monitor and debug a running MAS, it is intentionally neutral on framework specific aspects like types of agency, the structure of messages, mobility, etc.

We have tested an approach to IDE construction in which the IDE is built in the form of its own MAS. This approach decouples the IDE from any particular agent platform i.e.: the agents it monitors can be built on different agent platforms. We have evaluated this resulting IDE by experimentation and found that it can be extended by adding new agents to provide additional system-level tools and easily linked to existing agent-level tools like editors and inspectors. In addition we have succeeded in using the IDE as a bridge between two, otherwise incompatible, agent frameworks.

While more discussion is needed within the research community to determine which system-level tools are most appropriate and how they should be presented, we believe that it is possible to deploy these as an extendible, generic and platform-independent IDE.

References

1. Bellifemine, F.L., Caire, G., Greenwood, D.: Developing Multi-Agent Systems with JADE. Wiley, Chichester (2007)
2. Benfield, S.S., Hendrickson, J., Galanti, D.: Making a Strong Business Case for Multiagent Technology. In: AAMAS, Hakodate, Japan. ACM Press, New York (2006)
3. Bernon, C., Cossentino, M., Pavon, J.: An Overview of Current Trends in European AOSE Research. Informatica 29, 379–390 (2005)
4. Bordini, R., Hübner, J.F., Vieira, R.: Jason and the golden fleece of agent-oriented programming. In: Multi-Agent Programming: Languages, Platforms and Applications. Kluwer, Dordrecht (2005)
5. Bordini, R., Braubach, L., Dastani, M., Seghrouchni, A.E.F., Gomez-Sanz, J.J., Leite, J., O'Hare, G., Pokahr, A., Ricci, A.: A Survey of Programming Languages and Platforms for Multi-Agent Systems. Informatica 30(1), 33–44 (2006)

6. Braubach, L., Pokahr, A., Bade, D., Krempels, K., Lamersdorf, W.: Deployment of Distributed Multi-Agent Systems. In: Gleizes, M.-P., Omicini, A., Zambonelli, F. (eds.) ESAW 2004. LNCS (LNAI), vol. 3451, pp. 261–276. Springer, Heidelberg (2005)
7. Dastani, M., Meyer, J.C.: A Practical Agent Programming Language. In: Dastani, M., El Fallah Seghrouchni, A., Ricci, A., Winikoff, M. (eds.) ProMAS 2007. LNCS (LNAI), vol. 4908. Springer, Heidelberg (2008)
8. Filho, A., Antonio do Prado, H., Pereira de Lucena, H., Pereira de Lucena, C.J.: A WSA-Based Architecture for Building Multi-Agent Systems. In: AAMAS, Hawaii (2007)
9. Flater, D.: Debugging agent interactions: a case study. In: ACM Symposium on Applied Computing, Las Vegas, Nevada, United States. ACM Press, New York (2001)
10. Fonseca, S.P., Griss, M.L., Letsinger, R.: Agent Behavior Architectures: A MAS Framework Comparison. In: AAMAS, Bologna, Italy. ACM Press, New York (2002)
11. Gutknecht, O., Ferber, J., Michel, F.: Integrating Tools and Infrastructures for Generic Multi-Agent Systems. In: Fifth International Joint Conference on Autonomous Agents, Montreal, Canada. ACM Press, New York (2001)
12. Lam, D.N., Barber, K.S.: Verifying and Explaining Agent Behaviour in an Implemented Agent System. In: AAMAS. ACM Press, New York (2004)
13. Luck, M., McBurney, P., Shehory, O., Willmott, S.: Agent Technology: Computing as Interaction (A Roadmap for Agent Based Computing), AgentLink (2005) ISBN 0854328459
14. Lynch, S.C., Rajendran, K.: Boris-A Framework for Developing Multi-Agent Systems in Lisp and Java. In: International Lisp User Group Meeting, New York, USA (2003)
15. Lynch, S.C., Rajendran, K.: Breaking Into Industry: Tool Support for Multiagent Systems. In: AAMAS, Hawaii (2007)
16. Massonet, P., Deville, Y., Neve, C.: From AOSE Methodology to Agent Implementation. In: AAMAS, Bologna, Italy. ACM Press, New York (2002)
17. Modi, P.J., Mancoridis, S., Mongan, W.M., Regli, W., Mayk, I.: Towards a reference model for agent-based systems. In: AAMAS, Japan. ACM Press, New York (2006)
18. Ndumu, D.T., Nwana, H.S., Lee, L.C., Collis, J.C.: Visualising and debugging distributed multi-agent systems. In: Conference on Autonomous Agents, Seattle, USA. ACM Press, New York (1999)
19. Poutakidis, D., Padgham, L., Winikoff, M.: Debugging Multi-Agent Systems Using Design Artifacts: The Case of Interaction Protocols. In: AAMAS, Bologna, Italy. ACM Press, New York (2002)

Implementing Organisations in JADE

Cristián Madrigal-Mora, Esteban León-Soto, and Klaus Fischer

DFKI GmbH
Stuhlsatzenhausweg 3 (Building D 3-2),
D-66123 Saarbrücken, Germany
{Cristian.Madrigal,Esteban.Leon,Klaus.Fischer}@dfki.de

Abstract. The representation of an agent organisation using a concrete computational entity is a frequently missing feature in platforms for multiagent systems, and it is normally left as a result of the emergent behaviour of interacting agents. This is also the case for JADE, one of the most used multiagent system platforms. This paper proposes an extension to JADE that addresses this missing concept, without disrupting the compatibility with previously developed systems nor the availability of JADE's platform services.

1 Introduction

The application of Multiagent Systems (MAS) in varied industrial and business environments has been increasing in recent times. It can be argued that this is the case, because autonomous agents enable the development of robust and scalable software systems, since they can complete their objectives while situated in a dynamic and uncertain environment, engage in rich, high-level social interactions, and operate within flexible organisational structures [1].

When a system has a large amount of jobs to be performed several times in coordination with several providers, it is inefficient to distribute the tasks among all the parties involved every single time. In this case, it makes better sense to establish this repeated coordination structure based on the previous successes. This provider grouping can be formalized by the concept of *Organisation*. Organisations are social structures that provide processes for conflict resolution, as a result from previously resolved problems or conflicts [2]. They institutionalise anticipated coordination, which is especially useful for medium and large-scale applications that require the delimitation of the agents communication behaviour.

Since the overall computation in MAS is obtained by the combination of the autonomous computation of every agent in the system and the communication among them [3], the coordination and communication between the agents is essential. Agents acting in an organisational structure can provide additional encapsulation, simplifying representation and design, and modularization, enabling code reuse and incremental deployment. Nevertheless, these coordination or organizational structures are not always explicitly supported by agent platforms, even when some agent metamodels and methodologies do present them.

R. Bergmann et al. (Eds.): MATES 2008, LNAI 5244, pp. 135–146, 2008.

This paper proposes the implementation of an organisation-oriented extension for the JADE agent platform [4,5]. JADE is a FIPA [6] compliant multiagent system middleware which also serves as agent platform and provides basic services like directories and messaging. Its framework supports the implementation of ontologies for the contents of messages and knowledge of agents. JADE is also one of the preferred platforms to implement conversation protocols between autonomous agents, because it provides a library of behaviours for performing FIPA interaction protocols. New conversation protocols and their corresponding behaviours can be produced from scratch or by combining protocols. In spite of addressing the problem of composition of agent groups, it does not provide explicit features for groups apart of the emergent behaviour obtained by manifesting the behaviours of each agent.

The article is structured as follows: Section 2 presents related works; Section 3 addresses the extension to JADE and its implementation; Section 4 discusses the benefits of our approach; the open issues are addressed in Section 5 and Section 6 presents our finals remarks and conclusion.

2 Related Work

This section presents a short overview of some related work in agent platforms, metamodels and methodologies with regard to agent organisations.

Regarding the analysis of organisations, the approach the we present on this paper falls under what [7] calls the perspective of computational organisation theory and artificial intelligence, in which the organisations are basically described at the role and group—composed of roles—levels. Under this perspective, we can also find works such as GAIA [8,9] and MOISE [10]. While other models, such as ISLANDER [11], define organisations as electronic institutions, in terms of norms and rules.

With respect to organisational structures, Holonic MAS [12] present particular pyramidal organisations where agents of a layer (having the same coordinator) are able to communicate and to negotiate directly between them [13]. This coordinator is also known as the holon's *head*. Any holon that is part of a whole is thought to contribute to achieving the goals of this superior whole. Apart from the head, each holon consist of a (possibly empty) set of other agents, called body agents. Holonic structures can be expressed quite naturally in terms of roles and groups, under the perspective described previously.

Besides our chosen agent platform, JADE, there are two other platforms that we consider relevant in this context. First, JACK Intelligent Agents [14] supports organisational structures through its Team Mode. In this mode, goals can be delegated to team member in order to achieve the team goals. JADEX [15,16] presents another interesting platform for the implementation of organisations. While JADEX doesn't currently have organisational structures, the approach presented here could be easily adapted to it, while gaining its BDI reasoning and the ability to do metareasoning on the organisation structures and behaviours.

Additionally, there has been previous work regarding organisations through agent middlewares, such as AMELI [17] and S-MOISE+ [18], while the support of these in the more broadly used agent platforms, like JADE, has been dependent on the way the platform deals with behaviour execution and message passing without enforcing policies and restrictions at the organisation level through run time computational entities.

3   Organisations and Roles

The definition of Organisation[1] that we propose to use in JADE is the *Agentified Group* in [19]: a set of agents that possesses all the features that any agent might possess. For example, just as an agent, it can send and receive messages directly and take on roles. For this purpose, the Organisation is a specialization of Agent.

An Organisation or a group in general is formed to attain new processes and results that were not available by individual members, therefore taking advantage of the synergies among them. Organisations may be defined statically—at design time by the system designer—or dynamically—at runtime—as a collective task or goal arises.

Also, since an Organisation basically consists of interrelated *Roles*, it is defined according to these roles within it. Correspondingly, the roles have a meaning only within the Organisation's context. Therefore, the Role's meaning is determined by and dependent of the Organisation to which it belongs. This is the biggest difference between role and a capability: capabilities represent a set of features an agent can have independently of its current scope, such as a set of behaviours. Agent capabilities can match one to one to a role, can exceed the requirements demanded by a role or need to be aggregated to match these requirements.

Concrete organisational entities enable the design of the interactions in a clear fashion, whether they take place between different organisations or between individual agents and organisations, instead of leaving the collectiveness implied through the emergent behaviour that results from their capabilities.

3.1   Requirements

The extension was designed to provide a Platform Specific Model (PSM) for JADE for the transformation of our Platform Independent Model for Agents: PIM4Agents. In this context, the JADE metamodel needed to be defined in the Eclipse Modeling Framework (EMF) [20] in order to take advantage of the transformation tools available for Eclipse and to fit the model driven approach we have presented in [21].

The metamodel started as an extraction of the JADE class model from JADE's source code and documentation. However, when coming to the definition of the transformations from PIM4Agents to the JADE PSM, we noticed that additional flexibility and adaptability could be provided to JADE if we represented Organisations and Roles from the PIM4Agents as computational entities in JADE instead of just mapping them directly in agents.

---

[1] Capitalized terms refer to classes or relevant concepts.

Therefore, we concentrate on the Organisation as a computational entity for execution purposes. Although we use the analogy of social organisation, given the parallelisms that exist with regard to the distribution of tasks and team-work, our Organisation concept is not intended to address directly the issues of implementing institutions, alliances or coalitions, although this work could potentially be used as a base to implementing them in JADE.

3.2 Implementation

The extension of JADE is centered around two concepts/classes: *Organisation* and *Role* (Figure 1). It is important to mention that the *Behaviour* class depicted only represents the base node of JADE's Behaviour hierarchy, not any particular Behaviour type.

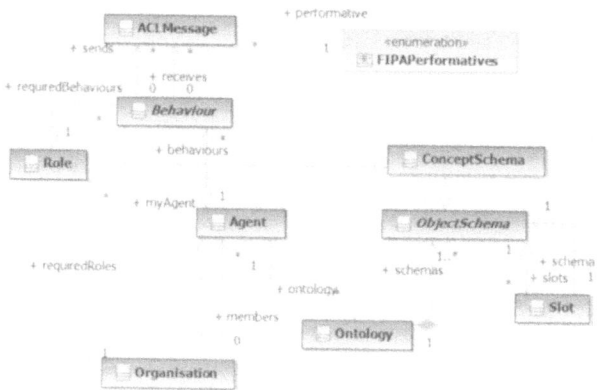

Fig. 1. Partial view of the core of the JADE metamodel

The Organisation contains references to all its members, as well as the Roles under which the membership relation is stated. The Organisation class extends the Agent class, given that we want it to be able to perform tasks and communicate with its members and other agents. As such, the Organisation is itself an Agent and possesses its own set of behaviours. Additionally, Organisation also provides the functionality of registration and deregistration of members as the Organisation changes over time. These tasks are performed using communication protocols that serve this purpose,and that will be described in detail further on.

The Role class is implemented as an Ontology Concept. It is part of the *OrganizationOntology* and groups the set of Behaviours that are allocated to it. Behaviours are, in principle, the basic mechanisms that manifest when their corresponding triggering event happens, usually an incoming message of a certain kind or with a certain content. The list of Behaviours can potentially be used (i) to verify that the agent is actually capable of fulfilling the Role or (ii) to allow the Agent to "learn" the Behaviours/Capabilities required to fulfill the role by adding them to its own, depending on the value of the Role's properties.

Additionally if an Agent is provided with new Behaviours/Capabilities when taking a Role, these can not be removed if the Agent leaves the Organisation since the Agent's autonomy has to be respected.

Behaviours inside a role can be *abstract* in the sense that they specify the normative requirements to fulfill the role, leaving unspecified how specific parts are to be resolved. This is particularly useful to delegate to the agents the concrete implementation of those parts of a protocol, where a decision of an agent is involved or where an agent has to provide a solution, in other words, where the agent contribution is expected. In the case that abstract behaviours in a Role are present, agents are expected to provide concrete matching behaviours.

Publishing to the Directory Facilitator. The Organisation structure can be determined at design time or at run time. For the ones setup in design time, the organisation establishment—initialization of the organisation structure—is already set; however, for those that are determined until run time, a selection of role fillers needs to take place. JADE already provides a directory service called the Directory Facilitator (DF). Through the DF, an agent/organisation can search for other agents/organisations that possess a given set of features, such as the protocols supported or the ontologies it can access.

In order to take advantage of the DF Service, we extend the class used to describe agents, namely *DFAgentDescription*, which is part of JADE's *FIPAAgentManagementOntology*. As depicted in Figure 2, we first extend DFAgentDescription by adding a list of of performed roles, creating the descriptor for Organisation members, *DFOrganisationMemberDescription*.

Since the Organisation requires and, as the agent that it is, performs roles, we create the Organisation descriptor, *DFOrganisationDescription*, by extending DFOrganisationMemberDescription with a list of required roles.

Organisation Establishment. Once the descriptions for Organisations and members are published to the DF, the organisation establishment can take place on the run time case. As a first step, a search for suitable agents/organisations is performed by quering the DF Service. For technical details on querying the DF

Fig. 2. Directory description class hierarchy of OrganizationOntology

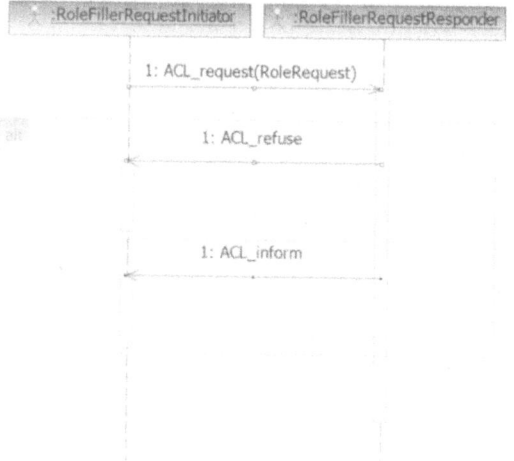

Fig. 3. RoleFillerRequest protocol

Service, please see [22]. When the list of prospective DFOrganisationMemberDe-
scriptions or DFOrganisationDescriptions is retrieved, the agent/organisation
initiates the RoleFillerRequest protocol (see Figure 3). The same protocol is
applied for the agent that wants to join an organisation or for the organisation
that wants to recruit a new member. In the first case, the organisation takes the
Responder role and a RoleRequest object is sent as content of the ACL_request;
and in the second case, the candidate agent is the Responder and a Member-
Request object is sent as content of the request. Once this request is received
by the Responder, an ACL_refuse message is produced if the request is denied,
or an ACL_inform message is produced if the request has been accepted. As it
can be expected, the decision process for accepting/denying these requests is left
to other internal behaviours of the agent/organisation. Depending on the design
policies, the decision process may include, for example, a verification that the requesting agent possesses all the behaviours necessary to fulfill the requested role.

Task Distribution. In order to allow the organization members to manage
their own work load, the distribution of tasks is performed through the simple
protocol presented in Figure 4. This protocol is basically a simplified version of
the FIPA Request Protocol [23] which provides the RequestResponder with the
option of refusing in case it is already busy.

3.3   Example: Product Sale with Personal Loan

As a concrete example on how Organizations that are created at runtime can
work, we present a Product Sale scenario. The basic interaction in this scenario
takes place between a *Buyer* and a *Seller* and it is depicted in Figure 5. The
interaction is initiated by the Buyer making a query about a certain product.
If the product is not in stock, the Seller sends an OutOfStock message and

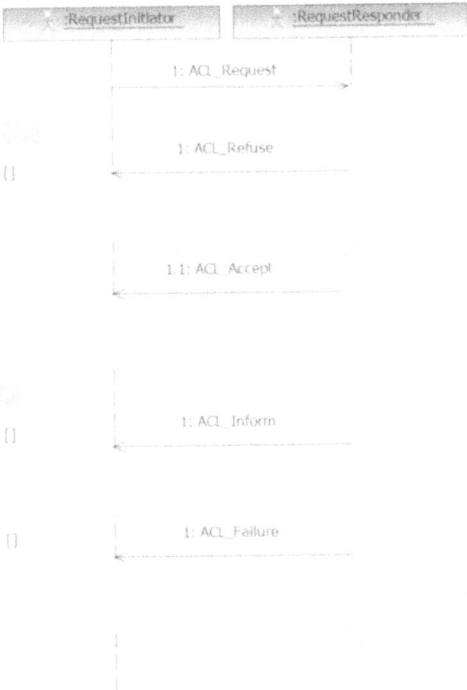

Fig. 4. TaskRequest protocol

the interaction terminates. If the product is in stock, the Seller replies with the product price. The Buyer receives the price and considers if it has enough money to pay for it. If it doesn't, the Buyer cancels the transaction. If it does have the money, it sends the payment to the Seller and, correspondingly, the Seller ships the product.

Under this scenario, if the Buyer doesn't have enough money, it has to find the means to get the necessary money. One solution would be to get a personal loan from a Bank. The *Personal Loan* is a collaboration or agreement between the *Bank* and the *Customer*, so that the Customer can obtain the product desired. The Personal Loan can be represented by an Organisation (see Figure 6). In order to instantiate this organization, the Buyer takes on the Customer role on the PersonalLoan Organisation, while the Bank takes the Loaner role. The organisation can be established following the previously presented RoleFillerRequest protocol, for example. Once the Organisation is established, PersonalLoan can take on the original Buyer role from the Product Sale protocol through the execution of the Financed Sale protocol, shown in Figure 7. PersonalLoan will persist as an organisation as long as the loan is valid.

The Financed Sale protocol, shows the best case scenario—no alternative paths—of the interaction between the PersonalLoan Organisation and the Customer and Loaner roles, in the case that the customer doesn't have enough money

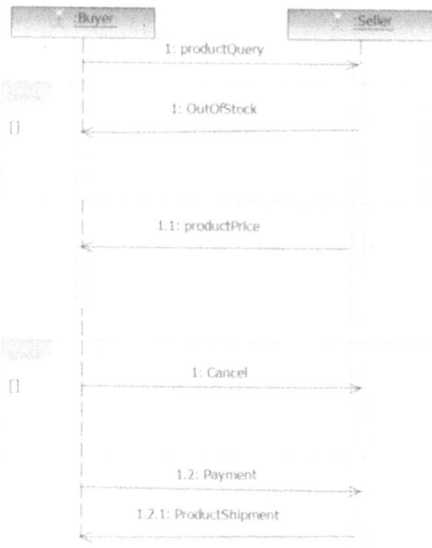

Fig. 5. View of the Product Sale Interaction Protocol

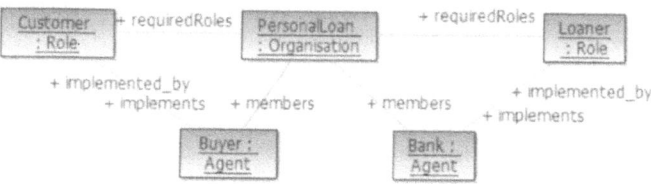

Fig. 6. View of the Personal Loan Organisation

to pay for the product. The interaction initiates with the Customer sending the product query to the PersonalLoan Organisation, who forwards it to the Seller, following the Product Sale protocol. When the reply with the product price is received from the seller, PersonalLoan forwards it to the Customer. Since the Customer doesn't have enough money to pay for the product, it requests a Loan from the Loaner providing the product information and price through the *re-questFinancing* message. When the financing is approved by the Loaner, it sends a financingApproved message to the Customer and asks PersonalLoan to forward the payment to the Seller.

This simple example shows that established protocols, such as Product Sale, do not need to be modified to allow additional interactions to be performed as part of the process. As a counter argument, it could be said that since JADE doesn't use the protocols per se, but projections of them, specified in Behaviours, the Organisation wouldn't be necessary. However, this argument is clearly

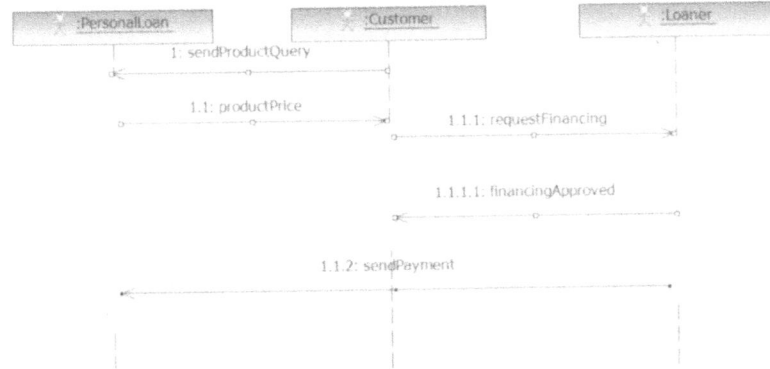

Fig. 7. Simplified View of the Financed Sale Interaction Protocol (best case scenario)

dependent on the protocol policies; for example, a Product Sale protocol could be very strict and require that the Agent that initiates the interaction has to provide the payment, while a Financed Sale protocol could require that the Loaner doesn't provide the money directly to the Customer, but directly pays for the product or service to the provider. In this scenario, the Organisation as an Agent would be required to intervene as a proxy to the transaction to allow reuse of the original Product Sale protocol by performing the Buyer role outside the Organisation and to be a proxy w.r.t. payment for the Seller. Of course, as the policies vary, the Organization's structure and its level of interference will vary accordingly, while still providing some additional flexibility in some cases.

4   Further Remarks on Organisations

In this Section, we present a discussion on the possible pros and cons of applying organisational structures like the ones proposed in this work to JADE and MAS, in general.

Organisations can be used easily to delegate tasks and simplify the modelling of interactions. For instance, in order to make interaction protocols more stable, some include interactions for validating features of their participants and control aspects. Through the use of clearly identified and properly managed organizations that take over these certification/authentication aspects, these tasks can be delegated. This way, agents do not have to start normal interactions by passing this evaluation/validation processes, instead they identify themselves as member of a "trusted certifying organization" proving that they fulfill the requirements.

Additionally, the predictability, reliability, and stability of MAS can be improved through the use of agent groupings [19], such as Organisations. The use of these groupings of agents allows the scoping of interactions, tasks and information accesses, therefore making each sub-organisation a specialist for a given scope and allowing the design, implementation, and testing of each scope in an incremental way, starting from the agents and their tasks/behaviours, up to the Organisation's behaviours and interactions.

In some cases, the gain of structure, provided by Organisations, can potentially come with a loss of autonomy to the individual agents. In one extreme case, the Organisation performs all the interaction with external parties, analogous to the the head of a holon, and the agent members lose part of their autonomy because of the restrictions and tasks that are imposed by the Organisation. In the other extreme case, an Organisation merely groups agents and provides the means to interact with them as one entity, so that any messages that the Organisation receives are merely forwarded to all members or to the designated handler of the given message, but the agents are not restricted from interacting directly with other parties. Our approach is generic enough to allow both extremes and cases in between of course. It is only necessary to provide the adequate behaviours to the Organisation, so that it can enforce/perform the policies and interaction patters desired.

5   Future Work

The concept of Organisation is currently being applied in the design of the prototypes for a supply chain management system for the steel industry, which are an extension to the work presented in [24]. In this context, there are several aggregates/devices in different factory locations that form a group to produce a specific customer order. Using the concepts provided in the present work, a customer order can be represented as an Organization of aggregates required for its production. This order-agents actively keep track of their progress by interacting with their member aggregate-agents, which at the same time go in and out of groups to represent the frequent changes in the production of an order.

Organizations, as described in this paper, serve also as behaviour containers for the behaviours required for each role. Agents entering an organization can fetch the set of behaviours that define their role. It is of crucial importance to study and compare how behaviours can be defined, how detailed they are required to be, which aspects are they expected to cover, how dependent they are of the definition mechanisms of each possible participating agent, and where is the most suitable place for the interface between the behaviour and the agents proper implementation.

In the case that the agents cannot fetch the set of behaviours for a given role, but are required to already possess behaviors that match the role's required behaviours, the appropriate matching mechanism has to be determined. At the moment, the extension of abstract behaviours has been used for simplicity, but other type of analysis, such as black-box need to be considered.

In order to support better design and easier management of organizations, the relationship between a conversation protocol and its corresponding role-behaviours has to be improved. This improvement could also impact the overall results significantly if the conversion could be automatized or the relation made at least more straightforward. Better proposals of definition that encompass both behaviours and global views of cooperations would serve this purpose better.

6   Conclusion

The representation of an Organisation using a concrete computational entity is a feature missing frequently in multiagent system platforms, as it is normally left as a result of the emergent behaviour of interacting agents. This is also the case for JADE, one of the most used multiagent system platform. The concept of an organization is proposed for this platform as a specific kind of agent. The fact that it is represented by an agent and not left as a virtual manifestation result of individual behaviours opens new options for collaborations modelling. Interaction protocols can be more easily modularized and, by scoping the aspects in complex interactions, the predictability, reliability, and scalability of such distributed systems are increased.

We have also discussed how there can be different types of organisations with respect to how much the group representation can intervene and how strict the protocols that rule the group are. Having a concrete representation entity for an organization also facilitates the definition of the policies, by making them explicit instead of implicit. Organisations provide not only advantage for design time, but also for enabling dynamic creation of organizations at run time.

References

1. Jennings, N.R.: Agent-based computing: Promise and perils. In: IJCAI, pp. 1429–1436 (1999)
2. Gasser, L.: Social conceptions of knowledge and action: Dai foundations and open systems semantics. Artificial Intelligence 47(1-3), 107–138 (1991)
3. Schillo, M., Fischer, K.: Holonic multiagent systems. KI 17(4), 54–55 (2003)
4. Bellifemine, F., Poggi, A., Rimassa, G.: JADE - a FIPA-compliant agent framework. In: Proceedings of the Practical Applications of Intelligent Agents (1999)
5. JADE: Java Agent Development Framework (2001), http://jade.tilab.com
6. Foundation for Intelligent Physical Agents: FIPA Abstract Architecture Specification. Document number SC00001L (2002),
   http://www.fipa.org/specs/fipa00001/SC00001L.html
7. van den Broek, E.L., Jonker, C.M., Sharpanskykh, A., Treur, J., Yolum, P.: Formal modeling and analysis of organizations. In: AAMAS Workshops, pp. 18–34 (2005)
8. Zambonelli, F., Jennings, N.R., Wooldridge, M.: Developing multiagent systems: The gaia methodology. ACM Transactions on Software Engineering and Methodology 12(3), 317–370 (2003)
9. Wooldridge, M., Jennings, N., Kinny, D.: The Gaia methodology for agent-oriented analysis and design. JAAMAS 3(3), 285–312 (2000)
10. Hannoun, M., Boissier, O., Sichman, J.S., Sayettat, C.: Moise: An organizational model for multi-agent systems. In: IBERAMIA-SBIA, pp. 156–165 (2000)
11. Esteva, M., de la Cruz, D., Sierra, C.: ISLANDER: an electronic institutions editor. In: AAMAS, pp. 1045–1052. ACM Press, New York (2002)
12. Schillo, M., Fischer, K.: A taxonomy of autonomy in multiagent organisation. In: Agents and Computational Autonomy, pp. 68–82 (2003)
13. Adam, E., Mandiau, R.: Roles and hierarchy in multi-agent organizations. In: CEEMAS, pp. 539–542 (2005)

14. AOS: JACK Intelligent Agents, The Agent Oriented Software Group (AOS)(2006), http://www.agent-software.com/shared/home/
15. Pokahr, A., Braubach, L., Lamersdorf, W.: Jadex: Implementing a bdi-infrastructure for jade agents. EXP 3(3), 76–85 (2003)
16. Braubach, L., Pokahr, A., Lamersdorf, W.: Jadex: A short overview. In: Main Conference Net.ObjectDays, pp. 195–207 (September 2004)
17. Esteva, M., Rosell, B., Rodrguez-Aguilar, J.A., Arcos, J.L.: AMELI: An Agent-Based Middleware for Electronic Institutions. In: AAMAS, vol. 1, pp. 236–243 (2004)
18. Hübner, J.F., Sichman, J.S., Boissier, O.: S-MOISE+: A Middleware for Developing Organised Multi-agent Systems. In: Boissier, O., Padget, J., Dignum, V., Lindemann, G., Matson, E., Ossowski, S., Sichman, J.S., Vázquez-Salceda, J. (eds.) ANIREM 2005 and OOOP 2005. LNCS (LNAI), vol. 3913, pp. 64–78. Springer, Heidelberg (2005)
19. Odell, J., Nodine, M.H., Levy, R.: A metamodel for agents, roles, and groups. In: Odell, J.J., Giorgini, P., Müller, J.P. (eds.) AOSE 2004. LNCS, vol. 3382, pp. 78–92. Springer, Heidelberg (2005)
20. Budinsky, F., Steinberg, D., Merks, E., Ellersick, R., Grose, T.: Eclipse Modeling Framework. Addison-Wesley, Reading (2003)
21. Hahn, C., Madrigal-Mora, C., Fischer, K.: Interoperability through a platform-independent model for agents. In: I-ESA (2007)
22. Bellifemine, F., Caire, G., Trucco, T., Rimassa, G.: Jade programmers guide, http://jade.tilab.com/doc/programmersguide.pdf
23. Foundation for Intelligent Physical Agents: FIPA Request Interaction Protocol Specification. Document number SC00026H (2002), http://www.fipa.org/specs/fipa00026/SC00026H.html
24. Jacobi, S., León-Soto, E., Madrigal-Mora, C., Fischer, K.: Masdispo: A multiagent decision support system for steel production and control. In: AAAI, pp. 1707–1714 (2007)

A Fair Mechanism for Recurrent Multi-unit Auctions

Javier Murillo, Víctor Muñoz, Beatriz López, and Dídac Busquets

Institut d'Informàtica i Aplicacions
Campus Montilivi, edifice P4, 17071 Girona
{jmurillo,vmunozs,blopez,busquets}@eia.udg.edu
http://iiia.udg.edu/

Abstract. Auctions are a good tool for dealing with resource allocation in multi-agent environments. When the resources are either renewable or perishable, a repeated auction mechanism is needed, in what is known as recurrent auctions. However, several problems arise with this kind of auction, namely, the resource waste problem, the bidder drop problem, and the asymmetric balance of negotiation power. In this paper we present different mechanisms to deal with these issues. We have evaluated the mechanisms in a network bandwidth allocation scenario, and the results show that the proposed mechanisms achieve higher benefits for the auctioneer, while also providing a fairer behavior.

1 Introduction

Auctions are becoming popular within the field of Artificial Intelligence due to its usefulness for resource allocation on competitive multi-agent systems [3], and its multiple types suitable for a wide range of situations.

However, auction mechanisms may have problems in some domains when renewable and perishable or consumable resources are being auctioned as pointed out by [8]. On one hand, having renewable resources means that the auctioneer offers the resources every time they become free (when the time of the contract expires). Then the auctioneer needs to allocate the resources to bidders again. On the other hand, perishable resources cannot be stored or left unused. That is, often, there is a free disposal condition in which the auctioneer can leave same resources unassigned if the benefit is maximized. Then, in a next auction, the auctioneer could re-sell the remaining resources. However, when the resources are perishable, these cannot be kept for a future auction. Related to these issues is the allocation of resources to bidders for specific time only [7]. In this domain, short-term contract is often used in those markets.

In these cases in which renewable and perishable resources are managed, the auction is repeated several times, in what has been called *recurrent* auction. A recurrent auction is an auction where the bidders are continuously competing for the resources. These kind of auctions have received little attention [6,12,7], but they are gaining importance, since there are many applications where this recurrence takes place, such as e-service oriented marketplaces.

R. Bergmann et al. (Eds.): MATES 2008, LNAI 5244, pp. 147–158, 2008.

Our research concerns these kind of auctions. Particularly, we are interested in recurrent multi-unit single-item auctions. On one hand, in single-item auctions an item is auctioned at a time (conversely to combinatorial auctions in which several items can be auctioned together). On the other hand, multi-unit auctions means that there is more than one unit of each item being auctioned. A typical example of the applicability of this kind of auctions in the e-service domain is the provision of network bandwidth. There is a single item to be sold: the network capacity, and there are several units of the item (depending on the capacity of the connection). Another example, regarding natural resource allocation, is the CO_2 emissions. In this scenario, there is a single item, the CO_2 capacity, that is divided into identical units called CO_2 credits [2].

In this paper we present various recurrent multi-unit single-item auction mechanisms to improve the final outcome of the auctioneer by getting fair or egalitarian solutions. The first mechanism is based on assigning priorities to the bidders; the second mechanism on defining variable reservation prices to pay for the use of the resource, and the third mechanism is a combination of the two previous ones. We experimentally show how the latter mechanism outperforms the former and the previous approaches found in the literature.

The paper is organized as follows first, we provide some basis on recurrent multi-unit single-item auctions (or recurrent multi-unit auctions for short) in Section 2. Next, in Section 3, we describe the new auction mechanism we propose. Then, we continue by describing our experimental scenario in Section 4 and explaining the results obtained in Section 5. Finally, we end with some related work and conclusions.

2   Issues in Recurrent Multi-unit Auctions

In a recurrent multi-unit auction, the auctioneer has some goods to be sold periodically. Then, auctions are repeated with the same bidders through time. In each auction, the auctioneer agent sends a message to all the bidder agents, offering the different units of the item to be sold. Then, the bidders send back to the auctioneer their bids, containing the price they would pay for a single unit of the item, sending as many bids as units required. Next, the auctioneer decides to which agents it will sell the available units of the item. In this process, three main components are distinguished:

- Bidding policies: how each agent decides the price it is willing to pay for the resources
- Market clearing or winning determination algorithm: how the auctioneer selects the agents that win the units of the item (or selects the winning bids).
- Pricing mechanism: how the auctioneer decides the price to be paid for the winners

Our research is concerned with the second one. The market clearing or winning determination algorithm poses an optimization problem to the auctioneer, which tries to maximize its benefits [4].

If there is the free disposal condition, then the auctioneer can keep some of the units if the benefit is higher. However, this free disposal condition has to be minimized when dealing with perishable resources, as it can produce what is known as the *resource waste problem*. Other problems related to recurrent auctions that should be tackled in the market clearing mechanism are the *bidder drop problem* and the *asymmetric balance of negotiating power*. We next describe in detail these problems.

2.1 Resources Waste Problem

Resources can be either static or time-sensitive. Static resources do not change their properties during a negotiation process [3]. On the other hand, a time-sensitive resource [7] is consumable or perishable. A resource is consumable if it gets worn out by constantly using it. For example, fuel is a consumable resource. A resource is perishable, if it vanishes or loses its value when held over an extended period of time. For example, network bandwidth is a perishable resource since the bandwidth not used is not accumulable for the future.

Perishable resources, present in many real-world scenarios, cannot be stored in warehouses for future sales; if the resources are not allocated, they lose their value or vanish completely. This is known as the *resource waste problem* in recurrent auctions, since if the auctioneer does not sell the resource in a round, it cannot sell it in the next round. On the other hand, it cannot give the resource for free. So a trade-off between the resource usage and the benefit of the auctioneer should be appropriately handled.

2.2 Bidder Drop Problem

This problem occurs when bidders participating in many auctions are always losing. They could decide to leave the market, since they are not getting any profit. This has bad consequences for the auctioneer: the reduction on the number of bidders gradually decreases the price competition, because the probability of winning increases for the remaining bidders. Hence, their attempts to decrease bid prices without losing the winning position will be successful, causing the overall drop of bid prices.

In order to avoid, or somehow decrease, the bidder drop problem, the recurrent auction process should have some degree of *fairness*.

2.3 Asymmetric Balance of Negotiating Power

In most of the traditional auction mechanism, the bid prices in an auction are dependent only on the customer's willingness to pay for the traded goods. This means that only the intentions of customers, but not of the auctioneer, are reflected in the auction winning prices [6]. At long run, the effect of this problem causes the collapse of the auction. For example, let us suppose that initially there are N bidders. A third of them, are poor and bid 1€; while the other two thirds are richer and pay some amount over 5€. After several rounds, the richer agents start lowering the price up to 3€, while the poor agents rise their bids up to 2€. At the end, the richer agents are the winners with a price close to the poor agents. In this case, the richer bidders have the power of fixing the price, not the auctioneer. In a recurrent auction, these prices can even go under the poor prices, if the poor agents have dropped out of the market. Note that this problem is different that the bidder collusion [13] although the effects are the same. In bidder collusion the bidders forms coalitions to force this situation, while the asymmetric problem is caused by the uneven wealth of the agents.

3   Mechanisms for Fair Auction Clearing

In the recurrent auction mechanism a fair solution means that at long term, all of the participants accomplish their goals in the same degree, independently of their wealth. The inclusion of this fairness can be somewhat acting against short-term optimality, since the result of an auction may differ from the optimal solution if a suboptimal solution is fairer. However, its mid or long-term effect produces an increase of auctioneer benefits, since it maintains the interest of bidders in continuing in the auction process [6].

We propose three different mechanisms based on the use of priorities and variable reservation prices for reaching fair solutions and solve the problems of recurrent auctions. The first mechanism is the priority auction that solves the resource waste and the bidder drop problem; the second one is the customizable reservation price auction that solves the asymmetric balance of negotiation power and the bidder drop problem; and finally, the last one is the customizable reservation price auction with priorities that achieves to solve the three problems.

3.1   Priority Auction (PA)

This mechanism takes into account the history of each agent in previous auctions. Each agent is assigned a *priority* value depending on the number of won and lost auctions. Thus, priority is defined in *[0,1]*. The more number of lost auctions, the higher the priority. The priority values are updated after each auction is finished, and they are used for clearing the next auction. The clearing algorithm could use them in very different ways: they could be transformed into new constraints to be satisfied by the solution, or directly designate the set of winning agents, among others.

Since the history of the agents in a recurrent auction scenario is long, a time window could be used to calculate the priorities instead. If the time window is very long, then the performance of PA is like the traditional auction (TA) (i.e. the typical auction where winners are the bidders with the highest bid) since the effect of the result of an auction is insignificant when the number of auction is high.

Thus, we propose to use this priority to modify the value of the bids and selects as winners the highest modified bids. More precisely, given a bid value v_i of an agent with priority w_i, a new bid valuation is computed as:

$$v_i' = f(v_i, w_i) \tag{1}$$

The priority is handled by the auctioneer, and this new value v_i' is the one used by the clearing algorithm to find an optimal solution. Note however, that the winner bidders will pay the original v_i price.

The function f can be designed in many ways, and it allows introducing different fairness facets in the auction solution. Thus, the function should increase the chances of winning of a high priority agent, while it should decrease the chances of a low priority one. For example, we are currently using the function: $v_i' = f(v_i, w_i) = v_i * w_i$.

Note that this mechanism does not produce any resource waste as it always sells all the available units and reduces the effect of bidder drop problem.

3.2   Customizable Reservation Price Auction (CRPA)

In this mechanism the idea is to have a reservation price for each bidder. We define the reservation price as the minimum price at which the auctioneer is willing to sell a good or service. That means that the auctioneer does not accept any bid of an agent under its reservation price. The reservation price is initially the same for all the bidders, but it gradually varies as the auctions succeed in the following way. For each agent, if a bid price is higher than the reservation price, then the reservation price for that agent is incremented. Otherwise, if the reservation price is higher than the bid's price, then the reservation price is decremented.

A parameter γ is defined indicating the minimum increment and decrement percentage of the reservation price. When a bidder bids with a value higher than its reservation price, then its reservation price is incremented by the half of the difference between the reservation price and the bid's value, except if the difference is lower than γ. In this case, the reservation price is incremented by γ. The algorithm of this procedure is shown in Figure 1.

$minimum = reservationPrice_i * \gamma$
$difference = abs(bid_i - reservationPrice_i)$
if $bid_i \geq reservationPrice_i$ **then**
    $reservationPrice_i = reservationPrice_i + max(difference, minimum)$
else
    $reservationPrice_i = reservationPrice_i - max(difference, minimum)$
end if

Fig. 1. Pseudo-code of CRPA reservation price's update

This mechanism is egalitarian since everybody can lose indistinctively of his wealth. In addition, it avoids that bidders with high wealth reduce their price to the minimum possible to win, and it obliges them to increase it to a minimum reservation price. Thus, this mechanism solves the problem of the asymmetric balance of negotiation. However, the use of reservation prices produces resource waste as it does not always allocate all the available resources.

3.3   Customizable Reservation Price Auction with Priorities (CRPA+P)

An idea to avoid the resource waste of the previous mechanism is to distribute the remaining resources among the non-winning bidders. Hence what we do is to give the surplus resources to the bidders with higher priority without considering its bid. This fact eliminates the resource waste problem and improves the level of fairness of the solutions.

Therefore, this method is a combination of the CRPA and the PA mechanism, since it is using the individual variable reservation price and the priority mechanism explained above.

4   Experimental Setup

In order to test the proposed mechanisms, we have used the experimentation scenario provided in [7] in which recurrent auctions are used to deal with the e-service networking markets. Thus, we use a previously used and tested scenario that corresponds exactly to the multi-unit single-item recurrent auctions.

4.1   Experimentation Scenario

The recurrent auction is formed by 2000 multi-unit auctions. There are 50 units of resources (i.e. time-sensitive e-service units) available for allocation in each auction round. There are 100 customers (bidders). The initial bidding price is randomly selected from the range $[t_i/2, t_i]$, where t_i represents the upper bound on customer i willingness to pay. There are three types of the standard distributions of the upper bound on willingness to pay among the customers, all with a mean of 5: (1) the exponential distribution, (2) the uniform distribution over the range *[0, 10]*, and (3) the gaussian distribution.

Based on the assumption that each bidder will maximize its expected profit, the following bidding behavior have been considered. If a bidder lost in the last auction round, it increases its bidding price by a factor of $\alpha > 1$ to improve its winning probability in the current round. The increase of bidding price is limited by the upper bound on bidder's willingness to pay. If a bidder won in the last auction round, then with equal probability of 0.5, it either decreases the bidding price by a factor β or maintains it unchanged. The decrease attempts to maximize the expected profit. α and β are set in the experiments to 1.2 and 0.8, respectively. The minimum bidding price of a bidder is 0.1.

In order to model the bidder drop problem a Tolerance of Consecutive Losses (TCL) have been defined. The TCL denotes the maximum number of consecutive losses that a customer can tolerate before dropping out of an auction. The TCL value of each customer is uniformly distributed over the range *[2, 10]*.

4.2 Other Auction Mechanisms

We have compared our mechanism with other previous ones: the traditional auction, the cancelable price auction, the reservation price auction, and the optimal recurrent auction. For such purpose, we have re-implemented them following the information given by the authors on the corresponding papers.

Traditional Auction (TA). In this mechanism the winners are the bidders with the highest bids.

Cancelable Auction (CA). In this type of auction, if the resulting revenue of an auction does not meet the minimum requirements of the auctioneer, the entire auction is canceled. Thus, the cancelation of an auction wastes the entire stock of resources [7].

Reservation Price Auction (RPA). In this mechanism the auctioneer defines a reservation price (the same for all bidders) that indicates the minimum price that the bidders should pay. Only bids higher than the auctioneer's reservation price are considered during the winner selection. In RPA, the reservation price restricts the number of winners and can produce waste of part of the resources.

Optimal Recurring Auction (ORA). Proposed by [7], it is a mechanism based on the demand-supply principle of micro-economics. The mechanism fixes a reservation price b_0 in each auction. This value is the maximum between the $(2R/3)th$ higher bid value in the current auction and the auctioneer's minimum desired benefit of the sold resource. R is the number of resources. Then, all bidders with a bid greater than b_0 become winners. The remaining resources are shared between the loser agents following the VLLF-BDC (Valuable Last Lost first Bidder Drop Control) algorithm [7].

4.3 Parameters

There are several parameters to take into account in the different methods implemented:

- CA. In the experiments the minimum requirements of the auctioneer is set to 250€.
- RPA. The value of reservation price is set to 5€.
- ORA. The auctioneer's minimum desired benefit is set to 5€.
- PA and CRPA+P. We have selected a time window of 10 auction rounds.
- CRPA and CRPA+P:
  - The initial reservation price is set to 5€.
  - The γ factor is set to 0.1.

5 Results

With the aim of measuring the fairness of the system we have used the following two measures:

- **Minimum Won Auctions (MWA):** It represents the utility of the worst bidder [3]. It is computed as the minimum percentage of won auctions of all of the agents that stay in all of the auctions. A high value of MWA indicates that the mechanism is fair, since the worst bidder is doing quite well.
- **Standard Deviation Won Auctions (DWA):** the standard deviation of the percentage of won auctions of all of agents. A low DWA indicates that the difference among the agents is low, therefore the fairness of the mechanism is higher.

Figures 2, 3 and 4 show the results obtained. On the right, there is a plot of the average bidding price of winners in each auction mechanism for the wealth distribution. On the right, a table provides some details of the results. The MWA and DWA columns show the values of the fairness metrics. The AWA column shows the Average Won Auctions, the BEN column indicates the total benefit obtained by the auctioneer along the 2000 auction rounds. The NB column shows the number of agents that stay in the auction at the end. Finally, RW shows the number of resources wasted during the recurrent auction.

The results of the plots and tables show that TA is affected in all distributions by the bidder drop problem, causing the decrease of the auctioneer's revenue down to very low values. RPA and CA maintain the auctioneer's revenue at higher values than TA because the balance of the negotiation power is maintained. However they are affected by the resource waste problem (especially RPA), and they are also affected by the bidder drop problem. The number of bidders at the end of the recurrent auction is lower than the bidders in TA.

ORA reaches better results than TA, RPA and CA because it is less affected by the bidder drop problem, the resource waste problem and maintains the balance of negotiation power.

The results of PA in uniform wealth distribution are better than RPA but worse than ORA. In the gaussian wealth distribution the results of PA are very similar to ORA and better than RPA, but in the exponential wealth distribution the results obtained show that the auctioneer's revenue falls to very low values because of the balance of negotiation power.

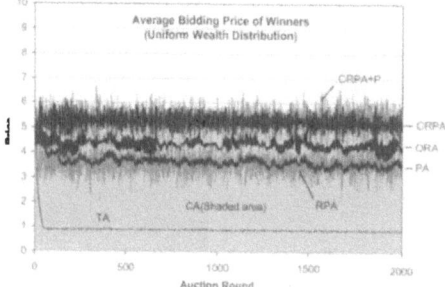

	MWA	DWA	AWA	BEN	NB	RW
TA	60.8	38.5	50.0	1862.3	66	0
CA	35.4	28.8	36.0	7608.1	57	29850
RPA	49.6	30.9	32.6	7100.3	53	34866
ORA	47.7	20.1	50.0	8697.2	87	0
PA	22.4	21.4	50.3	7311.3	85	0
CRPA	53.5	17.7	47.8	10659.7	88	4435
CRPA+P	52.6	6.3	52.2	10526.7	91	0

Fig. 2. Results for the uniform wealth distribution. *Left*: Average bidding price of winners. *Right*: performance measures.

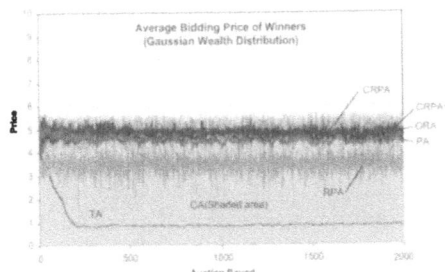

	MWA	DWA	AWA	BEN	NB	RW
TA	61.0	42.6	50.0	1827.3	61	0
CA	58.1	29.0	33.4	6479.3	50	40100
RPA	49.3	29.5	21.9	4780.5	36	56166
ORA	49.7	17.7	50.0	5617.1	90	0
PA	51.8	26.3	50.0	2933.0	79	0
CRPA	54.0	21.4	43.9	9421.1	81	12080
CRPA+P	47.1	2.9	51.6	9455.3	95	0

Fig. 3. Results for the exponential wealth distribution. *Left*: Average bidding price of winners. *Right*: performance measures.

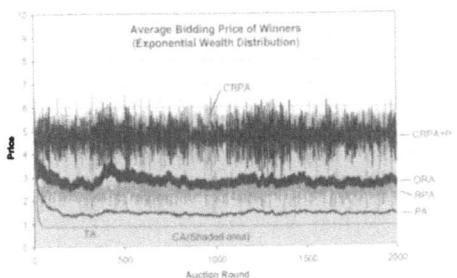

	MWA	DWA	AWA	BEN	NB	RW
TA	60.8	28.3	50.0	2026.2	77	0
CA	31.2	27.0	35.8	7032.5	57	30400
RPA	49.8	30.0	32.3	6965.0	54	35391
ORA	47.8	16.9	51.8	9192.6	87	0
PA	25.9	14.0	53.0	9040.3	87	0
CRPA	53.3	18.4	47.2	9713.5	87	5505
CRPA+P	52.7	1.8	53.5	9726.1	91	0

Fig. 4. Results for the exponential wealth distribution. *Left*: Average bidding price of winners. *Right*: performance measures.

CRPA and CRPA+P show the better results in all the distributions. These mechanisms merge fairness with a strategy to maintain the higher prices that each bidder can pay and consequently obtains very good revenues. The benefits reached by these methods are very similar but CRPA+P maintains a higher number of bidders and does not produce resource waste. Note that CRPA produces resource waste although it is less than CA and RPA. The improved version of CRPA, CRPA+P does not produce any resource waste.

Regarding the fairness measures, the best MWA values are for the CRPA method, followed by the CRPA+P, even thought they are quite close. That means that the variable reserved price helps in guaranteeing the amount of times that an agent wins an auction. On the other hand, the values of DWA are similar for the ORA, PA and CRPA and they are fairer than CA, RPA and TA. The fairest method is CRPA+P. That is, using our CRPA+P mechanism all the agents are winning in a more egalitarian way, while maintaining the benefits of the auctioneer.

Finally, the highest AWA value obtained is when using our CRPA+P method. Since the DWA is also the lowest, we are increasing the number of times any agent wins an auction.

6 Related Work

Regarding auctions, it is important to distinguish between recurring, continuous and iterative auctions. Recurring auctions, as the one described in this paper, are related to auctions that are repeated over time, getting a solution in each execution. Continuous auctions [5] are auctions that accept bids anytime, and clear the market as soon as offers arrive. Finally, iterative auctions are the ones that are repeated, but in each round, the solution is considered an approximation. The auction ends whenever the agents repeat the bids or each agent wins some bid [11].

There are few previous works related to egalitarian behavior in auctions, since most researchers have been focussed on an utilitarian point of view. More recently, due to the problems caused by recurrent auctions, this social welfare criteria has started to be a matter of study. For example, in [7] a mechanism based on reservation prices is proposed. In fact, our variable reservation price mechanism is based on it. Another interesting work is [1], where the authors propose the use of leximin preorder in order to establish a trade-off between utility and egalitarian approaches. In this case, however, the scenario considered is a combinatorial auction instead of a recurrent one.

Finally, regarding our priority mechanism, it has been tested in a wastewater treatment plant domain in [10,9].

7 Conclusions and Future Work

Auctions are becoming a popular method for dealing with resource allocation in multi-agent systems. When resources are either renewable or perishable, recurrent auctions are required. These auctions are known to have several problems: the resource waste problem, the bidder drop problem and the asymmetric balance of negotiating power. All these problems have been discussed in this paper, and three new recurrent auction mechanisms have been proposed to cope with them: the use of priorities (priority auction), the use of a variable reservation prices (customizable reservation price auction), and a combination of both (customizable reservation price auction with priorities). We have compared the new mechanisms with well-known auction mechanisms and the results show that our customizable reservation price auction with priorities mechanism achieves the highest benefits. This is due to the fact that the mechanism avoids the resource waste problem, maintains the balance of negotiation power and minimizes the effects of bidder drop problem thanks to the fair solutions. The fairness of the mechanism incentivizes the participation of bidders and consequently improves the auctioneer benefits.

Our future work includes two main directions, one related to the experimentation scenario, and the second one to the auction mechanism. Regarding the experimentation scenario, we are first planning to allow bidders to have a variable demand. In this sense they could bid for different amount of resources (currently only one unit is allowed) or in some auction rounds they could not bid for any resource. Secondly, we want to consider the resource provider (auctioneer) to not have always the same amount of resources, consequently the experimentation scenario could be extended to allow a variable resource supply. This fact can affect the auction mechanism in time of resource scarcity. Regarding the auction mechanism, we are considering to extend it in order to be combinatorial. That means that several items can be considered in a single auction.

Acknowledgments. This research project has been done with the support of the Commissioner for Universities and Research of the Department of Innovation, Universities and Enterprises of Generalitat of Catalonia and of the European Social Funds and DURSI AGAUR SGR 00296 (AEDS).

References

1. Bouveret, S., Lemaitre, M.: Finding leximin-optimal solutions using constraint programming: new algorithms and their application to combinatorial auctions. In: Proc. COMSOC (2006)
2. Burtraw, D., Palmer, K., Bharvirkar, R., Paul, A.: The effect on asset values of the allocation of carbon dioxide emission allowances. The Electricity Journal 15(5), 51–62 (2002)
3. Chevaleyre, P.E., Dunne, U.Y., Endriss, U., Lang, J., Lemaître, M., Maudet, N., Padget, J., Phelps, S., Rodríguez-Aguilar, J.A., Sousa, P.: Issues in multiagent resource allocation. Informatica 30(1), 3–31 (2006)
4. Cramton, P., Shoham, Y., Steinberg, R. (eds.): Combinatorial Auctions. MIT Press, Cambridge (2006)
5. Kalagnanam, J., Parkes, D.C.: Auctions, bidding and exchange design. In: Simchi-Levi, D., Wu, S.D., Shen, Z.M. (eds.) Handbook of Quantitative Supply Chain Analysis: Modeling in the E-Business Era, pp. 143–212. Springer, Heidelberg (2004)
6. Lee, J.-S., Szymanki, B.K.: A novel auction mechanism for selling time-sensitive e-services. In: Proc. 7th International IEEE Conference on E-Commerce Technology (CEC 2005), Munich, Germany, pp. 75–82 (July 2005)
7. Lee, J.-S., Szymanki, B.K.: Stabilizing markets via a novel auction based pricing mechanism for short-term contracts for network services. In: Proc. 9th IFIP/IEEE International Symposium on Integrated Network Management, Nice, France, pp. 367–380 (May 2005)
8. Lee, J.-S., Szymanki, B.K.: Auctions as a dynamic pricing mechanism for e-services. In: Hsu, C. (ed.) Service Enterprise Integration, pp. 131–156. Kluwer Academic Publishers, New York (2006)
9. Muñoz, V., Murillo, J., Busquets, D., López, B.: Improving water quality by coordinating industries schedules and treatment plants. In: AAMAS workshop on Coordinating Agents Plans ans Schedules (CAPS), pp. 1–8 (2007)
10. Murillo, J., Muñoz, V., López, B., Busquets, D.: Dynamic configurable auctions for coordinating industrial waste discharges. In: Petta, P., Müller, J.P., Klusch, M., Georgeff, M. (eds.) MATES 2007. LNCS (LNAI), vol. 4687, pp. 109–120. Springer, Heidelberg (2007)
11. Parkes, D.C.: Iterative Combinatorial Auctions: Achieving Economic and Computational Efficiency. Dissertation proposal, University of Pennsylvania (2000)

12. Payne, T.R., David, E., Jennings, N.R., Sharifi, M.: Auction mechanisms for efficient advertisement selection on public displays. In: ECAI, pp. 285–289 (2006)
13. Sandholm, T.W.: Distributed rational decision making. In: Weiss, G. (ed.) Multiagent Systems: A Modern Approach to Distributed Artificial Intelligence, pp. 201–258. The MIT Press, Cambridge (1999)

Multi-Agent Reinforcement Learning for Intrusion Detection: A Case Study and Evaluation

Arturo Servin and Daniel Kudenko

Department of Computer Science, University of York
Heslington, York. YO10 5DD, United Kingdom
{aservin,kudenko}@cs.york.ac.uk

Abstract. In this paper we propose a novel approach to train *Multi-Agent Reinforcement Learning* (MARL) agents to cooperate to detect intrusions in the form of normal and abnormal states in the network. We present an architecture of distributed sensor and decision agents that learn how to identify normal and abnormal states of the network using *Reinforcement Learning* (RL). Sensor agents extract network-state information using tile-coding as a function approximation technique and send communication signals in the form of actions to decision agents. By means of an on line process, sensor and decision agents learn the semantics of the communication actions. In this paper we detail the learning process and the operation of the agent architecture. We also present tests and results of our research work in an intrusion detection case study, using a realistic network simulation where sensor and decision agents learn to identify normal and abnormal states of the network.

1 Introduction

Intrusion Detection Systems (IDS) play an important role in the protection of computer networks and information systems from intruders and attacks. Despite previous research efforts there are still areas where IDS have not satisfied all requirements of modern computer systems. Specifically, *Denial of Service* (DoS) and *Distributed Denial of Service* (DDoS) attacks have received significant attention due to the increased security vulnerabilities in end-user software and bot-nets [12]. A special case of DoS are the *Flooding-Base DoS* and *Flooding-Base DDoS* attacks. These are generally based on a flood of packets with the intention of overfilling the network resources of the victim. It is especially difficult to create a flexible hand-coded IDS for such attacks, and machine learning is a promising avenue to tackle the problem. Due to the distributed nature of this type of attacks and the complexities that involve its detection, we propose a distributed reinforcement learning (RL) approach.

In order to evaluate our technique we explore its use in *Distributed Intrusion Detection Systems* (DIDS). Distributed Intrusion Detection Systems (DIDS) is a group of IDS or sensors coordinated to detect anomalies or intrusions. The system can be homogeneous with every sensor of the same kind and type or

R. Bergmann et al. (Eds.): MATES 2008, LNAI 5244, pp. 159–170, 2008.

heterogeneous with a mixture of types. We build our DIDS approach by training a group of heterogeneous sensor agents that must identify normal and abnormal states of the network resulting from Flood-Base DoS and DDoS. We have used the detection of these attacks to test our learning approach for the following reasons:

- Some researchers [2,19] note that a variety of sensor information is required to detect attacks with high levels of confidence.
- The type of attacks disrupt the operation of the network by modifying state information. Spotting these abnormal states can lead to the detection of a flooding attack.
- The abnormal states are characterised by several factors that are normally present in different part of the network and they are only visible to specific networks devices. To identify these events, it is not possible to use a single device or entity.
- To identify events around the network that are visible to only some type of agents it is necessary to use distributed specialised agents. These agents only have partial observability of the whole environment (network).

In addition to proposing a distributed RL approach for intrusion detection, we adapt and evaluate it in a realisic network simulation using the *ns-2* [20] simulator. In this way, we are able to demonstrate the practical applicability of our approach.

2   Technology Overview

Flood-Base DoS and DDoS attacks change the normal behaviour of the network in different ways and spotting these differences could help us to detect the presence of attacks [14]. The distributed operation of these attacks brings on the opportunity to use a distributed and adaptable platform to detect them. We propose to use an architecture based on MARL agents.

IDS are commonly divided in two functional categories; *Anomaly Intrusion Detection* and *Misuse/Signature Intrusion Detection*. Anomaly IDS states that intrusions are deviations of normal traffic. These systems create profiles of different variables over time to get a usage pattern. The difference between the pattern and the current activity triggers an alarm. The advantage of these systems is that they are capable of detecting unknown attacks, however non-malicious activity that does not match normal behaviour can also trigger the intrusion mechanism. This results in a high rate of *false alarms*. On the other hand misuse or signature intrusion detection systems use rule matching to detect intrusions. These systems compare system activity with specific intrusion rules that are generally hard coded. When the observed activity matches the intrusion pattern an intrusion is detected and an action is executed. The flaw of these systems is that regardless of their accuracy and reliability they lack the ability to detect new types of attacks.

Anomaly Intrusion Detection Systems use a variety of schemes to detect normal user patterns from simple statistical to complex machine learning methods.

Although most of the research on IDS using machine learning has been done under an Anomaly Intrusion Detection approach, recent research work incorporates *Machine Learning* to automatic rule generation on misuse/signature intrusion detection. IDS using machine learning try to learn a function that maps input information into different categories. The learning process can be supervised, unsupervised or reinforced.

In Reinforcement Learning an agent learns to act optimally via observations and feedback from the environment in the form of positive or negative rewards [23]. A widely used RL technique is *Q-learning* [24]. In Q-learning the agent iteratively tries to estimate a Q value function that tells the agent how good it is to perform a specific action in a given state. In Q-learning the agent chooses an action a in any given state s, observes the reward r and the next state s'. Then it updates the estimated Q value denoted by $\hat{Q}$ in Eq. 1.

$$\hat{Q}(s,a) \leftarrow (1 - \alpha)\hat{Q}(s,a) + \alpha(r + \gamma\ max_a\ \hat{Q}(s',a')) \qquad (1)$$

In order to discover which actions lead to the best rewards over time, the agent needs to *explore* and to *exploit* actions. In our experiments we have used *Boltzmann* or *softmax action selection rules* as the exploration/exploitation strategy. When RL is used in real world applications, it is not feasible to store values for all states individually. To tackle this problem we use Tile Coding, a *function approximation* technique.

MARL has shown promise in solving distributed problems, but there are many challenges to overcome when applying it in a realistic network domain, e.g., feature selection, communication, and synchronisation. In a DIDS architecture we require a large number of distributed agents collecting complex network information and coordinating their action under restricted communication.

3   Agent Architecture

In previous research [17], we used a highly abstract IDS scenario to test how a group of agents learn to interpret and coordinate their action signals to detect normal and abnormal activity. We proposed a hierarchical architecture of agents composed by groups of agents or cells. These cells were composed by *sensor agents* (SA) and *decision agents* (DA). SA collect and analyse state information about the environment. Each SA receives only partial information about the global state of the environment and they map this local state to communications action-signals. These signals are received by the DA and without any previous knowledge it learns their semantics and how to interpret their meaning. In this way, the DA tries to model the local state of cell environment. Then it decides which signal-action to execute to a higher level agent outside the cell or in single cell environments the final action to trigger (in our case study it triggers an alarm to the network operator). To expand the number of agents we used hierarchical multi-cell architectures composed of cells of DAs. In these multi-cell environments each DA inside the cells sends an action-signal to a central DA, which in turn sends an action-signal to a higher level DA. When the top agent in the hierarchy triggers the appropriate action, all the agents in the cell receive a positive reward. If the action is not correct, all the agents receive a negative reward. The goal is to coordinate the signals sent by the SA to the DA in order to represent the global state of the environment. After a certain number of iterations every agent must know the action that they need to execute in a specific state to obtain positive rewards.

This agent architecture may be used in a diverse set of environments to solve different kind of problems. In our past research work we designed a highly abstract simulation of a distributed sensor network. This environment gave us the opportunity to test the basic feasibility of the agent learning architecture using an abstract environment containing simple network agents. However, the question remained open how the approach would work with more complex and realistic network topologies, traffic patterns and connections. In order to evaluate our learning architecture of agents and to add elements and the complexity of real applications, in this paper we used the network simulator *ns-2* [20], a specifically designed library for ns-2 and the *Tile Coding Software* [22].

To detect the abnormal states that DoS and DDoS generate in a computer network we have slightly modified the original agent architecture as shown in Fig. 1. This architecture is composed by single cell with a Congestion Sensor Agent (CSA), a Delay Sensor Agent (DSA), a Flow Sensor Agent (FSA) and the Decision Agent (DA). We need this diversity of sensor information to develop more reliable IDS. The idea is that each sensor agent perceives different information depending on their capabilities, their operative task and where they are deployed in the network. Furthermore not all the features are available in a single point in the network. Flow and congestion information may be measured in a border router between the Internet and the Intranet whilst delay information may be only available from an internal router. What is more, Flood-Based DDoS attacks are launched from several remote controlled sources trying to exhaust a target's key resource. A stand-alone IDS does not have all the information to accurately identify sources and destinations of DDoS attacks.

In our test domain, the CSA analyses link information on a particular node in the network. It is advisable to use a representative node inside the network topology such as a backbone router or a border router in front of the node or service to protect from intrusions. Specifically this agent samples link utilisation in bytes per second, the size of the queue in packets and the number of packets drop by the queue. These three metrics (link utilisation, queue size and packets drop) are what we call our *feature domain*. To obtain a state representation of the network according with these features we use *tile coding*. The DSA monitors TCP connections between nodes. As previously stated DoS and DDoS attacks modify the normal behaviour of the network in many ways. Some of these changes can be spotted analysing TCP information from connections in the path of the attack. This agent has the same internal structure than the CSA but its feature domain is different. The features analysed for the TCP connections are the average number of ACK packets received, the average window size and the average Round Trip Time (RTT).

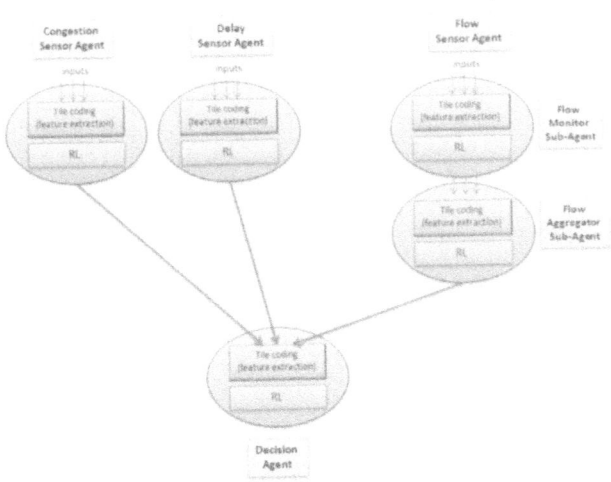

Fig. 1. Agent Architecture

The FSA has a different internal structure than the other sensor agents as can be seen in Fig. 1. This agent is composed by two logical sub-agents, the Flow Monitor (FM) and the Flow Aggregator (FA). The FM analyses the traffic flows that pass through the FSA and its feature domain is composed by protocol number, port number and the average packet size of the flow. Using this information the FM learns which flows are normal traffic and which ones may lead to an attack. The FA aggregates flow information by keeping a flow table with the signals reported by the FM. The feature domain of the FA is very simple. It is the number of attack flows reported by the FM. Finally the original DA described previously does not suffer any modification in its structure, functionality or operation.

4 Tests

To find out whether the agent architecture along with the proposed learning process were capable of detecting abnormal states of the network we performed a series of tests. To add some realistic elements and the complexity of real applications, in this paper we used the network simulator *ns-2* [20]. We generated the network topology of Fig. 2 composed by 7 agents or nodes. Node 0 generates normal FTP-like traffic while node 1 produces normal UDP traffic. Node 4 is an attacker producing a flood of UDP traffic. Node 5 is logically divided in two RL sensor agents, one CSA and one FSA. Their tasks are to forward traffic and collect data about the network. Node 6 is the DA and it solely works as a RL agent. Finally Node 3 is the DSA. It receives valid data from nodes 0 and 1 and it is the node under attack as well.

To measure the success of the performed tests we used a variety of metrics (See Table 1). The most common metrics used to measure the detection performance

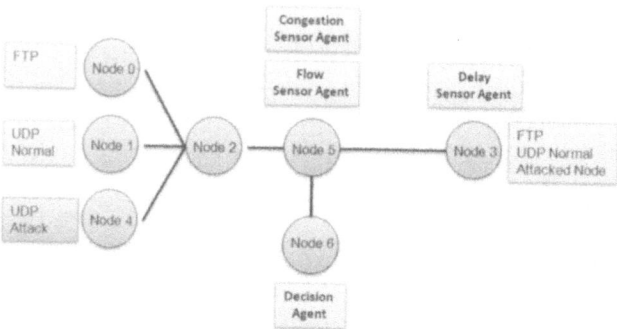

Fig. 2. Tested Network

of IDS are the *false alarm* rate and the *attack detection rate*. The false alarm rate is the fraction of the total alarms that do not represent an intrusion. We will refer to them as *False Positives* (FP) as well. *False Negatives* is the fraction of the total number of intrusions that were not categorized as intrusion. The intrusion detection rate or precision is the fraction of the total number of alarms that were identified as intrusions. To assist us in the design and evaluation of our results we also introduced other prediction metrics commonly used in bioinformatics and machine learning. *Recall* is introduced to show the number of malicious events that the IDS fail to categorise as negative instances. To verify that the IDS is learning how to detect attacks this measure is important to observe. In a similar fashion, accuracy relates all the variables together to an intuitive idea of the performance of the IDS system in relation with the number of correct events categorised. It is important to mention that all the described measures will not properly reflect performance well where the probability of intrusion is very low.

We set up several tests to verify the learning capabilities of the agents as shown in Table 2. We used a control test (Baseline) to train the agents to categorise

Table 1. Performance Metrics 1

Measure	Formula	Meaning
False Positive Rate	FP / (TP + FP)	The fraction of non negative instances that was redicted as negative
Intrusion Detection Rate	TP / (TP + FP)	The percentage of negative labeled instances that was predicted as negative
Events	TP + TN + FP FN	The total number of events
Accuracy	(TP + TN) / (TP + TN + FP + FN)	The percentage of positive predictions that is correct
Recall	TP / (TP + FN)	The percentage of negative labeled instances that was predicted as negative
Specificity	TN / (TN + FP)	The percentage of predictions that is correct

basic normal and abnormal activity in the network. To simulate the normal traffic we randomly started and stopped connections from node 0 (TCP/FTP) and node 1 (UDP stream). Using another random pattern of connections we used node 4 to simulate the attacks to the network characterised by a flood of UDP traffic. At time $t = 0$ each one of the agents started gathering information from the network and learning as previously explained. At time t_{final} we stopped the learning process and we stored the values of the weight array w in order to use them in each one of the tests of Table 2.

To evaluate the adaptability of the agents we ran test 2 to 8. During these tests the agents are not learning anymore and they are exploiting the knowledge acquired during the training with the baseline test (test 1). Test 2 considers an identical network topology as in test 1 but with different traffic patterns. In this test we modify the start-stop times of the data traffic from the no-attack and attack nodes. Tests 3 to 5 were designed to create a more complex scenario where the attacker changes its attack to mimic authorised or normal traffic. Test 3 simulates when the attacker changes the attack port to any other given port while in test 4 we change the attack port to be the same as the authorised application. In test 5 we simulated when the attacker goes further and changes the attack port and the packet size to mimic the no-attack application. Tests 6 to 8 modify the network topology adding more sources of traffic. These test are important because they modify some of the features that the learning process uses to detect intrusions such as link information, number of flows, packets transmitted per flow type, etc. Specifically in test 6 we added multiple UDP sources and in test 7 we added multiple FTP sources, both of them are valid applications. Finally in test 8 we added multiple attackers as UDP sources to simulate a DDoS attack.

Table 2. Tests

Test Description	
1	Baseline test
2	Traffic pattern change
3	Attack port change
4	Attack port same as no attack application
5	Attack port and packet size same as no attack application
6	Multiple valid UDP sources
7	Multiple valid FTP sources
8	Multiple attack sources

5   Results

Unless stated otherwise, we have performed our entire set of tests using the feature domains for sensor and decision agents described in section 2. In Fig. 3 we show the performed tests (1 to 8) evaluated using false positive rate, recall and accuracy. A low false positive rate indicates that our agents will not overwhelm the network operator. A high recall indicates that the agents are able to identify attacks while

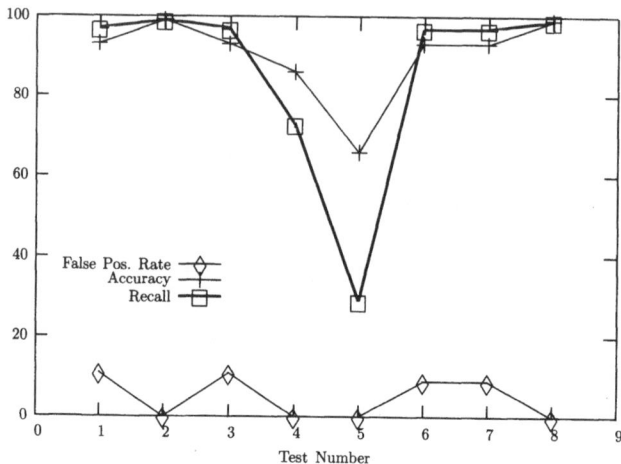

Fig. 3. Test 1-8 and Flow Feature Domain 1

they maintain a low number of false negatives (unidentified attacks). Finally a high level of accuracy indicates that the system is capable of identifying attacks while generating few false positives. The intrusion detection rate (IDR) is another important metric but it can be misleading given a certain type of traffic (e.g. the IDR can be high when the system recognises few attacks but the number of FP is low). Excluding test 5, the remaining tests show acceptable levels of all the intrusion detection metrics including accuracy and recall. Test 2 shows remarkably good levels of accuracy and recall as result of the modified traffic pattern with longer and fewer *no-attack/attack cycles*. A smaller number of no-attack/attack cycles means a small number of FN and FP due to the synchronisation issue between the DA and the collected network information. Contrary to test 2, tests 5 shows a low level of accuracy and recall. Remember that test 5 simulates when the attacker changes the information of the IP packet (protocol, port and packet size) of its attack to mimic a valid connection. In this case when there is an attack the FA interprets the flow information as a no-attack. However the CSA and DSA interpret the network information correctly. When the action signals are transmitted to the DA any of these scenarios may happen:

1. Even though the FA is reporting a no-attack, the signals for the CSA and DSA activate the DA weights that trigger an alarm-action.
2. The signals for the CSA and DSA are not strong enough to activate the alarm-action and the DA triggers a no-alarm-action.
3. The signals from the sensor agents activate weights with similar values for both actions and the DA trigger a *do-not-know action*. In other words, a do-not-know action denotes that the DA does not have enough evidence to trigger a committed action such as an alarm or no-alarm.

In test 5 when the attacks start the congestion and delay value measured by sensor agents are similar to the no-attack states causing the DA to trigger an incorrect action generating a FN. As the attack progresses the congestion and delay information make the current state appear to the DA as a no-attack but not strong enough to trigger a no-alarm action. Instead, the DA triggers the do-not-know action. Finally when the attack is at its peak, the signals from the DSA and CSA make the value of the alarm action better than the no-alarm and the DA triggers the alarm. A similar behaviour takes places when the attacker slows down its attack.

Trying to improve the intrusion detection metrics we ran more tests changing the feature domain of the sensor agents. This task showed the difficulty of choosing an optimal set of features, as in many applications of machine learning. While some sets improved the metric for some tests, they also showed worse results for other tests. The set of features presented in the past section yielded the best results overall.

In order to compare our learning IDS to alternative approaches, we implemented two common hand-coded (i.e., non-adaptive) IDS techniques. The first hand-coded approach (Hand-Coded 1) emulated a misuse IDS. In this case the IDS is looking for the patterns that match an attack in the same way that some commercial misuse IDS do in real world networks, e.g. Snort [21] and Checkpoint [6]. To evaluate a more complex IDS implementation the Hand-Coded 2 approach integrates the same variety of input information as our learning algorithm. This approach is similar to the one employed in some commercial Intrusion Protection System (IPS) such as the Cisco Intrusion Prevenstion System Sensor [7]. These type of devices search for intrusions through signature and anomaly detection methods. We evaluated the learning and hard-coded approaches using test 2 and test 5. We used test 2 because it only changes the traffic pattern of the attack and it must be very simple to detect. Attacks in test 5 are the hardest to detect because they emulate some of the signatures of normal traffic. The learning curves of the test are shown in Fig.4.

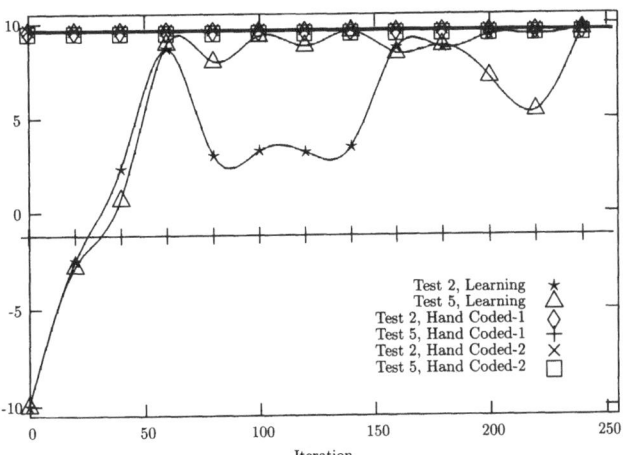

Fig. 4. Learning Curves

The Hand-Coded 1 approach had no problem to identify attacks and had low false negatives for test 2 but it completely failed to detect attacks in test 5. This is the same problem that misuse IDS have when the signature of the attack changes or when they face unknown attacks. The results for Hand-Coded 2 and our learning approach confirm our argument that for more reliable intrusion detection we need a variety of information sources. On test 5 the learning and the Hand Coded 2 approaches were capable of detecting the attacks even though one of the sensors was reporting incorrect information. This scenario also could be seen as the emulation of a broken or comprimesed sensor forced to send misleading signals.

Both the Hand-coded 2 and learning approaches present very good results regarding the identification of normal and abnormal states in the network. Hand-coded 2 reaches maximum performance from the beginning of the simulation. Nevertheless it has a major drawback, it requires in-depth knowledge from the policy programmer about the the network traffic and patterns in order to detect intrusions. While the learning algorithm requires some time to learn to recognise normal and abnormal activity, it does not require any previous knowledge about the behaviour of the network or exactly which features to observe. Although different sets of features show different results, the learning approach's flexibility allows the use of any (large enough) set of features to achieve some reasonable level of detection. The learning approach automatically will use the interesting features to detect attacks and it will ignore the ones that do not represent different states.

6   Related Work

Problems such as the curse of dimensionality; partial observability and scalability in MARL have been analysed using a variety of methods and techniques [15,18] and they represent the foundation of our research. More recent work related with our research include the use of Hierarchical Reinforcement Learning [10], learning automata [13] and game theory [16]. An application of MARL to networking environments is presented in [3] where cooperative agents learn how to route packets using optimal paths. Using the same approach of flow control and feedback from the environment, other researchers have expanded the use of RL to explore its use to control congestion in networks [8,11], routing using QoS [9] and more recently to control DDoS attacks [25].

The use of RL in the intrusion detection field has not been widely studied and even less in distributed intrusion detection. On IDS with RL research we found [4,5] where the authors trained a neural network using RL and aplied CMAC as the function approximation technique and [1] where game theory is used to train agents to recognise DoS attacks against routing infrastructure. Other recent research work include the use of RL to detect host intrusion using sequence system calls [26] and the previously mentioned [25].

7   Conclusion and Future Work

In this paper we have shown how a group of agents can coordinate their actions to reach the common goal of network intrusion detection. During this process decision agents learn how to interpret the action-signals sent by sensor agents without any previously assigned semantics. These action-signals aggregate the partial information received by sensor agents and they are used by the decision agents to reconstruct the global state of the environment. In our case study, we evaluate our learning approach by identifying normal and abnormal states of a realistic network subjected to various DoS attacks. Overall the following conclusions can be drawn:

- We have successfully applied RL in a group of network agents under conditions of partial observability, restricted communication and global rewards in a realistic network simulation.
- The use of a variety of network data has generated good results to identify the state of the network. The system presents high reliability even in cases when some sensor information is missing or compromised.
- The learning approach yields better results than the simple hand coded alternative. It also yields similar results to a more complex hand coded alternative using a variety of sensor information. The main advantage of the learning approach is that it does not need a trainer with prior knowledge of the network environment.

Future work includes evaluating on-line learning (i.e. during deployment of the IDS) and scaling up our learning approach to a large number of agents using the hierarchical approach from our previous work on abstract networks. This will allow us to create more complex network topologies emulating geographical cells of agents, security domains composed by cells or groups of cells, complex DDoS attacks and eventually the emulation of real packet streams inside the network environment.

References

1. Awerbuch, B., Holmer, D., Rubens, H.: Provably Secure Competitive Routing against Proactive Byzantine Adversaries via Reinforcement Learning. John Hopkins University, Tech. Rep. (May 2003)
2. Barford, P., Jha, S., Yegneswaran, V.: Fusion and filtering in distributed intrusion detection systems. In: Proceedings of the 42nd Annual Allerton Conference on Communication, Control and Computing (September 2004)
3. Boyan, J., Littman, M.: Packet routing in dynamically changing networks: A reinforcement learning approach. Advances in Neural Information Processing Systems 6, 671–678 (1994)
4. Cannady, J.: Applying CMAC-based on-line learning to intrusion detection. In: Proceedings of the International Joint Conference on Neural Networks, vol. 5, pp. 405–410 (2000)
5. Cannady, J.: Next Generation Intrusion Detection: Autonomous Reinforcement Learning of Network Attacks. In: Proc. 23rd National Information Systems Security Conference (2000)

6. CheckPoint. CheckPoint, N.G.X.: Firewall SmartDefense (June 2008),
   http://www.checkpoint.com/products/ips-1/index.html
7. Cisco. Configuring Anomaly Detections (June 2008),
   http://www.cisco.com/en/US/docs/security/ips/6.1/configuration/guide/
   cli/cli_anomaly_detection.html
8. Dowling, J., Curran, E., Cunningham, R., Cahill, V.: Using feedback in collaborative reinforcement learning to adaptively optimize MANET routing. Systems, Man
   and Cybernetics, Part A, IEEE Transactions on 35(3), 360–372 (2005)
9. Gelenbe, E., Lent, M., Su, R.: Autonomous smart routing for network QoS. In:
   Proceedings of International Conference on Autonomic Computing 2004, pp. 232–
   239 (2004)
10. Ghavamzadeh, M., Mahadevan, S., Makar, R.: Hierarchical multi-agent reinforce-
    ment learning. Autonomous Agents and Multi-Agent Systems 13(2), 197–229
    (2006)
11. Hwang, K., Tan, S., Hsiao, M., Wu, C.: Cooperative Multiagent Congestion Control
    for High-Speed Networks. Systems, Man and Cybernetics, Part B, IEEE Transac-
    tions on 35(2), 255–268 (2005)
12. Institute, S.: Sans top-20 2007 security risks, 2007 annual update (2008)
13. Katja Verbeeck1, P.V., Nowe, A.: Networks of learning automata and limiting
    games. In: Adaptive Learning Agents and Multi Agent Systems 2007, pp. 171–182
    (2007)
14. Mirkovic, J., Reiher, P.: D WARD, A Source-End Defense against Flooding Denial
    of Service Attacks. Dependable and Secure Computing, IEEE Transactions on 2(3),
    216–232 (2005)
15. Panait, L., Luke, S.: Cooperative multi-agent learning: The state of the art. Au-
    tonomous Agents and Multi-Agent Systems 11(3), 387–434 (2005)
16. Powers, R., Shoham, Y.: New criteria and a new algorithm for learning in multi-
    agent systems. Advances in Neural Information Processing Systems 17, 1089–1096
    (2005)
17. Servin, A.L., Kudenko, D.: Multi-agent Reinforcement Learning for Intrusion De-
    tection. In: Tuyls, K., Nowe, A., Guessoum, Z., Kudenko, D. (eds.) ALAMAS
    2005, ALAMAS 2006, and ALAMAS 2007. LNCS (LNAI), vol. 4865, pp. 211–223.
    Springer, Heidelberg (2008)
18. Shoham, Y., Powers, R., Grenager, T.: If multi-agent learning is the answer, what
    is the question? Artificial Intelligence 171(7), 365–377 (2007)
19. Siaterlis, C., Maglaris, B.: Towards multisensor data fusion for dos detection. In:
    Proc. of the 19th ACM Symposium on Applied Computing, Nicosia, Cyprus, pp.
    439–446 (2004)
20. N. Simulator. 2 (NS2) (January 2008), http://www.isi.edu/nsnam/
21. I. SourceFire. Snort (June 2008), http://www.snort.org/
22. Sutton, R.: Tile Coding Software, Version 2.0 (2007)
23. Sutton, R., Barto, A.: Reinforcement Learning: An Introduction. MIT Press, Cam-
    bridge (1998)
24. Watkins, C., Dayan, P.: Q-learning. Machine Learning 8(3), 279–292 (1992)
25. Xu, X., Sun, Y., Huang, Z.: Defending DDoS Attacks Using Hidden Markov Models
    and Cooperative Reinforcement Learning. In: Yang, C.C., Zeng, D., Chau, M.,
    Chang, K., Yang, Q., Cheng, X., Wang, J., Wang, F.-Y., Chen, H. (eds.) PAISI
    2007. LNCS, vol. 4430, p. 196. Springer, Heidelberg (2007)
26. Xu, X., Xie, T.: A Reinforcement Learning Approach for Host-Based Intrusion
    Detection Using Sequences of System Calls. In: Proceedings of the International
    Conference on Intelligent Computing (2005)

Teaching Distributed Artificial Intelligence with RoboRally

Ingo J. Timm, Tjorben Bogon, Andreas D. Lattner, and René Schumann

Information Systems and Simulation
Goethe University Frankfurt am Main
Robert-Mayer-Str. 10, 60325 Frankfurt, Germany
{timm,tbogon,lattner,reschu}@cs.uni-frankfurt.de

Abstract. Teaching Artificial Intelligence (AI) or multi-agent systems is a challenging task as algorithms are in question which are advantageous in highly complex and dynamic environments. Explaining multi-agent systems (MAS) in lectures requires interactive approaches accompanied by exercises. The key challenge in using practical exercises within lectures on MAS is to establish an environment for testing which is extremely time consuming. It is not reasonable that students do this work as they do have not enough time focussing on the important aspects. In this paper, we introduce a system which supports experimenting with AI and Distributed Artificial Intelligence (DAI) algorithms concurrently to the lecture. Our system is based on a board game called *RoboRally*. Different issues from the field of AI and DAI can be implemented and tested in a kind of challenge.

1 Introduction

Teaching students is an essential part in academic work. Teaching artificial intelligence (AI) or multi-agent systems (MAS) is a challenging task, as algorithms are in question which are advantageous in highly complex and dynamic environments. In order to ensure successful learning, it is useful that students can practise different aspects of the lecture. Explaining MAS in lectures requires interactive approaches accompanied by exercises. With exercises students can explore multiple approaches and configurations of AI algorithms, for instance. The challenge here is the design of exercises which address the core of the topic. Most topics rely on an environment or existing infrastructure, for example an exercise addressing coordination requires a communication infrastructure. Therefore, a specific framework is used in the course, often. Programming and testing within such an environment can be extremely time consuming. Therefore a key challenge in using practical exercises within lectures on MAS is to establish such an environment.

If it is desired to use such a learning environment, it has to be either implemented by the students themselves or it has to be provided by the lecturer. It is not reasonable that the students do this work as they have to do redundant work and do have not enough time focussing on the important aspects of the lecture.

R. Bergmann et al. (Eds.): MATES 2008, LNAI 5244, pp. 171–182, 2008.
© Springer-Verlag Berlin Heidelberg 2008

The main idea of this paper originates from the Artificial Intelligence group at the University of Bremen in 2004 in order to motivate students attending to AI and DAI courses. To do so two effects are addressed: Using a framework that supports the lectures and lets the students implement some tasks to get a more practical access to the content and additionally to motivate students with a game and some competition while evaluating different strategies of AI systems.

During our evaluation of different kinds of board games (Junta, Risk, Cluedo etc.) we found one game that fulfilled our requirements. The board game Rob-oRally[1] offers both aspects. In this board game, robots are "programmed" by players who select actions from a given set of options. We present the game in section 4 in detail. The task of the player, selecting and sequencing actions from a given set, allows a simple interface students have to implement. While the complexity how to implement the interface can be varied by the specified task and environment the robot is acting in.

The first experience teaching Artificial Intelligence with RoboRally was gained during winter term in 2004/05. Recently, the entire environment has been reworked and is used in current lectures. The application of RoboRally within the exercises enabled tasks which are focussed on the key subjects of the lectures only.

The rest of this paper is organized as follows. We address our vision of using a system in teaching in section 2. In section 3 we discuss previous work of teaching systems. We present the current state and first experiences in sections 4 and 5 before the paper ends with a conclusion and ideas for future work.

2   Vision of a Board Game for Lectures

As already mentioned our vision using a board game supporting lectures is to improve the efficiency of learning and teaching as well as to increase the motivation of the students. An experimental approach to the subject taught should enhance comprehensibility and enable learning effects for the long-term memory. Students should be motivated to invest their time, their attention, and their skills in the intense learning of the subject matter of the lecture. The learning effect will therefore be much higher than simply memorizing the contents of slides or scripts [1].

The learning environment should provide an interface which is open for exploring big variety of different MAS and AI techniques. It should be possible to implement every assigned task within an agent. The agent structure can provide a communication interface, a BDI structure [2] and if needed complete or partial world knowledge. Attributes of the game should be changeable to allow for adapting to different exercises.

Search strategies, for instance, are subject of one of the first lectures in AI. There exist different search strategies, each of them with advantages and disadvantages. The lecturer can point out the characteristics to his students but it is hard to understand why some strategies solve some kinds of problems better

---

[1] The board game RoboRally is currently published by Avalon-Hill, see http://www.wizards.com/avalonhill

than others. Using a learning and experimental environment, like the *RoboRally* framework presented here, students can implement different search strategies easily. The environment should offer access to all needed information. Students have only to implement a pathfinding algorithm and should see, presented at a graphical user interface, the consequences of their implemented decision taking, here search strategy. It has to be emphasized that the graphical representation of the programmed behavior is an important factor for the learning effect of the students. Additionally, students can understand the different search strategies better and especially the different characteristics on the basis of their own implementations.

As the subjects have a wide range in the lecture of MAS, it is important that the learning environment is flexible and customizable to support the lecturer during the entire course. At least it should be possible to configure the environment in a way that most problems of the fundamental AI[2] and MAS can be covered by the environment.

Cooperation, for instance, is an important issue in the field of DAI. The fundamentals of cooperations are communications, of course. If students want their programs to cooperate they need a communication infrastructure. Communication should be realizable in form of a centralized blackboard architecture or using message passing concepts, allowing directed communication among the players. The students can either implement these basics on their own or the learning environment provides possibilities therefore.

In this context, one could argue that one could use already existing agent frameworks, like JADE [4], for instance. These frameworks offer already a basic infrastructure but are not designed for teaching in the first place. In consequence, they do not offer the controlled, sandbox like, experimental settings as it is possible in a specific learning environment. An environment focussed on teaching AI therefore has to provide the infrastructure for communication as well.

An aspect that is not that obvious, but as well important is that exercises have to be evaluated and corrected. For the learning success it is important that students get a quick feedback to their solution ideas. Ideally, the students should receive the feedback online without a delay. Unfortunately, during the work students have no chance to evaluate their solutions and estimate if they are on the right track. It would be desirable to have an online system that makes it possible for students to upload their interim solution and to get an immediate report on the solution's degree of task satisfaction, like finding a specified place in our search example. This is helpful because they can see if there are aspects missing in their solution. Additionally, correcting exercises becomes much easier for the lecturer. If all programs are automatically pre-controlled by a program, the testing phase will be less time consuming, if necessary at all. If the evaluation of the exercises is done automatically, it will be possible to hold complete lecture online. For instance, the lectures could be broadcasted by

---

[2] Of course, aspects like natural language processing and computer vision are not covered by our approach. We assume that these subjects are not in the standard curriculum of an introducing AI course (cf. [3]).

video streams and the exercises could be sent by e-mail or published in a web based learning management systems like Blackboard[3], StudIP[4] or Ilias[5]. The exercise solutions can be uploaded by the students and the online evaluation tool revises the solutions. Using these techniques a complete online course can be offered that allows students to learn asynchronously from official lecture hours and independently of their current location.

3 Related Work

In Artificial Intelligence, there is a strong history in playing games. In the beginning of AI, chess was used for many approaches to test and evaluate algorithms. The area of knowledge acquisition and representation initiated different scenarios for benchmarking of approaches (Sisyphus, [5]). Here, there was a task provided which should be solved by the different approaches. Within the priority research program on intelligent agents in business applications funded by the DFG (SPP 1083), there has been a benchmarking of modeling techniques for multi-agent systems in a health-care scenario [6]. In the Artificial Intelligence Group at University of Bremen RoboCup [7] scenarios were used to motivate students. In Summer of 1999, there has been a first course on RoboCup as application area for teaching AI in Bremen.

Surely, RoboCup is one of the most famous teaching platforms for Artificial Intelligence today, as more than hundred teams from elementary schools up to groups of students from universities all over the world are involved in programming soccer teams trying to win the world championship [8]. But actually there is one problem with the *RoboCup* as a learning environment. Due to the actual progresses the technical level is comparable high and thus there exist high barriers to enter for new teams. A new team has to write many lines of code to achieve the premises of a special league. One single lecture is too short to develop a robot where we can test different AI tasks.

There are many other tools where a game is used for teaching. *ROBO-CODE* allocates an environment in *Java* where students can develop robots for a better understanding of *Java* techniques [9]. The program teaches the students in the fields of event-driven programming, object-oriented programming, and the usefulness of inheritance. Furthermore, they can learn something about learning and some higher level AI techniques. The students see their robots on a Graphical User Interface (GUI) where the robots fight against each other. But the environment is too simple to test high level AI tasks like learning systems and the focus is set to learn programming.

Teaching simple agent systems for undergraduate students is the appreciation of *FLEEBLE*. In this system, simple agents can communicate and demonstrate how a MAS works. It is easier to understand how a MAS works if all attributes and procedures of an agent are visualized by a program [10]. The communication,

---

[3] http://www.blackboard.com/us/index.bbb
[4] http://www.campussource.de/software/studip/
[5] http://www.ilias.de/

beliefs and states of the agents are presented in *FLEEBLE* as a scene. But this system is designed to demonstrate multi-agent systems and does not allow to integrate AI. The aim is to show how agents work together.

Another part of teaching is the area of e-learning. An example for an intense way of e-learning is the Virtual Atlantis University[6]. This university provides courses all over the internet. People can study from home and do their exercises online. The lectures are also available online. A lot of partners provide project-based offers and support this university. Our system is the next step for online lectures and could be integrated in this virtual university easily. In combination with a virtual lecture on video a complete class could learn AI techniques theoretically and practically.

The last project we want to present is *Sisyphus*. *Sisyphus* provides a uniform modeling environment which allows different software engineering projects to collaborate together building one model [5]. The underlying idea is to establish a benchmarking environment to various knowledge acquisition and representation techniques. For the use in teaching AI especially supporting exercises *Sisyphus* is not covering a sufficient range of AI or DAI.

The approaches we introduced above deal with specific tasks in supporting courses or benchmarking research. However, the complexity or initial barrier to take part is not adequate with respect to our course design. Thus, we aim at combining the advantages of the approaches and realize our vision of an innovative learning environment supporting nowadays AI and DAI lectures.

4   Current State of the RoboRally Framework

4.1   RoboRally – The Board Game

RoboRally is a racing game where different robots located in one plant try, apart from survival, to pass a number of checkpoints. The plant is represented by a map and is the environment the robots act in. The map seems like a simple grid but many tiles on the map have an effect. If there is no wall between two tiles, a robot can make a step. An example of such a map is shown in figure 1. In this environment obstacles, like walls, and traps, like laser beams or bottomless pits exist. Robots have a health state and a limited numbers of lives. Initially, the health state has a value of nine. If its health state drops to zero, the agent will lose a life, and will start again from the tile it started the game with full health state. If all lives are lost, the robot is taken out of the game.

The agents can move with predefined actions represented by program cards. A card defines a movement behavior, like drive ahead, drive reverse, turn left, turn right or U-turn. Each program card has a unique priority value. Some examples are shown in figure 2. The game is split into two phases:

Phase 1: According to the current health state, each player gets a set of randomly chosen program cards (nine cards at highest health; for each missing

---

[6] http://www.aida.h-da.de/projects/atlantis_university.html

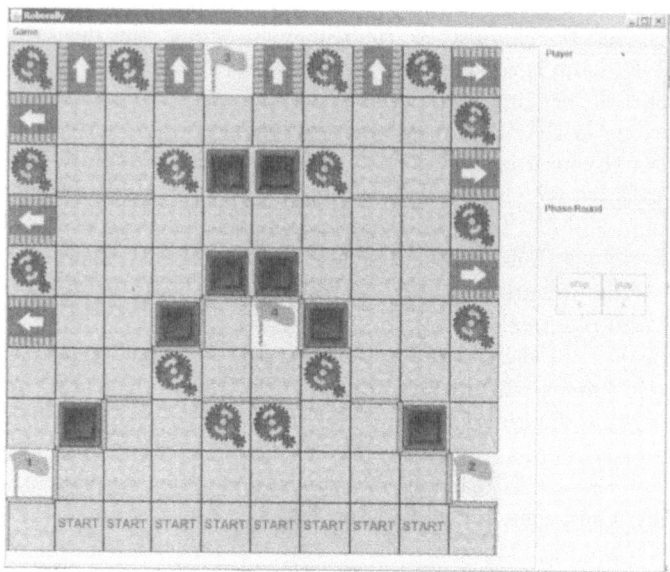

Fig. 1. An exemplified *RoboRally* map

Fig. 2. A set of program cards

health point one card less). Each player programs its robot by selecting and sequencing a subset of five program cards out of the card set he received. If he gets less than five cards, the last movements of the previous movement phase are frozen and cannot be replaced.

Phase 2: In this phase, the program of each robot is executed. This phase is divided into five turns. In each turn one program card is executed for each robot. So all first cards of the robots have to be executed in the primary turn, then all second and so on. Within one turn the sequence of execution is defined by the priority of the cards. A card with higher priority is executed first. If all robots have executed a movement, the robots fire their own laser in their direction. If a laser hits a robot, the health decreases by one. After this step, the map tile effects are executed (conveyors, lasers, bumpers etc.).

So even if it seems a trivial task to pass all checkpoints, the complexity in the game is still quite high. The different kinds of map tiles have effects on the robots. These effects can be predicted by the player but if more than one robot plays in the same game, the behavior of this robot is not predictable. The reason is that if a robot makes his move and goes to a map tile where another robots stands, he pushes this robot one tile (or more tiles) away into his move direction. The problem is that no replanning is possible in the next turn. The (expected) perfect order of the movement cards is not perfect anymore if the robot is not at the predicted position. This case could only be prevented if the agent considered possible moves of the other agents.

4.2 RoboRally – The Learning Environment

In *RoboRally* the challenge aspect is supported inherently. If each agent is programmed by a group of students, they can compete against each other within one race. Furthermore in *RoboRally* every aspect of the game itself (setup, rules, rounds) can be implemented without programming the intelligence, namely the behavior control of the robots. In the board game, the player is setting the cards in each round. This allows to design a framework with a simple interface which can be used by the students. Moreover, the environment of *RoboRally* is determined and all states are well known except the next moves of the other robots. Another point why *RoboRally* is adequate for teaching is that the complexity of the tasks is highly configurable by small changes of the environment and the task to achive. It is possible to define tasks that have a lower complexity than playing the entire game, search for a checkpoint for example. If the robot has a full spectrum of movements or only a few different moves, the complexity of building the best path to the goal changes immediately.

We have developed the *RoboRally* system in Java from scratch and have built an *eclipse* plug-in. This plug-in allows an easy integration in a state-of-the-art IDE[7], offers the students the option to focus on the core of the exercise (see figure 3).Most of the framework is hidden from the student by design. Only the API of some public classes and the agent class, presented in more detail below and in code-listing 1.1, is available for the students.

```java
public class agent implements AITask {
    public String getName(){
        // TODO: add your group name here
        return "your_group_name_here";
    }
    public Card[] generateTurn(Card[] useableCards){
        // TODO: add your code here
        return useableCards;
    }
}
```

Listing 1.1. Simple student interface to build their agents

To configure the environment, a typically *eclipse* run dialog is preferred to specialize some tasks for some cases or to run a normal game. Different kinds of maps can be loaded and can be built with the map editor. In the map editor

---

[7] http://www.eclipse.org

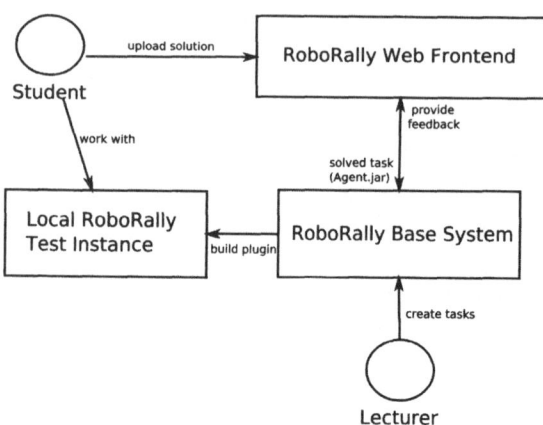

Fig. 3. Workflow of the *RoboRally* system

the map size and all tiles of the map can be defined by a simple "point and click" mechanism (see figure 4). Thereby new challenges or exercises are simply designed by editing a new map. Within the run-dialog other options, like activating the laser beams or the available program card set for each round is defined. This eases the task of specifying the problem instances needed to present specific exercises for different problems in AI. In order to develop an agent, students only have to implement the agent interface (figure 1.1). All decisions for the behavior can be made in the procedure *generateTurn*. The robot gets program cards from the game instance and has to observe the actual game state to find a solution for selecting and sequencing the program cards. In the current version, all map tiles are known and the robot has a complete world model without noisy perception.

After the agent has been implemented by the students our system offers different options how to proceed next. From the user's perspective our system is split into three parts:

Compute a game: The student can run a game with different settings and maps. The game takes the implemented agents and computes their steps. All actions are recorded and stored in a log file in an XML format.

Play a log file: A stored game can be loaded from a log file. The *RoboRally* environment contains a log file player. With this player it is possible to visualize all the movements of the agents and their interference.

Build a map: To create an environment for robots, either for creating a new exercise or for testing a solution strategy in different environments, a map builder can be used.

The integration of the different agents is very simple. The agent's source must be built as a *jar* file. The program scans a specific folder on the system and searches for new *jar* files. If there are some files, the files are loaded to build a new agent in *RoboRally*. The students have to copy their *jar* file into the right folder manually for testing. Our system allows to declare the position of the file and integrate it automatically.

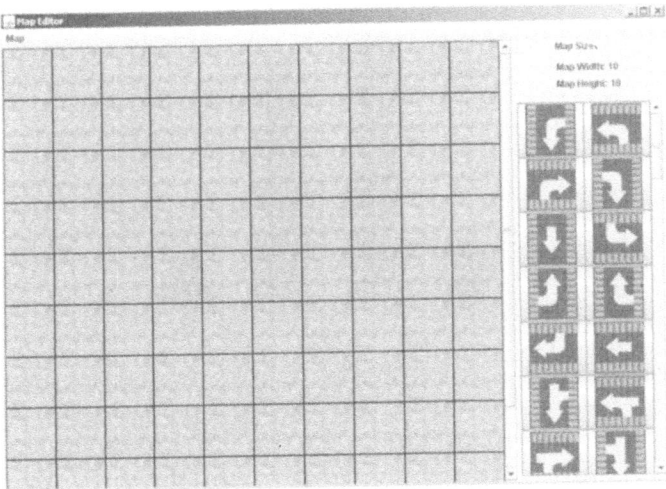

Fig. 4. The *RoboRally* map editor

5 First Experiences

Our first tests using *RoboRally* in a lecture started in the winter term 2004/05. In this test phase a very early version of *RoboRally* was used which contained no GUI and only one agent could exist on the map at the same time. Of course, this limited the range of exercises the framework could be used for. The API was in a beta-stage as well. In the course evaluation (see figure 5), the students evaluated the usage of *RoboRally* as good (with a score of 2.4 in average by 33 persons; good = 1 and bad = 4). Thereby, they criticized the missing GUI and the lack of documentation. From personal comments of the students we could see that the idea of using such a platform like *RoboRally* is helpful and motivating.

The current version of the *RoboRally* framework is used in a course called "Simulation of autonomous systems" in summer term 2008. The GUI has been reworked entirely. A lot of updates enhance the game. Up to ten different robots programmed by students can play against or with each other at the same time. Different exercises can be chosen by the run dialog of our plug-in. This enhances the possibility of creating specified exercises. At the moment five different tasks can be chosen.

1. ***Regular game***: This is the standard game. The robots have to chose the right cards and drive through all check points. Another variation of this game type is to find the shortest way to one check point.
2. ***Last man standing***: In this game mode, the agents have to challenge against each other. The goal is to be the last robot alive. All robots can fire once every move.
3. ***Capture the flag***: This is a variation of the shortest way version from the regular game. The game finishes after all robots have arrived at the goal flag. In this mode, it is possible to see the ranking of all robots.

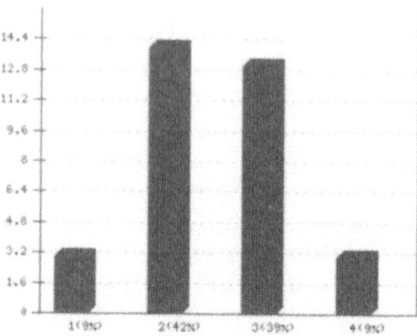

Fig. 5. Evaluation by the students (Question: How is your experience using RoboRally in the course?)

4. ***Build a chain***: At the moment the sole cooperative mode. All robots build up one team and have to create a chain from the start point to the goal point with there body. If they got one chain continually without a leak the game will finish.
5. ***Sokuban***: The goal of the Sokuban mode is to push a dummy robot (who does not move) from his position to the goal position.

Another way to specialize the exercises is to change the world environment. Every game can be played with laser or without shooting. The lives of the robots and different kind of cardsets[8] can be chosen. Combined with different maps there are a lot of possibilities to create motivating challenges. The students of the course had a lot of fun and learned how to build agents with AI or how to cooperate with other agents. The reply of the students was great. The students have tested many algorithms to find the best strategy for their agents. One special positive effect is that copying of solutions seems to be quite low. Every student keeps his strategy secret and does not share it because he wants to win the challenge.

As the framework is still under development the documentation is still subject of changes.

6   Conclusion and Future Work

Learning environments, like the *RoboRally* framework presented here, can support both, students and lecturers.

In our vision we point out that learning environments for exercises are needed to support successful learning. As we did not find an existing environment that can support exercises in an appropriate way, we searched for a motivating board game that can be easily implemented and explained to students. *RoboRally* meets all our requirements. So we are developing the *RoboRally* learning environment which we presented here.

---

[8] There is the normal *RoboRally* card set and a normalized card set providing all possible cards.

In the current version different game types could be realized, like pathfinding, survival of the fittest, align the robots in a chain of heterogenous programmed robots without direct communication and of course, play the game according to the official rules. As our preliminary evaluation indicates the motivation of the students is higher and they understand complex problems easier. Another aspect is that the evaluation of solutions to exercises can be done more rapidly.

RoboRally is currently used in our lectures and evolves very quickly. In the next steps the communication interface will be integrated in the framework to allow different robots to communicate with each other. This implies that the different robots compute their plans and actions in parallel to ensure an adequate communication behavior of the robots. In such a scenario one could think of implementing a marketplace or negotiation on program cards. Thereby one could demonstrate different properties of auction protocols here. The aspect of automated exercise correction will also be addressed in upcoming extensions of the framework which will allow faster feedback for students. One could think of a pre-controlling before the submission of a solution, and easier work for the lecturer who can spend more time to evaluate the relevant parts of the solutions and give more sophisticated feedback to the students.

Acknowledgment

The first version of *RoboRally* has been developed in the AI research group (Prof. Dr. Otthein Herzog) at the University of Bremen by Arne Hormann under supervision of Thorsten Scholz and Ingo J. Timm. The e-learning fund of the Goethe-University of Frankfurt is supporting the current developments of the *RoboRally* project. We would like to thank our student research assistants Tim Föller, Moritz Jäger, Erik Rohnfeld, and Markus Schmid for their great work on *RoboRally*.

References

1. McConnell, J.J.: Active learning and its use in computer science. In: ITiCSE 1996: Proceedings of the 1st conference on Integrating technology into computer science education, pp. 52–54. ACM, New York (1996)
2. Rao, A.S., Georgeff, M.P.: BDI Agents: From Theory to Practice. Technical Node 56, Australian Artificial Intelligence Institute (April 1995)
3. Russell, S., Norvig, P.: Artificial Intelligence: A Modern Approach, 2nd edn. Prentice Hall, Pearson Education, Inc., Upper Saddle River (2003)
4. JADE: Jade - java agent development framework (accessed on April 23, 2008) (2008), http://jade.tilab.com/
5. Dutoit, A.H., Wolf, T., Paech, B., Borner, L., Ruckert, J.: Using rationale for software engineering education. In: CSEET 2005: Proceedings of the 18th Conference on Software Engineering Education & Training, Washington, DC, USA, pp. 129–136. IEEE Computer Society, Los Alamitos (2005)
6. Kirn, S. (ed.): 2. Kolloquium zum DFG-Schwerpunktprogramm Intelligente Softwareagenten und betriebswirtschaftliche Anwendungen, TU-Ilmenau (2000)

7. Kitano, H., Asada, M., Noda, I., Matsubara, H.: RoboCup: Robot world cup. Robotics & Automation Magazine, IEEE 5(3), 30–36 (1998)
8. Lakemeyer, G., Sklar, E., Sorrenti, D.G., Takahashi, T. (eds.): RoboCup 2006: Robot Soccer World Cup X. LNCS (LNAI), vol. 4434. Springer, Heidelberg (2007)
9. Hartness, K.: Robocode: using games to teach artificial intelligence. J. Comput. Small Coll. 19(4), 287–291 (2004)
10. Pantic, M., Grootjans, R.J., Zwisterloot, R.: Fleeble Agent Framework for Teaching an Introductory Course in AI. In: CELDA, pp. 525–532 (2004)

Refactoring in Multi Agent System Development

Ali Murat Tiryaki, Erdem Eser Ekinci, and Oguz Dikenelli

Ege University, Department of Computer Engineering,
35100 Bornova, Izmir, Turkey
ali.murat.tiryaki@ege.edu.tr, erdemeserekinci@gmail.com,
oguz.dikenelli@ege.edu.tr

Abstract. The need for XP-like agile approaches that provide evolutionary development in a flexible way has been widely acknowledged in the AOSE area. Such approaches improve acceptability of agent-technology by industry. Evolutionary development of multi agent systems-MASs can only be applied successfully, if designs of the MASs being developed are improved throughout the development process. In this paper, we introduce a refactoring approach that can be used during evolutionary MAS development. The proposed refactoring approach makes it possible to develop MASs in an evolutionary way by managing the changes between the iterations of the evolutionary development process. Also, a case study that shows application of a refactoring technique during the evolutionary MAS development is introduced in the fifth section.

1 Introduction

Based on the experiences on agent-based system development, AOSE research community has realized that it is almost impossible to develop a complex system such as multi agent system - MAS in a sequential manner [15,4]. The solution is the iterative approach which has been accepted as one of the best practices by software development community and integrated to all recent software development methodologies such as rational unified process - RUP [11] and extreme programming - XP [1].

Managing the continuous evolution of the software architecture and related design is one of the key issues in iterative development. XP introduces two critical practices to manage the evolution of the architecture: test driven development [9] and refactoring [7]. Test driven development produces test code for each class developed during iteration and provides a protection shield against the breaks that can occur as a result of changes made on the working code by guaranteeing the functional accuracy of this code via the tests. On the other hand, refactoring defines a process for improving the structure of the software system without altering the external behavior.

An iterative and incremental development life-cycle approach is quite appropriate for developing dynamic systems such as MASs. For agent-based development, XP-like agile processes, that introduce light-weight practices for iterative and incremental development in a controllable way, are needed to improve acceptability of the agent-technology by the industry [4,15]. However, traditional

R. Bergmann et al. (Eds.): MATES 2008, LNAI 5244, pp. 183–194, 2008.
© Springer-Verlag Berlin Heidelberg 2008

testing and refactoring approaches and their supporting tools cannot be re-used directly in MAS development, since MASs are built using different abstractions and techniques. So we need to re-define these practices for MAS development.

In this paper, we propose a refactoring approach that makes evolutionary MAS development possible. This refactoring approach follows the route of traditional refactoring and provides some new refactoring patterns for MAS development. To transfer refactoring practice to AOSE, the proposed approach introduces three refactoring levels on the refactorable entities encountered during MAS development, some common problems called "bad smells" experienced during the development of such systems (such as role overloading and too big agent behaviors) and the maintenance strategies called "refactoring patterns" to overcome these bad smells. Each of the refactoring patterns defined in the proposed approach focuses on overcoming one or more than one bad smell(s) encountered during MAS development.

2   Related Works

In the literature, there are some pioneering works which try to apply agile practices to MAS development.

Knublauch [8] used practices of extreme programming (XP) [1], which is the one of the most known agile development processes used for MAS development. Although, this work proves the effectiveness of XP practices in terms of MAS development, refactoring is not explained in detail. Since the agent development framework and process meta-model, which are used during development, are very simple, refactoring operations on agents seem as very simple processes and refactoring practice is applied on agents. However, an agent that is developed by using a realistic development framework can play many roles in MAS and those roles have many goals, responsibilities and abilities. So, we believe that agents are not small; on the contrary they are too big entities for testing and refactoring.

In another important work has been introduced by Chella et. al. [5], well known Passi methodology is transformed to Agile Passi. The testing framework developed by the Agile Passi research team provides an automated testing approach for testing multi-agent systems [3,6]. Agile Passi approach does not introduce an iterative or evolutionary style for MAS development. Therefore, a refactoring approach that makes agile MAS development possible is not introduced in this work.

In [12], an iterative and incremental development approach called agent oriented test driven development - AOTDD is proposed to handle the complexity and continuously changing nature of the requirements in MAS development. In AOTDD, developers follow the development cycle with adding the new functionalities to the system between iterations, just like all other agile & iterative development approaches. Also, the life cycle of proposed test driven approach and a testing tool that supports the proposed test driven approach are introduced in this work. Since this work is focused on the testing part of test driven development, the refactoring step that is very critical for iterative and incremental development is not discussed in detail.

3   Refactoring in Evolutionary MAS Development Process

We introduce an agile development approach called agent oriented test driven development - AOTDD that supports evolutionary MAS development in [12]. AOTDD is based on the test driven development and refactoring practices of extreme programming [1]. The iterative and evolutionary development cycle of AOTDD is shown in figure 1. This section only focuses on the "improve the design by applying refactoring" step of this cycle and aims to explain the place and importance of refactoring in evolutionary MAS development.

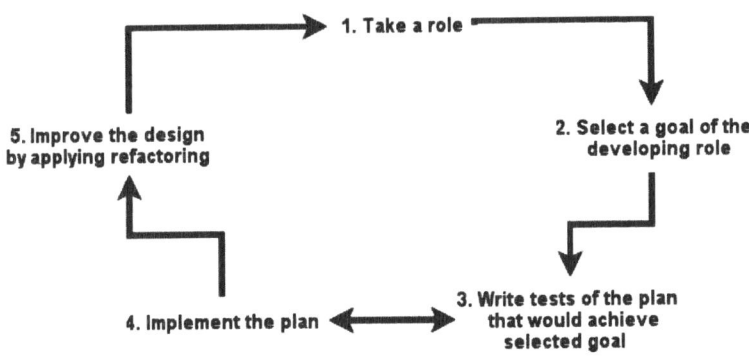

Fig. 1. Agile MAS development cycle

Until the refactoring step, tests that verify the selected goal are written in the third step and the plan that passes the defined tests and achieves the goal at hand is implemented in the fourth step. However, design of the system being developed may be deteriorated during plan implementation, since developers only concentrate on the functionality of the plan at hand. If the refactoring step is skipped, this deterioration prevents MAS design from meeting new requirements after a few cycles.

Developers have to protect the design from getting worse by evaluating the possibility of good design opportunities such as reusable plan fragments and flexible design on the developed artifacts. This process called refactoring is handled in the fifth step of the AOTDD cycle.

In the refactoring step, developers may improve the initial design decisions by using the pre-defined refactoring patterns. For example, a previous plan structure can be transferred to a better structure by identifying reusable task(s) within the plan and/or new roles or interactions between roles can be identified to improve modularity or robustness of the system.

Some refactoring operations may cause the refactoring of some pre-defined tests that have writen dependently to the internal structure. In such a condition, developers have to start a new cycle for the same goal of the same role or another goal of another role that has been affected by the refactoring operation and reorganize these test cases in the third step. If the plan code that has been written in previous cycles does not pass these reorganized tests, developers also have to implement code that passes the tests in the fourth step. Also, the design of the system may need to be refactored again since these changes can deteriorate system design. Therefore, a refactoring operation can initiate many development cycles.

4   Refactoring in MAS

There are three basic questions that should be answered in order to transfer refactoring practice into AOSE. These questions are:

- Which development artifacts in MAS development are refactorable?
- When and how do we decide to refactor during MAS development?
- What are the refactoring patterns that can be applied in MAS development?

In the following sub-sections, answers to these questions are discussed in detail.

4.1   Refactoring Levels in MAS Development

To identify refactorable development artifacts in goal oriented MAS development, we have to define a generic meta-model (called as metaphor in XP) that includes the common abstractions for all of the proposed goal oriented MAS development methodologies. So, we defined a basic meta-model for the target MAS model in order to apply the evolutionary MAS development process. Our meta-model which is shown in figure 2 is the synthesis of the meta-models of some of the well known goal oriented methodologies such as Gaia [14], Tropos [2] and Passi [5] and includes only common abstractions (they can be mentioned by different names in different methodologies) in these methodologies. For each MAS development scenario, an instance of the proposed meta-model is created and the steps of our agile development cycle is applied on this meta-model instance.

We separated the concepts in our meta-model into three vertical layers to specify the refactorable ones. These layers are goals, run-time artifacts and run-time supports. System goal and agent goal concepts are situated in the goal layer. The entities in the run-time artifacts layer are developed to achieve system and agent goals. The entities situated in run-time supports layer help the execution of the run-time artifacts defined.

Goal oriented development methodologies are based on identifying the goals that come from user requirements, decomposing high level goals to smaller goals during analysis and identifying run-time artifacts such as plan and role that achieve identified goals collaboratively during the design phase. Run-time artifacts that are defined to achieve goals are implemented using the run-time support entities.

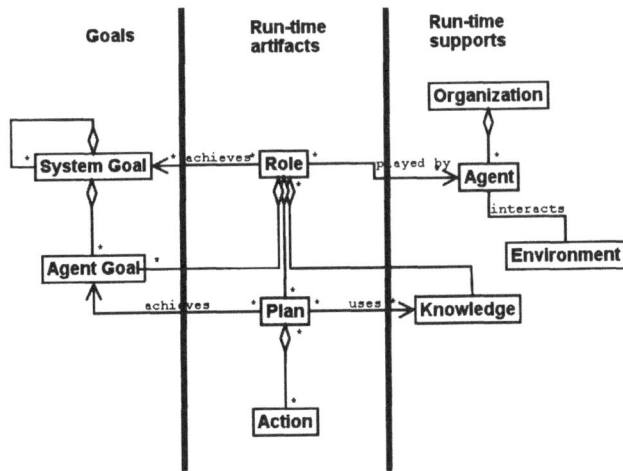

Fig. 2. MAS meta-model

From the testing perspective, developers have to test run-time artifacts in order to verify the correctness of goals that are achieved by these artifacts. For example, one or more than one plan(s) is/are implemented to achieve each agent goal. So, one has to test the execution of the plan(s) in order to understand whether related agent goal is achieved or not. Therefore, we need a testing infrastructure to write tests that verify to achievement of goals by releated run-time artifacts. We developed such a testing infrastructure [12] to write automated tests for run-time artifacts of our MAS meta-model. This testing infrastructure also provides a foundation for our refactoring approach.

Although refactoring is not change the external functionality of refactored component, other design components depend on the internal structure of this refactored component may be affected from the refactoring operation. So, refactoring may affect the faultlessly running code and breaks the system. To apply refactoring practice, system reliability has to be guaranteed with the pre-defined automated tests. Therefore, refactoring can be applied on the concrete and testable artifacts in the run-time artifacts layer of our MAS meta-model. Refactoring operations on run-time artifacts should not affect the achievement of goals achieved by these artifacts.

Based on the meta-model shown in figure 2, we defined three refactoring levels that focus on testable run-time artifacts for MAS development. In the following, these refactoring levels are explained in detail.

Role level: Roles are architectural elements which satisfy system goals collaboratively. Each role has some responsibilities (agent goals), abilities (plans), authorizations and rules all of which are based on system goals. During the deployment phase, each role is assigned to agent(s) on the verge of their execution. Therefore, all features of an agent come from the roles that are assigned to it. Agent is only container used to execute developed roles like object in traditional object oriented development - OOD.

Responsibilities and abilities of roles may change in dynamic and open MASs frequently. Hence, role is one of the most critical elements for refactoring in such systems. At this level, refactoring techniques such as moving responsibilities which are related with the role are needed to improve the role structure of MAS at hand. Several roles cooperate to achieve a common system goal of the system being developed. Since refactoring techniques applied on the roles do not change external behavior of the roles, achievement of system goals is not affected from the refactoring operations.

Plan (task) level: Agents achieve their own goals through the plan execution. Plans are the smallest testing and refactoring units like classes in traditional OOD. Plan testing verifies the valid execution of a goal in a single agent context. An agent context may include an agent knowledge base and the external environment that agent directly interacts. Hence, refactoring on agent plans may affect the agent knowledge base and/or external environment that is related with the refactored plan(s).

Agent plans are developed using a planning paradigm such as HTN [13]. Refactoring techniques at this level are dependent on the planning paradigm used. However, most of the refactoring techniques in this level can be generalized to other similar planning paradigms.

A sub-part of a plan can be used within another plan to satisfy a different goal. So, plans should be structured in a reusable way to reduce duplication of same task fragment in different plan structures. Refactoring techniques at this level aim to improve internal structure of plans. Since external behaviors of the plans do not change, tests that are written for an agent goal are still applicable to verify the correctness of the new structure after the refactoring operation.

Action level: Plans are composed of sequences of executable tasks called actions using a planning paradigm. We can consider actions as methods of classes in OOA.

Although plans are the smallest testable units in MAS development, sometimes actions can be considered as testable units like methods in OOD. An action can be used in different plan structures and there can be many actions that have similar executable code and/or structure like the actions "register a bookstore agent to DF", "register a user agent to DF", and "register a negotiator agent to DF". So, developers have to write reusable actions to avoid duplicated action code and structure. For this purpose, they can apply action level refactoring techniques to avoid duplicate action code. For example, the duplicated code and structure problem in the mentioned case can be overcame by moving the common code and structure of the actions to an abstract action called "register an agent to DF" and extending this abstract action from the others.

4.2   Bad Smells in MAS's

Some common design problems are encountered by developers during system development process frequently. Fowler named these common problems as bed smells in [7] and introduced refactoring techniques to overcome these bad smells in software design. Each of the defined refactoring patterns is introduced to overcome one or many bad smell(s). Similarly, we have to define bad smells for MAS development to decide when the refactoring process is started and then define their related refactoring patterns that overcome these bad smells.

Based on our experiences in MAS development gained during the development of Seagent platform by our research group, we have identified the bad smells shown below for each refactoring level in MAS development mentioned in the previous sub-section.

Action level bad smells: Duplicated action code, duplicated action parameters, big action, flow decision in action, long output list, long input list, unnecessary action group,

Plan level bad smells: Duplicated plan structure, big plan, execution decision in a plan, multiple intervention, long output list, long input list, continuous changing plan structure, speculative abstraction, plans in a plan, incoherent plans.

Role level bad smells: Overloaded role, wrong responsibility, unnecessary role.

In an evolutionary development process such as test driven development, developers only focus on writing the code that passes pre-defined tests during the implementation of each development iteration. Hence, it is unavoidable that some bad smells can occur in system design during the implementation. These bad smells can be captured at the end of the iteration. In our AOTTD process, bad smells are captured by the developers at the final step ("improve design by applying refactoring") of the development cycle.

4.3   Refactoring Patterns for MAS Development

Now, we can define refactoring patterns that can be used, while the run-time artifacts in the refactoring levels are refactored, in order to overcome the bad smells defined in the previous sub-section. Refactoring patterns were defined by using the Fowler's definition standard [7] that includes five parts: name, abstract, motivation, mechanics and sample. Some refactoring patterns that were defined based on our experiences with its initiator bad smell(s) are shown in figure 3.

We can not give detailed definitions for all refactoring patterns defined here because of the page limitation. Detailed definitions of all refactoring patterns defined are accessible on the following internet address:

http://etmen.ege.edu.tr/wiki/index.php/refactoring_agent_systems

However, to give an inside about our refactoring patterns, brief definitions that include the name and abstract for some refactoring patterns are listed below.

Move responsibility (role level): You have a plan that should be executed by another role. Move the plans to target role with the knowledge used by the plan and reorganize original plan(s) of the source role to interact the moved plan.

Merge plans (plan level): You have some incoherent plans that should be executed for a common objective. Create a new plan named by considering the common objective and move the tasks in original plans into the new plan.

Level	Refactoring	Bad smell(s)
Role level	Move responsibility	Wrong responsibility
	Split role	Overloaded role
Plan level	Extract plan	Plans in a plan Execution decision in a plan
	Extract superplan	Duplicated plan structure
	Merge plans	Incoherent plans
Action level	Extract superaction	Duplicated action code Duplicated action parameters
	Split action	Big action Flow decision in action
	Combine provisions	Long input list

Fig. 3. Some of the refactorings for MAS development

Extract superaction (action level): You have some actions that have the same executable code and/or parameters. Create an abstract action that holds duplicated code and/or parameters and extend this abstract action from the original action.

Some high level refactoring patterns can include some of the other refactoring patterns that are situated at lower or same refactoring level(s) in their mechanics. For example, mechanics of the "split role" refactoring pattern at the role level includes another refactoring called "move responsibility" at the role level.

5   Case Study

This section introduces an example that shows application of one of the most common refactoring techniques called "extract plan" on an actual plan structure during the evolutionary MAS development. This plan structure is in a conference management system that has been developed by Seagent group and achieves the "sending call for paper" goal of the "organization" role in this system. The initial HTN structure of this plan that was obtained at the end of the fourth step of the AOTDD cycle for "sending call for paper" goal is shown in figure 4

In HTN formalism, there are two kinds of task; complex task (we call plan) and primitive task (we call action). Complex tasks hold the structure of its sub-tasks. Primitive tasks have directly executable code. Information requirements of tasks are illustrated as provisions. Outcomes are result states of tasks. Data is transferred to other tasks through inheritance, disinheritance and provision-outcome links. An inheritance link is used to transfer a provision of a parent complex task to a sub task. Disinheritance links are used to transfer outcomes of sub tasks to parent complex task. And finally, the information flow between outcomes and provisions of the tasks in the same level is provided by provision-outcome links. Details of HTN formalism can be found in [13,10].

The simple plan in the figure 4 takes the conference topic as a provision. This provision is passed to the "create suitable researcher profile" action through an

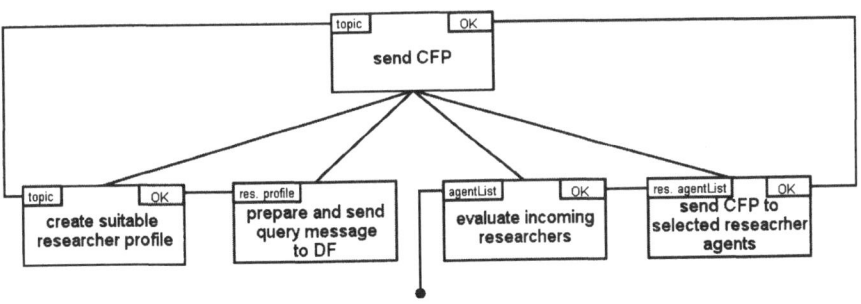

Fig. 4. The initial plan structure

inheritance link. In this action, a researcher profile object is created, the interested_topic field of this profile is set with the topic that is received as a provision and this researcher profile is returned through the "OK" outcome. The other action called "prepare and send query message to DF" takes the researcher profile, creates a query message by using this profile and sends this message to directory facilitator - DF. The "evaluate incoming researchers" action has an external provision called researcherList. This provision includes agent descriptions of the researcher agents that are sent by the DF. In this action, the description of the researcher agents are filtered according to the preferences and suitable researchers are selected. The final action called "send CFP to selected researchers" has the responsibility of sending call for paper of the conference to selected researchers using the agent descriptions that are received as a provision.

In the testing step of AOTDD cycle, we wrote the tests that check functionality of the whole plan and each of the executable actions that are situated in the lower level of this plan structure.

During the refactoring step of the AOTDD cycle, we realized that some tasks in the plan structure have a common objective called "finding the suitable researcher agents". This objective could also be part of the other plan structures such as "create program committee" in the system. This was a bad smell called "plans in plan". So, we decided to collect "create suitable researcher profile", ""prepare and send query message to DF" and "evaluate incoming researchers" actions into a new plan that achieves the common objective by applying "extract plan" refactoring technique on these actions.

In the following, the definition of the "extract plan" refactoring pattern is given. This definition includes all parts of the Fowler's refactoring pattern definition standard. The sample part of the definition is the case mentioned above.

Name: Extract Plan

Abstract: You have a task fragment that can be grouped together. Turn the task fragment into a plan whose name explains the purpose of the plan.

Motivation: Extract plan is one of the most common refactoring types used in agent systems development. This refactoring should be applied, when a plan includes reusable sub-plan structure. In such a condition, a group of these tasks is collected in a new plan to create a reusable plan structure.

Small plans introduce several advantages in the development of multi agent system scenarios. Firstly, they increase the re-usability of the tasks in other plan structures. Secondly, changing and maintenance of plans become easier with reusable plan structures. Another advantage is that plans composed using reusable plan structures are more understandable and more manageable.

Mechanics:

1. Create a new plan and name it depending on the intention of the task.
2. Scan the tasks to be extracted for references to other tasks that are defined in the main task structure as senders for the provision definitions. If there are such provision definitions, add each of these provisions to new task.
3. Scan the tasks to be extracted for the outcomes that are not linked to any tasks that are to be extracted. If there are such outcome definitions, add each of these outcomes to the new task.
4. Copy the tasks to be extracted to the new plan.
5. Add an inheritance link for each of the provision that are expected from other tasks in the main plan to new task structure.
6. Add a disinheritance link for each outcome that isn't linked to any tasks in the new plan structure.
7. Compile and test the new plan.
8. Replace the task group to be extracted to to the newly created plan and reorganize provision-outcome links in the main plan structure.
   (a) Scan the new plan's provisions. If there is any provision whose sender is one of the other tasks in the main plan structure, add a provision-outcome link between the new plan's provision and the other task's related outcome.
   (b) Scan the provisions of the tasks in the main plan structure, if there is any provision whose sender is the one of the extracted tasks, add provision-outcome link between new plan's related outcome and this provision.
   (c) Modify the each inheritance and disinheritance link between the main plan and an extracted task in the main plan structure as between main plan and new plan.
9. Compile and test main plan.

At the end of the "extract plan" refactoring, we obtained a new plan called "find researcher agent" that can be re-used in the other plan structures. This plan has the responsibility of finding agent descriptions of the researchers that work on the conference topic according to the topic provision. The "find researcher agent" plan was simply used in some other plans in conference management system. The plan structure of our "send CFP" plan after the "extract plans" refactoring is shown in figure 5.

After this refactoring operation, all tests that had been written to verify functionality of the whole "send CFP" plan passed without any change, since refactoring did not affect external behavior of the plan.

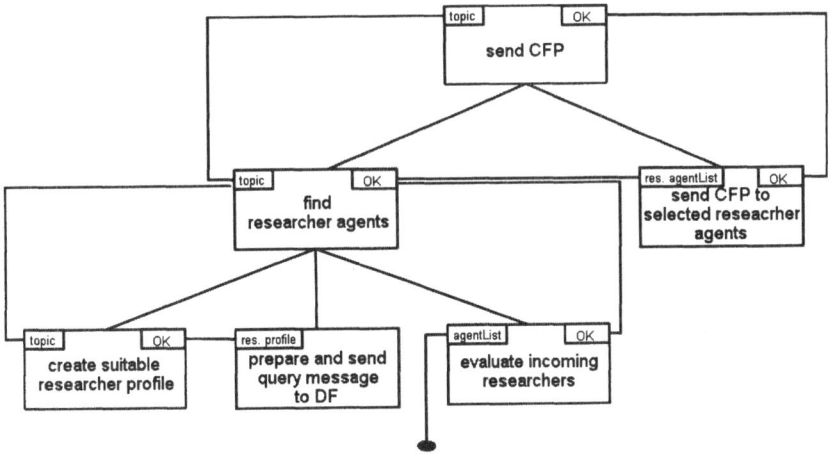

Fig. 5. The final plan structure after the "extract plan" refactoring is applied

6   Conclusion and Future Works

In this paper, a refactoring approach that makes evolutionary MAS development possible has been proposed. This approach introduces some refactoring patterns that overcome some common problems (called as bad smells in this paper) that are encountered during the MAS development. During the development activities of our research group, we observed that refactoring patterns become necessary frequently in evolutionary MAS development. Moreover, we also realized that applying refactoring practice creates more reusable and easily manageable plan structures.

Currently, we have been developing a refactoring tool that supports the proposed refactoring approach at all of the proposed refactoring levels and simplifies the refactoring process in evolutionary MAS development.

References

1. Beck, K., Andres, C.: Extreme Programming Explained: Embrace Change, 2nd edn. Addison-Wesley, Reading (2004)
2. Bresciani, P., Perini, A., Giorgini, P., Giunchiglia, F., Mylopoulos, J.: Tropos: An agent-oriented software development methodology. Autonomous Agents and Multi-Agent Systems 8(3), 203–236 (2004)
3. Caire, G., Cossentino, M., Negri, A., Poggi, A., Turci, P.: Multi-agent systems implementation and testing. In: From Agent Theory to Agent Implementation, Fourth International Symposium (AT2AI-4) (2004)
4. Cernuzzi, L., Cossentino, M., Zambonell, F.: Process models for agent-based development. Journal of Engineering Applications of Artificial Intelligence 18 (2) (2005)
5. Chella, A., Cossentino, M., Sabatucci, L., Seidita, V.: From passi to agile passi: Tailoring a design process to meet new needs. In: IEEE/WIC/ACM International Joint Conference on Intelligent Agent Technology (IAT-2004) (2004)

6. Cossentino, M., Seidita, V.: Composition of a new process to meet agile needs using method engineering. In: Choren, R., Garcia, A., Lucena, C., Romanovsky, A. (eds.) SELMAS 2004. LNCS, vol. 3390, pp. 36–51. Springer, Heidelberg (2005)
7. Fowler, M.: Refactoring: Improving the Design of Existing Code. Addison-Wesley, Boston (1999)
8. Knublauch, H.: Extreme programming of multi-agent systems. In: AAMAS 2000, pp. 704–711. ACM Press, New York (2002)
9. Link, J., Frolich, P.: Unit Testing in Java: How Tests Drive the Code. Morgan Kaufmann Publishers Inc., San Francisco (2003)
10. Paolucci, M., Kalp, D., Pannu, A.S., Shehory, O., Sycara, K.: A planning component for retsina agents. In: Lecture Notes in Artificial Intelligence, Intelligent Agents VI (1999)
11. Rational Software. The rational unified process (1998)
12. Tiryaki, A.M., Öztuna, S., Dikenelli, O., Erdur, R.C.: Sunit: A unit testing framework for test driven development of multi-agent systems. In: Padgham, L., Zambonelli, F. (eds.) AOSE VII / AOSE 2006. LNCS, vol. 4405, pp. 156–173. Springer, Heidelberg (2007)
13. Williamson, M., Decker, K., Sycara, K.: Unified information and control flow in hierarchical task networks. In: Theories of Action, Planning, and Robot Control: Bridging the Gap: Proceedings of the 1996 AAAI Workshop, pp. 142–150. AAAI Press, Menlo Park (1996)
14. Zambonelli, F., Jennings, N.R., Wooldridge, M.: Developing multiagent systems: The gaia methodology. ACM Trans. Softw. Eng. Methodol. 12(3), 317–370 (2003)
15. Zambonelli, F., Omicini, A.: Challenges and research directions in agent-oriented software engineering. Autonomous Agents and Multi-Agent Systems 9(3), 253–283 (2004)

Autonomous Scheduling with Unbounded and Bounded Agents

Chetan Yadati[1], Cees Witteveen[1], Yingqian Zhang[1],
Mengxiao Wu[2], and Han la Poutre[2]

[1] Delft University of Technology, Delft
[2] Centrum voor Wiskunde en Informatica, Amsterdam

Abstract. Autonomous scheduling deals with the problem - how to enable agents to schedule a set of interdependent tasks in such a way that whatever schedule they choose for their tasks, the individual schedules always can be merged into a global feasible schedule? Unlike the traditional approaches to distributed scheduling we do not enforce a fixed schedule to every participating agent. Instead we guarantee flexibility by offering a set of schedules to choose from in such a way that every agent can choose its own schedule independently from the others. We show that in case of agents with unbounded concurrency, optimal make-span can be guaranteed. Whenever the agents have bounded concurrency optimality cannot be guaranteed, but we present an approximation algorithm that ensures a constant make-span ratio.

Keywords: Scheduling, autonomous agents, flexible scheduling, algorithm, make-span optimality.

1 Introduction

Autonomous scheduling aims to provide autonomous agents with a set of minimal constraints on tasks such that each agent is able to make a schedule for its tasks independently from the others. This independent scheduling capability should hold even if the tasks of an agent are dependent upon the completion of tasks given to other agents. The construction of such constraints can be viewed as the result of a coordination mechanism that ensures the existence of a joint feasible schedule whenever each of the individual agent's schedules meets its constraints. In particular, such coordination mechanisms are useful whenever a set of tasks has to be completed by a number of autonomous agents who are not willing, or not able, to communicate and negotiate about the schedules for the tasks they have to process.

Autonomous scheduling problems differ from classical (distributed) scheduling problems in the sense that besides efficiency criteria like minimal makespan, also *flexibility* criteria that aim to maximize the freedom of scheduling choice (autonomy) of the participating agents play a role: Instead of forcing each agent to comply to a given schedule, autonomous scheduling offers them a choice from a *set* of schedules for the tasks proposed.

R. Bergmann et al. (Eds.): MATES 2008, LNAI 5244, pp. 195–206, 2008.

To represent such a set of possible schedules, in autonomous scheduling a set of (time) constraints for each of the tasks is constructed in such a way that each agent can choose a schedule itself, provided that it satisfies all the task constraints. Of course, such a set of constraints should be such that *(i)* whatever schedule is chosen by an agent, it never interferes with the choice made by other agents and *(ii)* the set of constraints should be *maximally flexible*, that is, it should not be possible to find a weakening of the original constraints that also satisfies the first condition. If a set C of constraints satisfies both conditions we say that it meets the criterion of *maximal flexibility*. Besides flexibility to meet the needs of autonomous agents, we are also interested in *efficiency* as a system value: In order to get the total set of tasks done by the agents, we would like to minimize the total *makespan*. One of the questions then to be answered is: Can we design a flexible makespan efficient autonomous scheduling method?

In this paper, we show that there exists a surprisingly simple makespan efficient autonomous scheduling algorithm, provided that the agents are capable to process as much tasks concurrently as possible, i.e., they have unbounded concurrent capacity. Often, however, this might seem quite unrealistic. Hence, we adapt the method to accommodate for such bounded concurrency requirements of agents. In particular, we consider the case where agents are strictly sequential. We then prove that in this latter case designing a makespan-efficient autonomous scheduling method is NP-hard. The good news, however, is that there exist good approximation algorithms for makespan efficient autonomous sequential scheduling, if we allow the tasks to be processed in a preemptive way.

The structure of this paper is as follows: In the next section, we first provide some background on distributed and autonomous scheduling. Then, the basic framework which we use to describe problem instances is presented. In Section 4, we develop an algorithm called the ISA for distributed scheduling for tasks with homogeneous durations and unbounded capacity. In Section 5, we deal with sequential agents. We summarize our findings, conclude and point to future directions for research in Section 6.

2   Background and Related Work

Distributed scheduling has been an active area for research in the past decade. Roughly speaking, one can distinguish between approaches that assume that the participating systems, or agents controlling these systems, are cooperative and approaches that assume that the participating agents/systems are non-cooperative. Examples of the former (classical) approaches are DLS [1], HEFT [2], CPOP [2], ILHA [3] and PCT [4]. All these approaches mainly focus on optimizing some performance criteria such as makespan and required communication between processors. Typically, these approaches assume that the participating systems are *(i)* fully cooperative in *(ii)* establishing a single globally feasible schedule for the complete set of tasks.

In quite a lot of applications, however, we simply cannot assume that the participating systems are fully cooperative. For example, in grid applications, jobs often have to compete for CPU and network resources, and each agent is mainly interested in maximizing its own throughput instead of maximizing the global throughput. Thus, several researchers have adopted a game-theoretic approach for solving scheduling problems with non-cooperative agents. For example, Walsh *et al.* [5] use auction mechanisms to arbitrate resource conflicts for scheduling network access to programs for various users on the internet. Another approach to non-cooperative scheduling is based on negotiation. Recently, Li in his PhD thesis developed both static and learning based dynamic negotiation models for grid scheduling [6].

In both approaches to non-cooperative scheduling, however, the effort is directed at developing a *single global* centrally computed schedule that meets some criterion. In situations where agents are exploring unknown or hostile territory, it might be very restrictive or even impossible to enforce rigid schedules on the agents. In other situations where agents participate in more than one such system, they would require a minimum set of constraints on their schedules rather than a single rigid schedule. Recently, Hunsberger [7] has developed a temporal decoupling method for Simple Temporal Networks (STNs) to decompose an STN into a number of independent sub-STNs, each of which can be scheduled independently from the others. Although the autonomous scheduling method we will apply is related to his decoupling method, we want to design such independent subnetworks directly from a given set of simple constraints. Moreover, even if such a common temporal network would exist, unlike in the temporal decoupling method, we would allow to modify one or more of its constraints in the decomposition process as, e.g., we will do in the sequential scheduling case. Finally, the principal aim of our method is to provide a decomposition method where flexibility as well as efficiency criteria play an important role.

3   Preliminaries and Framework

We assume a finite set of tasks/operations $T = \{t_1, \ldots, t_m\}$, each of which takes finite time $d(t_i) \in Z^+$ for processing. Furthermore, these tasks are interrelated by a partially ordered precedence relation $\prec$, where $t_i \prec t_j$ indicates that t_i must be completed before t_j can start. We use the transitive reduction $\ll$ of $\prec$ to indicate the immediate precedence relation between tasks, i.e., $t \ll t'$ iff $t \prec t'$ and there exists no t'' such that $t \prec t''$ and $t'' \prec t'$. We use a directed acyclic graph (DAG) $G = (T, \ll)$ to represent the task structure of T.

We assume that T has been assigned to a set of autonomous agents $A = \{A_1, \ldots, A_n\}$ according to a pre-defined task allocation $\phi : T \to A$. We denote the set of tasks allocated to agent A_i by $T_i = \phi^{-1}(A_i)$ Note that $\{T_i\}_{i=1}^n$ is a partitioning of T. Likewise, the precedence relation $\prec_i$ is the precedence relation $\prec$ induced by T_i and $d_i()$ is the duration function restricted to T_i. We also assume that there is a function $c : \{1, 2, \ldots n\} \to Z^+ \cup \{\infty\}$ assigning to each agent A_i its concurrency bound $c(i)$. This concurrency bound is the upper bound on the number of tasks agent A_i is capable of performing simultaneously. We say that $\langle \{T_i\}_{i=1}^n, \prec, c(), d() \rangle$ is a *scheduling instance*.

Given such a scheduling instance $\langle\{T_i\}_{i=1}^n, \prec, c(), d()\rangle$, a global schedule for it is a function $\sigma : T \to Z^+$ determining the starting time $\sigma(t)$ for each task $t \in T$. Obviously, to be a feasible solution, σ should satisfy the following constraints:

1. for every pair $t, t' \in T$, if $t \prec t'$, then $\sigma(t) + d(t) \le \sigma(t')$;
2. for every $i = 1, \ldots, n$ and for every $\tau \in Z^+$, $|\{t \in T_i \mid \tau \in [\sigma(t), \sigma(t) + d(t)]\}| \le c(i)$, that is the concurrency bounds for every agent A_i should be respected.

Of course, we prefer a schedule σ which minimizes *makespan*, i.e., among all feasible schedules σ', we prefer a schedule σ such that $max_{t \in T}\{\sigma(t) + d(t)\} \le max_{t \in T}\{\sigma'(t) + d(t)\}$. Since we are dealing with autonomous agents, we would like to offer them the possibility to choose a most adequate schedule from a set of feasible schedules in such a way that their individual choices do not interfere. More in particular, we want to guarantee that a feasible global schedule σ can be obtained by imposing upon each agent a (minimal) set of additional constraints C_i, such that if C_i is specified for the scheduling instance $\langle T_i, \prec_i, d_i(), c(i)\rangle$ of agent A_i, then all *locally feasible* schedules σ_i satisfying their *local* constraints C_i can be merged into a globally feasible schedule σ for the original total scheduling instance. More precisely, for each $i = 1, 2, \ldots, n$, let Σ_i be the set of all locally feasible schedules σ_i that satisfy C_i. Given any locally feasible schedule $\sigma_i \in \Sigma_i$ of any agent $A_i \in A$, we require the merging $\sigma = \bigcup_{i=1}^n \sigma_i$ to be a globally feasible schedule for $\langle\{T_i\}_{i=1}^n, \prec, c(), d()\rangle$.

In this paper, the set of constraints C_i that we will add to each local scheduling instance for each agent A_i, is a set of *time intervals* $[lb(t), ub(t)]$ for the tasks in T_i, where each interval $[lb(t), ub(t)] \in C_i$ with $lb(t), ub(t) \in Z^+$ specifies that any individual schedule σ_i agent A_i might choose has to satisfy the constraint $lb(t) \le \sigma_i(t) \le ub(t)$.

Example 1. Consider a simple example shown in Figure 1, where there are three agents and 7 tasks with precedence constraints. Here, a direct precedence constraint $t \ll t'$ is represented as an arrow from t pointing to t'. The task durations $d(t)$ are indicated below the circles representing the tasks t. Suppose that each agent can perform two tasks simultaneously, that is $c(1) = c(2) = c(3) = 2$. Clearly, the minimal makespan of processing these tasks is 11. To achieve this minimal makespan, the following schedules for the agents are possible: $\sigma_1(t_1) = \sigma_1(t_2) = 0$; $\sigma_2(t_3) = 2; \sigma_2(t_4) = 3$ and $\sigma_3(t_5) = 3; \sigma_3(t_6) = 7; \sigma_3(t_7) = 9$. However, prescribing these schedules is unnecessarily restrictive to the agents. In fact, several other schedules also result in the same global makespan. For example ,A_1 could start task t_1 in the interval $[0,2]$ while starting task t_2 starting in the interval $[0, 0]$. Agent A_2 can process tasks t_3 in the interval $[4, 7]$ while starting t_3 in $[2, 2]$. Similarly, agent A_3 can process task t_5 in the interval $[8,10]$ with task t_6 starting in the interval $[7, 7]$ and task t_7 in $[9,9]$. Notice here that any schedule produced by the agents such that these intervals are honoured will always lead to a global makespan of 11. Thus, by introducing the additional constraints in the form of these intervals, agents have some amount of flexibility on deciding their local schedule without affecting the minimal makespan.   ∎

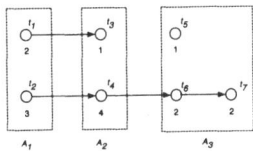

Fig. 1. A set of tasks t_i with their durations $d(t_i)$ to demonstrate the possibility of developing several makespan optimal schedules. Task durations are indicated as numbers within the circles representing the tasks.

Our goal is to design a minimal set of constraints C_i for each agent A_i, such that the merging of individual schedules σ_i that satisfy C_i always is a globally feasible schedule. Moreover, we would like the merging to be also makespan efficient. In the next sections, we consider two scenarios: the first, where agents can perform an unlimited number of tasks simultaneously and the second where they can perform only a single task at any given point in time.

4   Autonomous Scheduling for Agents with Unbounded Concurrency

In this section, we discuss a simple method to specify additional constraints for each agent in order to guarantee that individual schedules σ_i meeting these constraints can always be merged into a global *makespan efficient* schedule. The central idea is to specify as the constraint for a task t an interval consisting of its earliest possible starting time and its latest possible starting time, taking into account the precedence constraints between the tasks and their duration. Once these intervals are computed, the agents can autonomously create any local schedule provided that it satisfies these intervals. Thus, they are offered the flexibility of creating more than one schedule but still be assured that the global makespan is optimal.

The idea of using these intervals is related to the way in which the CPOP [2] algorithm by Topcuouglu *et al.* computes the priority of a task for scheduling on a machine. In CPOP, a combined value of the *depth* and the *height* of a task is used to compute the priority. We build upon this idea and compute intervals instead of priorities, within which each agent/machine is free to schedule its tasks.

To define the interval $[lb(t), ub(t)]$ for the starting time of a task t in the given partial order $\langle T, \prec, d() \rangle$, we first compute, for each task $t \in T$ its $depth(t)$ and its $height(t)$. We will need both measures to determine the earliest and the latest possible time at which a task can be started. To aid in our computation of the depth and height of a task t, we further define two sets: $pred(t) = \{t'|\ t' \ll t\}$ and $succ(t) = \{t'|\ t \ll t'\}$.

The depth of a task t is defined as follows: $depth(t) = 0$ if $pred(t) = \emptyset$ and $depth(t) = max_{t' \in pred(t)}\{depth(t') + d(t')\}$, otherwise. Note that the depth of a task t is the maximum duration of any chain of tasks preceding it, hence it directly determines the earliest time task t might start. The depth $depth(T)$ of the set of tasks T is defined as the maximum duration required to complete all tasks taking into account the precedence relation $\prec$: $depth(T) = max_{t \in T}\{depth(t) + d(t)\}$. So $depth(T)$ defines the minimal makespan of T.

The height $height(t)$ of a task t in a partial order $\langle T, \prec, d() \rangle$ defines the time that has to pass before all tasks occurring after t and including t have been completed: So $height(t) = d(t)$, if $succ(t) = \emptyset$ and $height(t) = max_{t' \in succ(t)}\{height(t') + d(t)\}$, otherwise. From the specifications of $depth(t), height(t)$ and $depth(T)$ the earliest $(lb(t))$ and latest $(ub(t))$ possible starting times for a task t can be derived as follows: $lb(t) = depth(t)$ and $ub(t) = depth(T) - height(t)$.

These intervals $[lb(t), ub(t)]$, however, are still not directly usable for autonomous scheduling. Since the length of task chains might differ, it can easily happen that the intervals of some precedence constrained tasks $t \prec t'$ might overlap, that is $lb(t') < ub(t) + d(t)$, while $t \prec t'$. Such an overlap might cause a violation of the first constraint on the joint schedule, namely that $t \prec t'$ should imply $\sigma(t) + d(t) < \sigma(t')$.

Example 2. Consider the set of tasks given in Figure 1. The depth of T is $depth(T) = 11$. Computing the depths and the heights of the tasks t_1 and t_3, we derive the constraints $C(t_1) = [0, 7]$ and $C(t_3) = [2, 9]$. Now, agent A_1 could decide to start t_1 at time $\sigma_1(t_1) = 5$, while A_2 could choose $\sigma_2(t_3) = 6$. However, if these schedules are merged, we violate the precedence constraint between t_1 and t_3 since then $\sigma(t_3) < \sigma(t_1) + 2$. ∎

This implies that, in case of overlap, the agents are not free to choose any point in the interval $[lb(t), ub(t)]$ as the starting point $\sigma(t)$ for t. Therefore, we have to remove such overlap as depicted in Figure 2: In order to satisfy the scheduling constraint we should ensure that whenever $t \prec t'$, the difference between $lb(t')$ and $ub(t)$ should be at least $d(t)$. Note that, in case of an overlap between two tasks $t \prec t'$, it is always possible to remove the overlap without creating empty intervals: If $t \prec t'$, we have $lb(t) + d(t) \leq lb(t')$ and $ub(t) + d(t) \leq ub(t')$. The existence of an overlap implies that $lb(t) < lb(t') < ub(t) + d(t)$. Hence, $ub(t') - lb(t) \geq ub(t) + d(t) - (lb(t') - d(t)) > -d(t) + 2d(t) = d(t)$.

Since we require $lb(t') - ub(t) \geq d(t)$, we set $ub(t) = lb(t) + \lfloor \frac{ub(t') - lb(t) - d(t)}{2} \rfloor$ and thereafter $lb(t') = lb(t) + \lfloor \frac{ub(t') - lb(t) - d(t)}{2} \rfloor + d(t)$. In both cases, since $ub(t') - lb(t) > d(t)$, the new constraint intervals are non-empty. The complete description of the algorithm is given in the ISA [1] Algorithm (see Algorithm 1).

Example 3. Consider again the set of tasks given in Figure 1. The "raw" constraints on the tasks are computed as $C(t_1) = [0, 7], C(t_3) = [2, 9], C(t_5) = [4, 10]$ while $C(t_2) = [0, 0], C(t_4) = [3, 3], C(t_6) = [7, 7]$ and $C(t_7) = [9, 9]$. Since there is overlap between the constraints of task t_1 and t_3 and t_3 and t_5, these constraints have to be adapted. The result is the following set of constraints: $C(t_1) = [0, 3]$, $C(t_3) = [5, 7]$ and $C(t_5) = [8, 10]$. It is easily verifiable that all local schedules that adhere to their constraints are feasible and also that all such local schedules can be combined to obtain a global schedule that is correct and has a makespan of 11. ∎

---

[1] Interval-based Scheduling Algorithm.

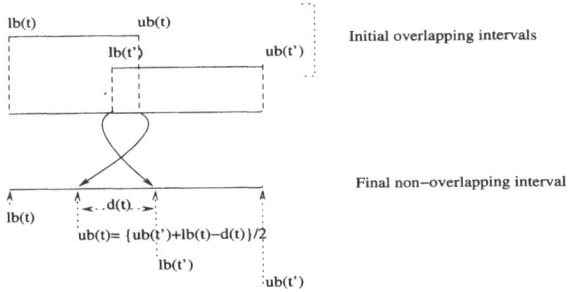

Fig. 2. Overlapping interval splitting procedure in ISA

Algorithm 1. Generalised Interval based Scheduling (ISA)

Require: Partially ordered set of tasks $(T, \prec)$, for every task $t \in T$ its depth $depth(t)$
  and its height $height(t)$;
Ensure: For every $t \in T$ its scheduling interval $C(t) = [lb(t), ub(t)]$;
1: $depth(T) := max_{t \in T}\{depth(t) + d(t)\}$
2: **for all** $t \in T$ **do**
3:    $lb(t) := depth(t)$ and $ub(t) := depth(T) - height(t)$
4: **end for**
5: **for all** $t, t' \in T$ such that $t \prec t'$ and $lb(t') - ub(t) < d(t)$ **do**
6:    $ub(t) = lb(t) + \lfloor \frac{ub(t') - lb(t) - d(t)}{2} \rfloor$
7:    $lb(t') = ub(t) + d(t)$
8: **end for**
9: return $C(t) = [lb(t), ub(t)]$ for all $t \in T$

Obviously, this algorithm runs in polynomial time. Note that each interval
$[lb(t), ub(t)]$ computed by ISA is always non-empty and for every $t \in T$, $ub(t) \leq$
$depth(T) - d(t)$. Moreover, for every pair t, t' of tasks, $t \prec t'$ implies $ub(t) + d(t) <$
$lb(t')$. Hence, it is not difficult to see that *(i)* every local schedule σ_i satisfying
the local constraints C_i will be a feasible schedule for the set of tasks T_i and *(ii)*
the merge of every set $\{\sigma_i\}_{i=1}^n$ of local schedules is a feasible global schedule,
thus ensuring the correctness and make-span optimality of the algorithm:

Proposition 1. *The interval-based scheduling algorithm (ISA) ensures a correct
global schedule and it is efficient in terms of makespan.*

With respect to flexibility of this autonomous scheduling method, it is not difficult
to see that it satisfies maximal flexibility. Here, we call a set $C = \{C(t) \mid t \in T\}$
of interval constraints for a a scheduling instance $\langle\{T_i\}_{i=1}^n, \prec, c(), d()\rangle$ maximally
flexible, if there does not exist any strict weakening[2] C' of C such that C' also allows for autonomous scheduling of $\langle\{T_i\}_{i=1}^n, \prec, c(), d()\rangle$ and is makespan efficient.
This property can easily be proven by noticing that the ISA algorithm generates

---

[2] A set C' is a strict weakening of C if every schedule σ satisfying C also satisfies C'
  but not vice versa.

a set of constraints $C = \{C(t) \mid t \in T\}$ such that *(i)* for every task t such that $succ(t) = \emptyset$ we have $ub(t) = depth(T) - d(t)$; *(ii)* for every t such that $pred(t) = \emptyset$ it holds that $lb(t) = 0$; *(iii)* for every pair of tasks t, t' such that $t \prec t'$ it holds that $lb(t') = ub(t) + d(t)$.

This implies that any strict weakening C' of C would contain a constraint $C(t) = [lb(t), ub(t)]$ such that either *(a)* $lb(t) < 0$ or *(b)* $ub(t) > depth(T) - d(t)$ or *(c)* there exists some t' such that $t \prec t'$ and $ub(t) + d(t) > lb(t')$ or *(d)* there exists some t' such that $t' \prec t$ and $ub(t') + d(t) > lb(t)$. Clearly, case *(a)* and *(b)* would imply that some C'-satisfying schedules are not make span efficient and if case c or d holds, some C'-satisfying schedules violate a precedence constraint. Hence, such a weakening cannot exist and we have the following proposition:

Proposition 2. *Any strict weakening the set C of constraints imposed by ISA either leads to a infeasible schedule or leads to a non optimal makespan.*

Summarizing, we have the following property:

Theorem 1. *ISA ensures a maximally flexible set of constraints and a makespan efficient global schedule.*

Note, however, that the minimal global makespan is ensured by the proposed algorithm ISA only under the assumption that the participant agents have capabilities to perform a potentially unbounded number of tasks at the same time. Often, this assumption is not realistic as agents may only have limited resources at their disposal. Therefore, in the next section, we study the case when every agent is capable of performing only a single task at any point in time (sequential agents).

5   Scheduling Sequential Agents

A scheduling instance $\langle \{T_i\}_{i=1}^n, \prec, c(), d() \rangle$ where $c(i) = 1$ for every A_i is called a sequential scheduling instance, abbreviated as $\langle \{T_i\}_{i=1}^n, \prec, 1, d() \rangle$. Like in the unbounded case, we would like to come up with a set C of constraints $C(t) = [lb(t), ub(t)]$ for each task $t \in T$ such that the agents are able to construct their *sequential* schedule independently from the others. Any individual schedule σ_i for a sequential agent A_i with the set of tasks T_i assigned to it, has to satisfy the following conditions:

- $lb(t) \leq \sigma_i(t) \leq ub(t)$ for every $t \in T_i$ where $C(t) = [lb(t), ub(t)]$;
- for every $t, t' \in T_i$, $t \neq t'$ implies $\sigma_i(t) - \sigma_i(t') \geq d(t)$ or $\sigma_i(t') - \sigma_i(t) \geq d(t')$.

While designing such constraints for autonomous scheduling if the agents are unbounded turns out to be a feasible problem, the equivalent problem for sequential agents turns out to be infeasible, mainly because we cannot ensure that, based on a given set of constraints delivered to the individual agents, they are able to find a sequential schedule satisfying all the constraints. More precisely, while in the unbounded case we were able to find a minimum makespan M for the total set of tasks and could guarantee that given a set C of additional task constraints any set $\{\sigma_i\}_{i=1}^n$ of locally feasible schedules would result in a makespan M complying global schedule, finding such a makespan complying schedule in the sequential case is an intractable problem:

Proposition 3. *Given a sequential scheduling instance $\langle\{T_i\}_{i=1}^n, \prec, 1, d()\rangle$ and a positive integer M, the problem to decide whether there exists a set of constraints C such that the scheduling instance allows for a solution with makespan M by autonomous scheduling is NP-hard.*

Proof. We reduce the PARTITIONING problem [8] (Given a set S of integers, is there a subset S' of S such that $\sum_{s \in S'} s = \sum_{s \in \bar{S}} s$, where $\bar{S} = S - S'$?) to the autonomous scheduling for sequential agents problem.

Take an instance S of PARTITIONING and let $d_S = \sum_{s \in S} s$. Without loss of generality, we can assume d_S to be even. Consider the following set of tasks $T = \{t_s | s \in S\} \cup \{t_a, t_b, t_c\}$. For every task $t_s \in T$, let $d(t_s) = s$, let $d(t_a) = \frac{d_S}{2}$, let $d(t_b) = 1$, $d(t_c) = \frac{d_S}{2} + 1\}$ and let $\prec = \{(t_a \prec t_b), (t_b \prec t_c)\}$. Furthermore, there are two agents A_1 and A_2, where A_1 has to perform the tasks t_a and t_b and agent A_2 has to perform all the remaining tasks $(T - \{t_a, t_b\})$. Finally, let $M = d_S + 1$.

If the agents are sequential, there exists a set of constraints C allowing for a makespan (M) efficient autonomous scheduling solution iff the PARTITION instance S has a solution: exactly in that case, agent A_2 is able to process one subset of its set of tasks in the interval $[0, d(t_a)]$, starts t_b in the interval $[d(t_a), d(t_a)]$ and completes the remaining subset of tasks in the interval $[d(t_a) + 1, d_S + 1]$. □

Note that the complexity is not dependent upon the number of agents: Already two agents suffice to render the problem hard and, in particular, the problem derives its hardness from the difficulty to determine for a *single* agent the set of constraints that would allow it to determine its own schedule without violating the global makespan.

Therefore, we have to rely on approximation algorithms for autonomous scheduling in the sequential agent case. As we have shown in some recent work [9], there exists a polynomial 2-approximation algorithm for constructing a set of constraints in the sequential agent scheduling case if all the tasks $t \in T$ have unit durations $d(t) = 1$. This algorithm constructs a maximally flexible set of constraints guaranteeing that the resulting global makespan is never more than twice the optimal makespan that can be realized by sequential scheduling agents. We will briefly discuss the outlines of this algorithm and reuse it (after some adaptations) to the general sequential agent scheduling case.

The basic idea in this algorithm is to first use the ISA algorithm to determine the set of constraints C for the unit duration tasks. As we have shown above, if the agents would be able to handle tasks concurrently, an agent would be able to find a schedule satisfying all the constraints. In the sequential agent scheduling case, this might not be possible. For example, if there are three unrelated tasks t_1, t_2 and t_3 of unit duration, where the first two are given to agent A_1 and the third to agent A_2, agent A_1 is not able to schedule both tasks given the constraints

$C(t_1) = C(t_2) = [0,0]$. There is, however, a simple way to tell whether a given agent is able to find a sequential schedule for all tasks $t \in T_i$ with the constraints $C(t)$ given to it: Consider the bipartite graph $G_i = (T_i \cup N_i, E_i)$ where N_i is the set of all time points occurring in the intervals $C(t) = [lb(t), ub(t)]$ of tasks $t \in T_i$ and $(t,n) \in E_i$ iff $n \in C(t)$.[3] It is not difficult to see that there exists a sequential schedule for agent A_i iff the graph G_i has a *maximum matching* [10] that includes every task $t \in T_i$.

If the (polynomial) maximum matching algorithm is not able to find a complete matching for T_i, i.e., some of the tasks could not be scheduled, there must be a *scheduling conflict* between a task t in the matching and a task t' not in the matching. Such a conflict can be resolved by adding a precedence constraint $t \prec t'$ between t and t' and calling the ISA algorithm again on the extended scheduling instance. Note that the result of such extensions of the precedence relation is twofold *(i)* the conflict between t and t' is removed and *(ii)* the global makespan $d(T)$ might be increased.

Continuing our last example mentioned above: consider the two tasks t_1 and t_2 agent A_1 was not able to handle. A maximum matching for G_1 contains either t_1 or t_2. If we add a precedence constraint $t_1 \prec t_2$ to the set of tasks, agent A_1 will receive the constraints $C(t_1) = [0,0]$ and $C(t_2) = [1,1]$ is able to find a suitable sequential schedule for its set of tasks.

This matching, extending the precedence relation, and calling the ISA algorithm is repeated until we are guaranteed that for each agent there exists at least one sequential schedule.[4] The result is a set of constraints C guaranteeing that any schedule resulting from independently chosen schedules realizes a makespan that is at most twice as long as the optimal makespan. One of the attractive features of the unit-duration sequential scheduling case is the existence of a polynomial decision procedure (the maximum matching algorithm) for deciding whether there exists a sequential schedule satisfying the constraints $C_i(t)$ for an agent A_i. The reduction from PARTITION given above shows that, unless P=NP, we cannot hope to find a solution for the same problem in the general sequential scheduling case.

There is, however, a possibility to reuse the approximation algorithm sketched above if we assume that, although the agents are strictly sequential, the tasks can be accomplished using *preemption*. This enables an agent to complete a part of task t, then to start some other tasks, process a next part of t and so on. If this is allowed, we can easily reduce a sequential scheduling instance $\langle \{T_i\}_{i=1}^n, \prec, 1, d() \rangle$ to a sequential scheduling instance with unit durations as follows:

Each task $t \in T$ is split in unit parts $t^1, \ldots, t^{d(t)}$, we add the constraints $t^j \prec t^{j+1}$ for $j = 1, \ldots, d(t) - 1$. Finally, every precedence constraint $t \prec t'$ is replaced by the constraint $t^{d(t)} \prec t'^1$. See Figure 3 for an illustration. Note that this assumption implies that the sequential scheduling case with arbitrary task durations can be reduced to the unit duration sequential case. Hence, we can reuse the approximation algorithm for this case, too, obtaining a 2-approximation al-

---

[3] Note that we assume integer values for schedules $\sigma(t)$.

[4] This procedure must halt because conflicts can never reoccur.

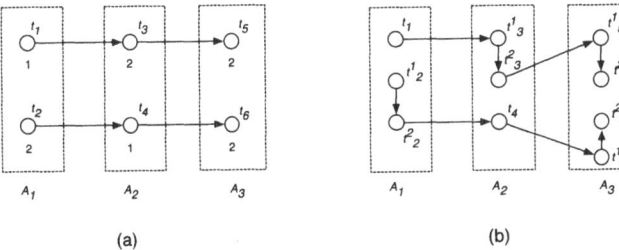

Fig. 3. A sequential scheduling instance (a) and its reduction to the equivalent unit-duration case (b) if preemption is allowed

gorithm for autonomous scheduling of tasks with arbitrary durations. There is of course a catch: The approximation algorithm is only polynomial for those instances where the durations $d(t)$ are not super-polynomial in the number of tasks $|T|$. Otherwise, the splitting of tasks in unit duration tasks would result in a super polynomial number of unit-duration tasks.

Example 4. Consider the problem instance in Figure 3. Here, the tasks are assigned to 3 agents $T_1 = \{t_1, t_2\}$, $T_2 = \{t_3, t_4\}$ and $T_3 = \{t_5, t_6\}$ with task durations $d(t_1) = d(t_4) = 1$ and $d(t_2) = d(t_3) = d(t_5) = d(t_6) = 2$. The precedence constraints are $t_1 \prec t_3 \prec t_5$ and $t_2 \prec t_4 \prec t_6$. The minimal makespan for the unbounded case is $d(T) = 5$. This implies that after task splitting of task t_2, agent A_1 will receive the constraints $C(t_1) = C(t_{2a}) = [0, 0]$ and $C(t_{2b}) = [1, 1]$. If t_1 is included in the maximum matching (and t_{2a} is not), an additional constraint $t_1 \prec t_{2a}$ is added to the set of tasks. As a result, the depth $depth(T) = 6$ and the new constraints are $C(t_1) = [0, 0]$, $C(t_2^1) = [1, 1]$ and $C(t_2^2) = [2, 2]$. Continuing the procedure with agent A_2 and agent A_3 in the same way will result in a joint schedule with makespan 7, while the optimal makespan for sequential scheduling agents is 6. ∎

6   Conclusions and Future Work

In this paper, we studied the distributed scheduling problem in the context of non-cooperative agents. Unlike traditional scheduling algorithms, which generate a single rigid schedules for the agents, our algorithms introduce constraints on the starting time of each task. In this way, we allow flexibility for each agent to choose among a set of allowable ones, while ensuring that the combined global schedule is feasible. We believe that for many real-world applications, specially those with uncertainty, such flexible scheduling for individual agents is highly desirable.

We have developed a polynomial time algorithm - ISA that generates a set of constraints on the possible schedules the agents can develop so that, any schedule that abides by these additional constraints is always feasible. The schedules generated by ISA also were proved to have maximal flexible and makespan efficient. We have also shown that in the the sequential case, it is NP-hard to find

a makespan optimal schedule. We then showed that preemptive task processing allowed us to reuse an approximation algorithm developed for sequential
scheduling of unit duration tasks. The makespan of the schedules resulting out
of using this approximation algorithm are at most twice that of the optimal.

As a follow-up of this paper first of all, we would like to use approximation
algorithms for the general bounded agent case without relying on the preemptive task processing assumption and without restricting attention to the strictly
sequential case. Next, we plan to formally analyze the minimal degree of flexibility that the proposed algorithms can ensure given different task structures.
Furthermore, we would also like to investigate the trade-off between the degree
of flexibility and the loss of the makespan efficiency. Such a study would enable
us to design algorithms that are better customized to specific applications.

References

1. Sih, G.C., Lee, E.A.: Scheduling to account for interprocessor communication
   within interconnection-constrained processor networks. In: ICPP (1), pp. 9–16
   (1990)
2. Topcuouglu, H., Hariri, S., Wu, M.Y.: Performance-effective and low-complexity
   task scheduling for heterogeneous computing. IEEE Trans. Parallel Distrib.
   Syst. 13(3), 260–274 (2002)
3. Beaumont, O., Boudet, V., Robert, Y.: The iso-level scheduling heuristic for heterogeneous processors. In: Proc. 10th Euromicro Workshop on Parallel, Distributed
   and Network-based Processing 2002, 9-11 Jan. 2002, pp. 335–350 (2002)
4. Maheswaran, M., Siegel, H.J.: A dynamic matching and scheduling algorithm for
   heterogeneous computing systems. In: HCW 1998: Proc. of the Seventh HCW, p.
   57 (1998)
5. Walsh, W., Wellman, M., Wurman, P., MacKie-Mason, J.: Some economics of
   market-based distributed scheduling. In: Proceedings of 18th International Conference on Distributed Computing Systems 1998, 26-29 May 1998, pp. 612–621
   (1998)
6. Li, J.: Strategic Negotiation Models for Grid Scheduling. PhD thesis, TU Dortmund
   (2007)
7. Hunsberger, L.: Algorithms for a temporal decoupling problem in multi-agent planning. In: Proc. of AAMAS-2003 (2002)
8. Garey, M., Johnson, D.: Computers and Intractability - a guide to the theory of
   NP-completeness. W.H. Freeman and Company, New York (1979)
9. Yadati, C., Witteveen, C., Zhang, Y., Wu, M., Putre, H.L.: Autonomous scheduling. In: Proc. of the FCS 2008 (2008)
10. Cormen, T.T., Leiserson, C.E., Rivest, R.L.: Introduction to algorithms. MIT
    Press, Cambridge (1990)

Author Index